for

Madhulika and Krittika

Rickie, Rachel and David

and

to the spirit of collaboration

M.B. *and* D.M.

The Sari

MUKULIKA BANERJEE
DANIEL MILLER

PHOTOGRAPHS
DIXIE
DESIGN
OROON DAS

For
James,
Best wishes,
Mukulika Banerjee
Daniel Miller

⊛ BERG

First published in 2003 by

Berg

Editorial offices:

First Floor, Angel Court, 81 St Clements Road, Oxford, OX4 1AW, UK

838 Broadway, Third Floor, New York, NY 10003-4812, USA

Berg is the imprint of Oxford International Publishers Ltd.

Library of Congress Cataloging-in-Publication Data

A catalogue record for this book is available from the Library of Congress.

British Library Cataloguing-in-Publication Data

A catalogue record for this book is available from the British Library.

ISBN   1 85973   732   3(Cloth)

Printed in Hong Kong by Hong Kong Graphics & Printing Ltd.

www.bergpublishers.com

TABLE OF CONTENTS

ACKNOWLEDGEMENTS

We are particularly indebted to Kathryn Earle of Berg Publishers who originally suggested a book on the sari to us and she and her team have been extremely supportive throughout the project.

We are extremely grateful to Garden Silk Mills, especially to Shilpa and Praful Shah, for their generous financial support which has made possible the extensive illustrations that are so integral to the book. Thanks also to Harshah Shah for administering the grant and the marketing team at Garden for providing advertisements reproduced here. Many thanks to Ebony who also helped us with a grant. Deborah Swallow and Rosemary Crill at the Victoria and Albert Museum, London put us in touch with potential donors. We would also like to thank Gauri Advani who saw the intellectual merit of this project and generously made us a grant.

We thank Panikos Andidoros for the generous loan to Dixie of his hi-tech camera; Chris Pinney for lending some relevant visuals from his personal collection; the Getty Images and *Outlook* magazine for photographs of Indian politicians and film stars; Verena Salzman for the loan of hardware; Michael Stewart for the loan of office space; Chris Hagisavva at the Department of Anthroplogy, UCL and Vipul Sangoi for technical IT support; and Frances Mather for preparing the index.

The following people read various versions of the manuscript and provided helpful comments: Veronique Benei, Rickie Burman, Joanne Eicher, Jo Entwhistle, Rachel Miller, Lucy Norris, Kaori O'Conner, Caroline and Filippo Osella, Audrey Prost, Emma Tarlo, Julian Watts, Sophie Woodward.

As with any ethnographic project this work has been possible only because our informants were so giving of their time, opinions, advice and address books, and so flexible in adjusting their schedules to ours. This overwhelming generosity reflects not only their own merits but also a wider ethic that makes Indian society, and others like it, such a delight and education.

For help with hospitality and contacts and for encouragement during fieldwork we would like to thank: Varsha Chopra, Suresh, and Partha Mukhopadhyay in Ahmedabad; Sanjeev and Susheela Ailawadi, Asha Baxi, Ira Bhaskar, Anjali Capila, Siddhartha Chatterjee, Nandita Das, Siddhartha Das, Jasleen Dhamija, Omkar Goswami, Rta Chishti Kapur, Subhash Malik, Kalyani Mukherjee, Ashok Matthew, Harminder Sahni, Rajiv Sethi, Patricia and Jit Uberoi, Kapila Vatsyayan and Yogendra Yadav in Delhi; Ruma Banerjee in Lucknow; Nandini Banerjee, Leela Das, Sukanya Ghosh, Kavita Panjabi and Milan Sen in Kolkata; V.P. and Shanta Dhananjayan, Mithilesh Kumar and Mr. Rajaram in Chennai; Ruchika Chanana and Apurva Sarin in Bangalore; Radha in Kovalam; Tanni Ganguly, Zubin Kabiraji, Subur Munjee,

Praful Patel, Kamlesh Punjabi and the fashion team at Express Textile, Om Puri, Amit Raje, Rakesh Sharma, S.Swaminathan, Soumya Venkatesh and all the staff at IRIS in Mumbai; Tahir Ahmed, Tanvi Amin, Prof. Balarajan, Devika Banerjee, Laura Bear, Imogen Butler-Cole, Nidhi Dalmia, Sangeeta Datta, Krishna Dutta, Vishal Gulati, Enamul Hoque, Nakul, Malavika Jayaram, Surina Narula, Dion Paragas, Andrew Robinson, Pradeep Ratnam, Verena Salzman, Suchi and Sandeep, Matt Snowden, Gail Thakur, Hiromi Uedain, Preeti Vasudevan and Michael Yorke in London.

Several people agreed to be interviewed and photographed as models. Our special thanks to all these individuals who shared their wardrobes and stories which enriched the testimonies in this book. In Ahmedabad: Mr. Narayan, Jayanti Ravi, Bhagyashree Patwardhan; in Delhi: Alka Agarwala, Ambika, Madhulika Banerjee, Krittika Banerjee, Shukla and Bishwa Ranjan Basu, Tripta Basu, Geetan Batra, Bindu, Keya Das, Sufi Dharma, Indrani, Kamayani Jalan, Mrs. Kapoor, Sheila and Dwey Lunkad, Suchet Malhotra, Malti, Monalisa Mishra, Riya Mukherjee, Pramod Nair, Jyoti Pandey, Bansuri Taneja and her family, Reeta Sahni, Kiran Segal, Zohra Segal, Rukmini Sekhar, Shanno, Meera and Kalpana Subramanian; in Kolkata Sati Choudhury, Nabanita Deb Sen, Dulari, Tapati Guha-Thakurta, Manish and Rini Gupta, Kasturi, Lolita, Tinni Sen, Jawhar and Nandita Sircar, and members of 'Doorbar'; in Shantiniketan, Kumkum and Ranjit Bhattacharya. To everyone in Madanpur and Chishti for their characteristic bemused but indulgent help; in Chennai Supriya Banerji, Vishnu Bharatheeyan, Deepti, Amishal Natarajan, Subhash Rajagopal, Meenakshi Ravi, Sreepriya Subramaniam, Vyshnavee; in Bangalore Ruchika Chanana, and staff and students at National Institute of Biological Sciences; in Mumbai Anurag and Archana, Beena Bhakta, Monica Correa, the late Deena Pathak, Arvind Poddar, Nandita Puri, Nim Sood Vandana; in Oxford Barbara Harriss-White and Nandini Gooptu; in London Begum Maitra, Shubhrasheel Roy Choudhury, Sangeeta Banerjee, John Harriss, Paulina Bozek and Barira Limbada.

Our special thanks to our families: Roma and Akshay Banerjee, Madhulika and Krittika Banerjee, Rickie Burman, Rachel and David Miller, Bob and Sue Dix, Keya and Ajit Das.

Finally, our very special thanks to Julian Watts whose contribution was way beyond the call of spousal duty. He read and edited the manuscript, poured drinks and tolerated endless sari-talk at the dinner table with mostly good humour.

Mukulika Banerjee, Daniel Miller, Dixie, Oroon Das
London

Note: Most of photos in this volume are by Dixie; the occassional less artistic ones are by the authors.

Imagine a piece of cloth lying stretched out in a display case, rectangular, lifeless. We could tell you that this is a sari, five meters long, made from cotton. We could add that it is hand-woven, in a pattern known as *ikat*, and go on to explain this pattern's history and origins in a particular region of India.

But now imagine encountering that same sari enveloping the body of a young woman – call her Mina. Suddenly the cloth comes alive: it exaggerates her vivacity as she turns around, her elegance as the pleats rustle at her ankles, her flirtatiousness as it slowly threatens to slide off her shoulder, her authority and dexterity as she controls its folds. Meanwhile, though we may not realise it, the sari is also scratching her with its home made rice starch, and scaring her with its constant threats to lose its shape. She remains anxious about whether it *really* matches the blouse she chose to team it with today. We may just note her look of triumph when she sees that her sari has a more original design than that worn by a rival…

As our evocation of Mina suggests, this is intended to be a different book about clothing, focusing on the sari not as an object of clothing, but as a *lived* garment. A catalogue of fabrics and designs conveys nothing of the anxiety and careful thought involved in selecting what we wear, the sense it brings us of our own bodies, of who we are and who we might become. The way Mina manipulates her sari and responds to its movements expresses not only her personal aesthetic and style, but also her ideals about what it is to be a woman in contemporary India. These ideals may incorporate patriarchal dictates about women's responsibility to preserve and embody Indian 'tradition'; or they may seek to challenge those dictates by adopting new styles of sari, or even alternative kinds of garment. When wearing a sari, Mina may be aspiring to look like a leading female politician, or a popular soap opera star.

an Ikat

A different kind of book about clothing must also be a different kind of encounter with India. In the early 1990s the Indian economy was substantially de-regulated, giving rise to an exponential increase in the availability – for some – of international consumer products, a proliferation of brands in cars, mobile phones and airline carriers, a jump from a single public television channel to a hundred private ones. Coupled with this has been a rise in the disposable income of the middle classes, a growing gap between rich and poor, and a wave of rural migrants to the cities.

Against this backdrop, almost everything that might have been taken for granted even a decade ago is now being challenged and re-config-ured. Women in villages may still live very different lives from the middle classes in the towns, planting rice and tending water buffalo, but now they too are often watching television and buying mascara, or arguing about the relative merits of synthetic saris versus cotton ones. Meanwhile, young urban women debate the merits of whether saris are practical garb for riding scooters to the office, where even a generation ago 'working' women were frowned upon. Older women watch bemused as their granddaughters choose each morning between a sari, a shalwar kamiz, or jeans and a T-shirt.

This book will not document the different ways of draping the sari still to be found in India,[1] not to mention elsewhere in South Asia. Within that region, the sari shares a wider landscape of draped and unsewn clothing used by both men and women including shawls, turbans, the *dhoti* and the *lungi*.[2] Some of the ways of tying the sari are so very different from one another that they hardly seem to form the same garment at all: for example, the sari is pulled between the legs in Maharashtra and Tamil Nadu, while in Bengal it is wrapped three times around the body. Neither will we add to the already ex-cellent reviews of the variety of types, colours and designs of the handloom sari.[3]

Rather, our encounter with the sari takes us to women's most private moments, to their points of doubt and creativity, and often in their

draping styles: (top) Tamil,
(below) Maharashtra

own voices. The careful concern women show for how they appear reflects tellingly on how they are coming to terms with a changing India. It is their practical assertion that the sari is not some antique or folk costume, but is instead a living and effective alternative to the stitched clothing of the West. As we argue, this can help challenge our own taken-for-granted assumptions about the nature of 'modern life'.

Our approach reflects our own previous interests and research. Mukulika Banerjee is a political anthropologist who has studied the rank-and-file beliefs of a non-violent anti-colonial movement in British India[4] and whose current work aims to explore popular Indian perceptions of democracy and their interaction with everyday village

draping styles: (top) Bengali,
                   (below left to right) Tamil, Kerala, Gujarati

life. Daniel Miller is a student of material culture who has written about ordinary peoples' experience of global capitalism and modernity, and has also carried out ethnographic studies of women's clothing in Trinidad and London.[5]

A common theme in our previous work has been a concern to draw together 'micro' perspectives based on ethnographic fieldwork with individuals, and 'macro' perspectives which are concerned with wider changes such as in politics or religion. Bridging the gap between these was one of our commitments in undertaking this project. When we read books about clothing, we felt their sometimes cold and analytical style lost touch with the importance of clothing as feeling and social experience. But the way the sari continues to flourish also clearly poses some 'big' cultural questions. We wanted to see if we could link these two spheres: specifically, could the way women feel about wearing their sari help account for its continued popularity and also tell us about their relationship to modern India?

We explored these themes by spending time in India making observations and conducting over a hundred extended conversations. This data was supplemented by Mukulika Banerjee's fieldwork over the last four years in villages in West Bengal. Often we have quoted our respondents verbatim. Sometimes we have drawn together shared comments and perspectives in a single notional spokeswoman or dialogue. We have sought to represent the perspectives of cities and countryside, producers and consumers, Hindus and Muslims, but we acknowledge that it would be wrong to claim that every statement we make necessarily applies to every part of that great cultural patchwork which is India. After all, each region has a distinct history of clothing, and in some cases the sari is itself a recent interloper.

Nonetheless, we are confident that the main portraits we present will be familiar and recognisable to the great majority of Indian women. This is in part because we are mostly concerned not with the regional handloom traditions but with the most common type of sari worn today. This is a mass-produced synthetic sari using generic floral, ab-

sari worn with a blouse

stract and other motifs promoted by companies such as Garden and Reliance, and associated with the rise of textile mills and subsequently with powerlooms. It bears no allegiance to any particular region, since there has been a homogenisation and an increasing self-consciousness about the sari as a pan-Indian garment, its ideals and images associated with such figures as Indira Gandhi and leading film stars. The style of draping has become dominated by the Nivi style, now ubiquitous in urban India and abroad.[6] Many of our observations presume this Nivi style.

As this historical trend suggests, the sari is a highly dynamic garment.[7] Over the past century it has also acquired accompanying garments, first petticoats and fitted tops followed later by underwear.[8] Although the emphasis throughout this book will be on the sari, there is another protagonist that makes a constant appearance: the shalwar kamiz, or suit. Originally a regional, mainly Punjabi, dress at a time when South Asia was politically divided, the shalwar kamiz went on to become the national dress for both men and women in Pakistan. But in recent decades it has defied political boundaries and become increasingly popular in India also. In the final chapter of this book, the story is told of how the shalwar kamiz developed an association with college education, then youth more generally, and emerged as an increasingly acceptable dress for women across India. This emerging contest between the sari and the shalwar kamiz can be seen as corresponding to, and acting out, a fundamental conflict between two versions of thinking about, and being, 'modern'.

Following Mina's 'autobiography' of sari wearing, which forms Chapter 1 of this book, Chapter 2 examines the intimate relationship between women and the sari, highlighting its dynamic and expressive relationship with the wearer. Chapter 3 then discusses the sari not as a single garment but as part of a trunk or wardrobe that reflects the various possibilities available to an individual. Next, a sequence of chapters explores the place of the sari in womens' life cycles, starting from the way in which young women first come to wear saris and gradually learn how to inhabit them. The focus then turns to the

sari worn without a blouse

many expectations and pressures concerning sari wearing that surround women in their roles as wives and mothers and as working women, and the poignant way in which older women and their saris are linked together by a deep-seated cosmology that expects them, literally, to fade away together.

Chapter 8 explores the case of a mistress and her maid as an illustration of the complex algebra of social and aesthetic considerations that can leave a woman who possesses three hundred saris convinced that she has nothing to wear, or a woman with only three still in agony over which would be best. Chapter 9 describes various adventures of sari shopping and collecting, while Chapter 10 briefly considers the structure of the contemporary market for designing and manufacturing saris. Chapter 11 looks at the arbiters of taste of the modern sari, notably the new fashion designers and the film stars they compete to adorn. The final chapter discusses recent developments in sari wearing, including what is at stake in its growing rivalry with the shalwar kamiz. We reflect on how the current trends are far from those which simplistic accounts of 'globalisation' and 'modernisation' might have predicted, and ask what the sari can teach us about alternative ways of being modern.

But first, to introduce the 'lived sari', we return to Mina. On a long Sunday afternoon, Mina told us her 'sari autobiography', which in retrospect encapsulated many of the themes we go on to explore. Like many of her contemporaries, she is not really a representative of any region, class or attitude. Her family comes from the southern state of Kerala, but her husband is from Bengal in the east, and she married much against the wishes of her parents, who would have preferred her to marry within her own community. She lives in Delhi, where her neighbours are mostly Punjabi. While reading her story, we would like you to forget much of what you know about India if you are Indian, or what you expect of life in India if you are not.

(left)   churidar kamiz (L) and shalwar kamiz (R)

(below) shalwar kamiz with dupatta

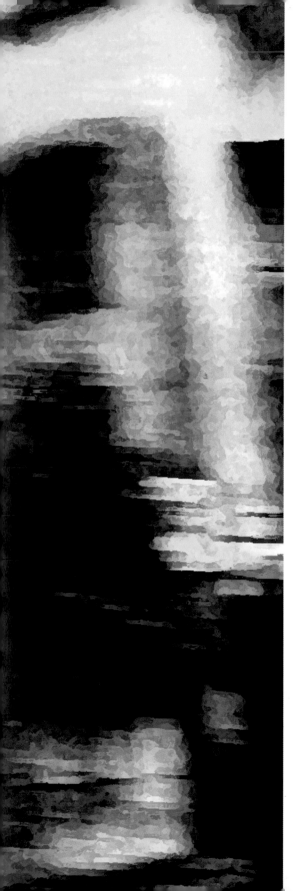

CHAPTER 1

Mina's Story

I don't have to wear a sari for my job, but I do wear one, because I am married and I live with my in-laws. I am a total outsider to the family, from a different caste, and a different community. I am a South Indian girl, Tamil and Malyali both, though born and brought up in Delhi, but my husband is Bengali. In Bengal you have to cover your head. My sister-in-law [her husband's older brother's wife] used to be after me all the time to wear a sari. Everything is totally different. My mother always wears saris. I have one younger sister who wears suits [shalwar kamiz][10] and jeans because she is in college.

The first time I wore a sari was for a school 'farewell' [graduation ceremony] – my parents went out and got me a new sari. It was a chiffon[11] sari with a lot of embroidery in the pallu.[12] Most of my friends wore cottons. I had pinned my sari to my blouse to cover my waist. Then my friends told me I looked weird. I said I felt awkward if my waist and stomach showed. So then they said well ours is showing too, if someone looks they will see ours and not only yours! They persuaded me to take off all the safety pins. I did that only after I arrived at the school. I was always overweight, which is why I preferred chiffon because it is slimming and because it stays the way you wear it. A cotton sari makes you look even fatter. I wanted a sari in which my body would look OK. My mother has lots of different kinds, and I knew how different she looked in different fabrics.

The next time (apart from a cousin's wedding) was at my own wedding three years ago. My wedding sari was a blue sari made of good silk. My parents boycotted the wedding, so it was my in-laws who arranged everything. Within a day we got married. In that one day they bought saris, jewellery, everything else. I did not have anything when I came from my mother's house, just a thin chain and some jewellery for my ears. My parents came only after two or three months. My in-laws went to the Bengal emporium and bought the best sari there for the ceremony. It was a blue sari rather than the usual red, because blue is my husband's favourite colour. So they agreed to have just a red veil and they bought a pink sari for the evening reception. Then there were two saris from my husband's older brother's family. They were kota,[13] not from Rajasthan, maybe from Orissa. These are small squares, but they are very colourful. They were in pure cotton.

After my wedding when I changed out of the finery (in which you will look good anyway with all the jewellery, etc.!) and washed off my make-up, I wore a lemon yellow sari. I saw myself in the mirror, with this sari, a simple bindi [forehead decoration] and red sindoor in my hair parting and I couldn't believe my own eyes at how beautiful I looked. It was a cotton. I always thought yellow would not suit me. My sister-in-law had got me that one. Earlier the blue colour was looking good on me but with all the make up and eyes done up I looked even darker. When I washed it all off and changed people were asking is this the same bride? They couldn't believe it. I consider my wedding sari my lucky sari. I have worn it two or three times to other weddings.

There is only one condition at my in-laws: 'Don't wear suits.' Up to today I have only one suit, which was given to me by my husband's younger sister. She gave me a suit because she realised I was very young (twenty-two). So she thought I should not be forced into a sari. I should be allowed to wear suits. But my sister-in-law wouldn't have that because I was staying with them and with my husband's older brother around. She used to say, 'I don't care which family she has come from but now that she is married into ours, she has to follow all our norms and customs.' I have to cover my head in front of my husband's older brother. I live with the oldest one and his wife. My mother-in-law, who lives in Bengal with one of the brothers, is more relaxed. Her attitude is that I am too young; I should be allowed to wear what I want. I used to wear maxis at home in front of her, I never went out of my room in them, but at least I could wear them. It may have been because my father-in-law is dead. I never had to cover my head in front of my mother-in-law.

I now always sleep in a sari. I used to wear nighties before marriage, but now I don't. If on certain days I am too hot or uncomfortable then I wear a maxi, otherwise it is always a sari. Now at least we live on our own, so I can take the top of the sari off. Earlier I had to cover my head in case anyone could see me in the candlelight during a power cut. It used to be stifling hot but that's what I had to do, even when in bed. No one used to come into the room, but in the morning my sister-in-law came in with tea and things. So that there would be no problem with her and I would be properly covered. I used to loosen the petticoat a bit but I would be always anxious about the sari at night, it should not ride up above the knees. In the early days I used to set the alarm for 5 o'clock every morning, and also warn my husband to wake me up, so that I could straighten my sari properly before she came in with the tea. Even then I couldn't sleep properly because

I used to feel such tension about whether I looked right. I couldn't do anything. After all, there was the young nephew in the house. We have a good relationship, but I used to feel uncomfortable just in case he came in by mistake and found me sleeping there, with my sari over my knees.

I used to tie my petticoat very very tightly always and the doctor told me not to. You see, I used to worry that my sari would come off. It happened once. I had gone out with my husband to one of his friend's house on the motorcycle. My sari felt very loose. My sister-in-law had helped me wear it that day. I was feeling a bit uncomfortable in it as I sat on the bike, but I ignored the feeling. I don't know how it happened. The knot had opened. It was too horrible. When we arrived my husband went and rang the doorbell but I kept sitting on the bike. The lady asked us to come in. I could see the table all laid out with the food which they had arranged, but I refused to get off and I wanted to just go home. So she asked what had happened, and I told her that my sari was going to fall off because it had become very loose. So she asked me to come in and retie it. But I did not know how I would get off or walk past all the guests. You see, my sister-in-law had tied the knot according to her estimate, and it wasn't tied tight enough, and all the pleats had come out and the pleats and the sari had spread all over, all five metres of it, and it was a cotton which I can't handle anyway.

So my husband said he would take me in through the back door, where I could then retie my sari. But my problem was I did not even know how to tie a sari yet, so how could I fix it myself? This was only three days after the wedding. In their house there were lots of people, and they were all there to see the new bride! So I begged the lady to help me in her bedroom. She retied the sari as best as she could. It was too horrible. She is Punjabi, and wore shalwar kamiz! She needed help to wear a sari herself! So I asked to borrow one of her shalwars and decided to take off my sari totally. When my husband came to check if I was OK, I told him my new plan, but he disagreed, because he said I was there for the first time and all these people had come to see the new bride. To appear in a suit would not be appropriate. So then my husband himself came to help. He knows how to tie a sari just from watching the women in his own family all of whom wear saris all the time, and I knew a bit by then too. So together we managed to put it back on, though I lost count of how many pins I put on my sari that day! About sixteen! That was too horrible. Plus two hair pins to keep my pallu on my head. I had never seen women covering their heads in my Tamil family, so I hadn't a clue how to keep it on my head.

Working in the kitchen used to be dangerous. They used to ask me to make chapattis. One day I was wearing a chiffon which someone had given me. For a long time I kept trying to keep it on my head, as my husband's older brother was hovering around there, but I just couldn't manage. So I finally held it with a clip at my shoulder and left the pallu free floating. Then it caught fire. When my husband's older brother saw this, he called my husband, who put the fire out by putting water on it. I couldn't learn these things from watching my sister-in-law, because as she is the oldest daughter-in-law she has never had to cover her head in front of anyone. So I am the only one who has to keep purdah. None of the others have to, because one lives with the mother-in-law and the other one is in America, and she of course even wears jeans and things. So I am the only one who has to keep her head covered. When I have too much trouble, I can't say anything...one has to adjust. My husband's older brother finally intervened and said if he had a daughter she would be about my age and he wouldn't impose this on her, so there was no reason to put me through it. So after that incident in the kitchen, I stopped keeping purdah.

It is better to be in a shalwar kamiz when on a bus than to be in a sari, because no part of the body shows in it. In a sari, sometimes your stomach shows, sometimes your waist shows, sometimes your bra – it is too horrible. The moment I enter the bus, I am aware of it, especially until one gets a seat. I try and cover myself as much as I can. I have got into the habit now, I have learned how to handle the sari. One feels very hot all covered up like that, but still it is better to cover up. The men don't even know what they are doing. I think it is worse in a sari because in a shalwar kamiz at least you know no one will be able to touch your body, your skin directly, but in a sari when you raise your left arm, everything is exposed so one can't even say anything because you are totally exposed to their gaze. But if someone does any slightly wayward thing, I raise a storm.

When I was pregnant, the doctor told me not to tie my petticoat so tight. After four months, the baby wasn't able to grow. When I went for my routine check-up, my doctor saw me taking off my sari and saw the mark of the petticoat on my waist and told me I was mad. I told her I couldn't wear a sari loosely. She also told my husband. She recommended I wear a maxi, so he went out and bought me four maxis. By then we lived separately from my in-laws, so inside the house I wore maxis. But when I had to go out, I still wore tight saris. Then the doctor gave me an ultimatum and told me she could give me no guarantee about my baby if I continued to tie the sari so tightly. So I started using at least six pins. In any case I wasn't travelling far in those days, and I wasn't travelling by bike anymore as it was risky. It was easier in an auto-rickshaw, as once one sat down one stayed there until getting off at one's destination. Initially, getting out of an auto-rickshaw was a terrifying experience. Also, I have slipped innumerable times on the two steps in my sister-in-law's house where my sari gets trapped under my sandals. When I sat behind my husband on the motorscooter, I used to bunch the sari up high and my husband used to tell me off and say what will people say if you sit like this, what will they think of you? I didn't care. But now, after continuously wearing saris for two years, I have got more used to them.

My sari does not fall even if my son is holding it. Cotton is like that. It stays on however one puts it. As I am usually alone at home even if it falls, I don't have to worry about it. He refuses to let go of my sari, and then he picks up an onion or potato and looks at me and says, 'mama out!', like a bowler in a cricket match. Sometimes he falls down if I move quickly and he can't keep up with me. Then I have to stop and console him.

I haven't really changed the way I wear a sari with my changing shape. I am aware now that I don't look the way I did in a sari on the day of the school farewell, but my husband insists that I haven't changed at all. Of course I have put on weight and my stomach has come out much more. Now it doesn't feel as comfortable in a sari, because the waist band rides up when you sit down, this didn't happen before. I have to keep checking in the mirror and have to pull down my sari every time I sit down. Now I have to tie the sari above my navel. I have put on weight, and however tightly you tie the petticoat, it looks odd. Besides, my son was born by a C-section. It used to look nice, though, when it was tied low.

I would wear the same sari on two consecutive days. But not to work. I wash and starch it myself, but send it out for ironing. It costs Rs7[14] per sari. You can wear it only once; never more than twice because it gets crushed very badly. We make rice water – instant starch is terrible, the sari becomes limp after you sit down once. I don't know how people use it! In our family rice is never made in a rice cooker, so there is always starch. The day I need starch I keep it for use that day. It is better to starch in the sun, otherwise the sari smells. So, I may keep the starch from the previous evening meal, or I cook the rice early before noon so that I get the starch to use while the sun is still hot. It takes me a long time to wash clothes. Every three days, it takes one and a half hours.

Sometimes I even wash my saris before leaving for work, in which case I tell my husband to starch the saris before leaving for his work because I run out of time. If he is in the mood, he does it. Otherwise I do it when I get back. Chiffons have none of this hassle. You can wash it in the evening and it would be dry by the morning, and it does not even need to be ironed. With cottons it takes a long time and you have to wait for it to return from the press-wallah. This is the reason why I totally prefer chiffons. I have to wash them each time I wear them in the summer. Maximum two wears. Otherwise they smell. Delhi is too horrible. Before I started this job I always wore only cottons. But it is commuting in buses that has made me wear chiffons. Earlier I did not even own any and if I wore them, it was only if I felt like it, but now I wear nothing else.

During the Durga Puja [the main annual Bengali religious festival] there are a lot of comments about other people's saris, it is normal. I have done it myself. There was a lady once in a silk shalwar kamiz. I asked if she was Bengali. She didn't look like one in her black *bindi* and shalwar kamiz. Now I have internalised all this, so I felt it looked odd. In my opinion now, if a woman is Bengali then at least for Puja she should wear a sari and a red *bindi*. She had a son of six or seven years old. I was saying to my niece, why has she worn a suit? She said why not? That evening there was a cultural show and she came in a beautiful Bengali sari and I thought she looked much more beautiful, not the ragamuffin she looked in the morning.

Yesterday when I was in my mother's house, I was hanging around in a shalwar kamiz of my sister's. But my sister said to me, do change, because you look so much better in a sari – it suits you more than a shalwar kamiz, and we have got used to seeing you only in a sari now. I refused to change, as I was hot. But then I looked in the mirror and agreed that I did look odd. My husband says I look at more like a woman in a sari, rather than a girl, and look more his age! He is quite tall and has a more mature figure and face. He says, I want a wife by my side, not a girlfriend. So I don't have a choice about wearing saris – I have to!

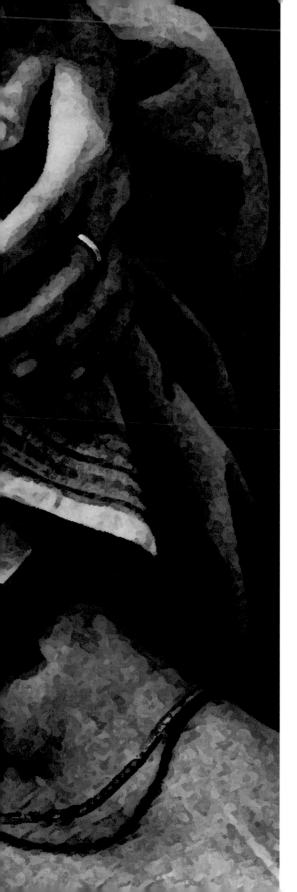

The Intimate Sari

Other clothing is on you, but it is not with you. But the sari is with me. I have to constantly handle it. I just can't let it lie. The whole thing creates movement and one is moving with it all the time. That is why the pallu is not stitched. And that is the grace of the sari.

— Deena Pathak, ACTRESS

The Sari: a roadmap

Pallu can be used to cover head

Where should the sari cross the blouse?
Potential for revealing cleavage

Pleats of pallu can be kept fixed on the shoulder by a safety pin

Left breast is more exposed from the side than the right breast which is totally covered

The blouse can be in matching or contrasting colour of the sari

Where to tie the petticoat?
Too high above the navel - she looks like a nun
Too low below the navel - she looks 'filmy'

Tightness of petticoat string causes itchiness

Navel feels crowded where pleats are gathered and tucked in. Sweaty, scratchy because of gold thread on sari border

The pleats are made by folding about one metre of cloth

Sweat tends to trickle down legs but is cooled by circulating air

The fall: additional strip of cloth attached to the inside bottom edge to strengthen the border

The petticoat, a skirt tied with a drawstring worn under the sari, from waist to ankle

Height of sari can be altered. The higher one ties it, the freer the ankles

The Intimate Sari [15]

The feel of the Sari

Clothes are among our most personal possessions. They are the main medium between our sense of our bodies and our sense of the external world. The sensual qualities of the sari, the way it feels on the skin, profoundly affects womens' experience of the garment as something simultaneously part of them yet outside of them.

To wear clothing is to be subject to different sensations with varying intensities, as we are conscious of only certain points of contact between flesh and cloth. In the now widespread Nivi style, the sari is draped from right to left, passing over the lower body twice – the second time in a cluster of fan-shaped pleats – and the upper body once. The pallu, the free end of the sari, falls over the left shoulder down to the waist. Given the asymmetry of the sari, no sensation in one part of the body is repeated in any other. The right leg does not feel like the mirror of the left. The two shoulders and the two breasts are touched by the garment in quite different ways. The right shoulder can remain untouched by the sari, while the left bears the weight of the pallu. The right breast feels the pressure of the pleats of the pallu pulled across the bosom, whereas the left one feels strangely exposed, covered from the front but visible from the side. The right side of the waist is hot from the pleats passing over it, but the left side is uncovered and cool.

The centre point of the sari – the navel – carries the sensation of being a focal pivot around which the security of the whole garment revolves. Here the pleats are tucked into the drawstring of the petticoat. About a yard of cloth is gathered, with a good five inches tucked inside the string, against the belly. This causes perspiration, and a *zari* [16] or starched cotton border may scratch, but these sensations also give reassurance that the pleats are not spilling out.

statuesque

The thighs help define the graceful folds of the pleats that fan out from between the legs. Here again the sensations are asymmetrical. The pleats often lie from right to left in such a way that the first pleat rests on the right leg while the last pleat rests against the left leg. It is how one holds the right leg and knee that defines the shape of the pleats, but it is from the left leg that the sari curves from mid-thigh around towards the back of the body, resting in folds on the back of one's waist to then be brought around from the right side as the pallu. So the curve of a woman's hip and waist is accentuated on the left side. A slight bend at the knee can create a horizontal break in the vertical folds of the sari, giving a woman a more feminine and statuesque look. The ankles always feel slightly crowded as the gathers of the folds of the sari rest against them, their touch made heavier by the 'fall'.[17]

When walking, the right leg determines the length of the stride, which is kept in check by the warning tension at the ankle when the stride is too long for the sari. The left leg needs to move a little bit out and forward so as not to trap the pleats between the knees. The pallu may slide off with the movement, in which case the right arm comes up to restore it to the left shoulder, but carefully so as not to crush the cloth. After a few strides the sari may slip down from the left waist, and the left arm needs to pull it back up in order to retain the fan shape of the pleats.

As they sit down, women invariably check that the pallu has not slipped from covering the right breast, and that the waist is not too exposed by the folding of the torso. The folding of the body upon sitting down in a rickshaw or a car tends also to crush the sari in front and threatens the sequence of the pleats. A series of adjustments is required to even out the part of the pallu which is visible in the front; the pleats need to be rearranged to help them retain their order, and the pallu needs to be freed from being trapped beneath the bottom.

Different sorts of weather create their own sensations and problems. The perspiration that accumulates where the sari is tucked in or densely bunched is mainly unseen. Indeed, the perspiration running down the legs meets the air circulating there, creating a pleasurable cooling sensation. When the waist becomes too damp and itchy, a woman can push the petticoat string to a fresh patch of skin on the waist. In wet weather the bottom of the sari tends to be soaked first, making it heavy and pulling the whole garment downwards. The sari loses its shape and is harder to control or feel comfortable in. A wet sari also clings to the body at various points, accentuating curves and dips of its own accord, rather than as intended by the wearer.

For most women today, the relationship between the sari and the body is mediated by the presence of undergarments.

blouse

exposed petticoat

Thinking of the sari as an unstitched garment, we might imagine it as particularly loose and comfortable. This may well have been the experience of women in the past, and indeed for some older women in rural areas today. But elsewhere the number of women who wear only a single unstitched piece of cloth is rapidly diminishing, and for the rest the desire to look modern involves tightly fitted stitched accompanying garments which are the very opposite of loose comfort. As a thirty-something advertising executive from Mumbai commented:

the petticoat and the fitting of the blouse has really to be tight. A thousand years ago, when the sari evolved, nobody wore a petticoat. It was just one piece of clothing and even the blouse was worn tied around, like a bustier. So it was perfect for the tropics. But the way we wear it today, thanks to the missionaries, is horrible.

The blouse is tight, has sleeves of varying lengths and ends near the waist. The petticoat is a full length skirt, tied at the waist with a drawstring. The sari is draped over these accessories. Many women who prefer to wear a shalwar kamiz cite its advantage as being loose-fitting compared to the tight-fitting sari blouse.

The sari wearer sees herself as engaged in a constant battle to make her 'second skin', that six yard piece of rectangular cloth, move, drape, sit, fold, pleat and swirl in a manner obedient to her will. What victory gives her, however, is a remarkable flexibility to accentuate, moderate or even hide features of her body. But this requires a constant, though unconscious, responsiveness to the way the sari moves with every gesture that she makes. This is in striking contrast to stitched clothing, which once put on in the morning is largely taken for granted for the rest of the day. The sari forces a continued engagement, a conversation, between a woman and her garment.

This conversation includes a subtle alternation between actions that become almost unconscious or automatic, and others that are highly self-conscious. This word is particularly appropriate, since an effect of the sari is often to give wearers a heightened sense of themselves. Recall how Mina, the neophyte sari wearer, lives in constant fear of embarrassment even within her home. She can hardly sleep because she is so afraid that loss of consciousness will lead to her head or knees being uncovered, and as a result she feels stifled in the summer nights. Her worry about the sari falling off leads her to tie her petticoat string so tightly that the doctor is convinced she will harm the baby growing inside her. Yet all the while she is also developing a familiarity with the garment, such that some of her actions become increasingly natural and automatic and she loses awareness that she is inhabiting the sari and its requirements. This process culminates symbolically in the moment when she criticises as 'disrespectful' a woman who has worn a suit rather than a sari during a Bengali festival.

Such self-consciousness is always experienced in the light of particular cultural ideals and fear of social disdain. An urban middle-class woman may strongly believe that the sari can and should command a particular grace or elegance, and be driven to strive to live up to this image of what we shall call the 'elevated sari'. A villager, in contrast, may be self-conscious about different aspects of her clothing: how can she walk in order best to prevent her sari's rents and faded patches from showing? What both women are likely to hold in common, however, is the continued and powerful belief in the special capacity of the sari to make a body more beautiful and womanly than any other garment.

This degree of intimacy in the relationship between wearer and sari may lead to a sense of the sari itself as animated: as having, in a metaphorical sense, a life of its own. This emerges even in the most unlikely areas, such as the maintenance of cleaning, starching

and pressing. Starching, for example, may in its own way be expressive of the intimate relationship between the sari and its wearer. A well-starched sari may look more beautiful and its pleats will stay in place, but it has none of the softness that makes well-worn unstarched cotton such a pleasure on the skin. As an old (and on that day frail) village woman told us:

Now I have a fever and don't feel good so I don't feel like wearing my new sari which I just received yesterday at this wedding I sang at. This old one feels much better as it is soft and old, and it's light. In general it is better to wear old saris when doing housework since it is soft and you know where it is. A new one is crisp and you can't control it and tie it around your waist, and then it might catch fire in front of the hearth.

This leads to a sense that the sari has a life that can be extended by proper starching: 'especially when they wore thin, I used to starch them lightly and then have them ironed before putting them away'. Further, the substance that gives them more life, the starch itself, is traditionally the water used for boiling rice. This becomes in turn a metaphor about feeding a sari. A villager notes:

if I could eat grapes and fruit then would I look like this, wasted and thin? I would have more blood in my body. But if I only eat stale rice, how can I have blood in my body? All the blood will dry up. It's the same with a sari.

This relationship becomes particularly poignant under conditions of poverty when rice is synonymous with food and survival. One of the enduring images of the Bengal Famine of 1943 is that of starving and desperate people drinking the waste starch water from wealthier homes. Feeding a sari with the rice water that was once needed for personal survival contributes to this sense that the sari itself has an animate element, which the owner will seek to keep alive as long as possible. From this develops broader metaphors linking the life of a person and her sari. Sixty-year-old Asma, when asked whether she still had her wedding saris, laughed, saying: 'How can I still have them? They have torn and disappeared years ago. Look at the way a person ages and gets old; how can a sari remain for so long?'

Between self and world: the pallu

There he stands – her betrayer! Not only has she compromised her virtue by agreeing to meet him unchaperoned in these deserted ruins, but now she has discovered that this was precisely the fate of her beloved sister (or at least the person who until three episodes ago she had thought *was her sister), who mysteriously disappeared. His lips quiver in rage at her discovery and it is clear from the evil look that furrows his brow that he is now contemplating her 'removal' too. She stands terrified, her hands clutching and unclenching her pallu. Then, desperate to somehow remove herself, at least for a moment, from this world too horrible to contemplate, she pulls her sari around her shoulders, enveloping herself in its folds. Now at least she will face her own anguish in this sealed-off sanctuary beneath the pallu. The thin polyester will hardly protect her from the violence that may be about to engulf her, and her shaking shoulders betray her fear, but at least she has preserved her dignity and prevented him seeing the true extent of the anxiety that wracks her face.*

The actresses who daily perform these tales of love, comedy and domestic strife in the television serials which entertain an ever-increasing segment of the Indian population do not need to be told that their most constant and effective prop in portraying melodramatic sequences of intense emotion is the pallu.

In this they are the inheritors of a long tradition of classical and folk acting. Deena Pathak, well-known in popular cinema for her portrayal of the 'mother figure', previously enjoyed an established career in the theatre where she learned from some of the great figures of the stage. She acted out for us the extraordinary range of emotions and scenarios that can be effected simply through shifting the position of the pallu.

The pallu may be used to characterise a coy young girl, peeping out from a small hole in the folded cloth that reveals one curious eye. In another scene, seizing the cloth in one hand and tucking it firmly into the waist signifies impatience or impending wrath. As Deena Pathak noted, in acting:

Deena Pathak

Mostly it is the pallu which is handled. It is more of the fiddling with the end of the pallu. That is usually the coy kind of handling with pallu. But there can be so many other ways. You can hold it in a particularly tight way in your fist and show anger. With a peasant woman – she would hold it in her teeth most of the time, thereby both hiding and revealing her face. The pallu is now a protection of sexuality, now used as an exposure. That pallu has got to fall at a particular time to show the boobs in a particular way, or the cleavage. That is something which may be an undercurrent, but equally it can become very obvious of course.

The many references to the pallu being used to veil and hide the face show its subtle relationship to decorum. A girl laughing just a bit too hard covers her mouth with the pallu. A woman dabbing with it at her tears thereby also screens her eyes. The pallu is a haven for an embarrassed face and a cover for unseemly emotion. But, as with so many gestures made with the sari, these ambiguities can in turn unintentionally give rise to an erotic element as when covering the mouth suddenly accentuates the eyes, or screening the eyes draws attention to the lips.

The pallu is able to portray tragedy, comedy and love with such economy because it is lifted so directly from everyday life and is so readily recognised by audiences. A middle-class informant in Delhi did not hesitate for a moment before providing an example of a woman incessantly fiddling with her pallu: 'A maid being interviewed for a job!' This conjures up just the right combination of anxiety and deference that such clutching, twisting and untwisting of the loose cloth conveys. But the pallu is equally effective at demonstrating authority. A schoolteacher noted:

I can't sit and teach, so I walk around and then when I write on the board, I find the pallu distracting for myself as well as for my students. So what I do is just pick it up and tuck it in the waist. There are very interesting connotations to this and the meaning is noted immediately by everyone. The gesture says: 'I am one of those whose pallu will be tucked in to her waist.' It is definitely a statement of being matter of fact – a no nonsense, non-fussy, 'take me seriously' kind of attitude.

Thus, while the series, plots and characters may change, the pallu's starring role remains constant.

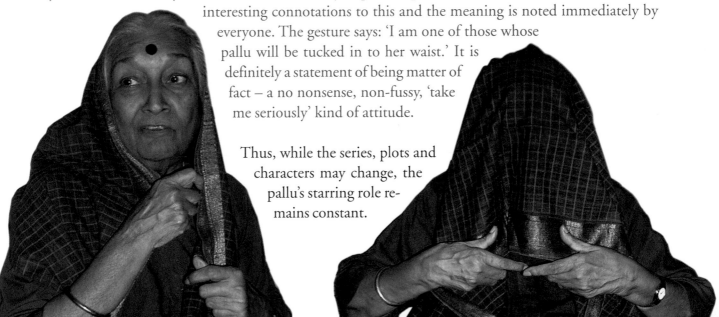

playing peek-a-boo

Most Indians have their first encounter with the sari as an infant, before the time of memory. Mothers use it as a multi-purpose nursing tool. When breast feeding they cradle the baby within it, veiling the operation from the outside world, and use the cloth to wipe the surplus milk from the baby's lips. The pallu retains this close association with the breast, as Mina observed of her son:

When he falls asleep he puts my pallu twisted around his thumb into his mouth. If I disengage my sari he starts wailing. Sometimes people give children pieces of cloth like a hankie or a scarf to get them out of the habit of their mothers' pallu. But I never have. Several neighbours have suggested it but I think – what is the harm if he holds my sari, why give him a separate piece of cloth? He plays peek-a-boo with my sari. He keeps hiding behind it and showing his face. He keeps doing this until I smile back. He thinks I may be angry otherwise. When we sleep next to each other, I cover my face and pretend to be asleep. So he moves the pallu away to see if I am smiling or laughing. If I don't register any emotion he starts crying and keeps calling 'Ma! Ma!' then I have to give in and he is happy. And he starts doing the same by covering his face and playing the same game himself. He learnt to walk holding not my finger, but my pallu.

— Mina

For the child, the pallu becomes a physical embodiment of their mother's love, a love they can literally take hold of. Like the Western idea of a 'comfort blanket' (like that carried by the character Linus in the cartoon *Peanuts*), the pallu serves as what the psycho-analyst Winnicott has dubbed a 'transitional object'.[18] A child takes time to understand that it is itself an individual thing, separate from the rest of the external world as first represented by the mother and her breast. The pallu helps bridge that awful separation and comforts the child during his growing awareness of it.

The value and pathos of the pallu in this respect is seen in the following story, recently told on Indian television by Jayalalitha, a leading politician, who briefly eschewed her usual regal aura to allow a rare glimpse of her early years. When she was a little girl, her mother was a busy cinema star, and she and her brother were brought up by her aunt in Bangalore. Between the ages of four and ten Jaya was able to see her mother only occasionally, as and when the latter could manage the time to come and visit from Madras. She missed her mother terribly. When her mother was around, one of the daily rituals she faithfully performed was to put little Jaya to bed. On such occasions, Jaya was in the habit of clutching her mother's pallu while she fell asleep. It was her comfort blanket, her insurance against her mother's disappearance.

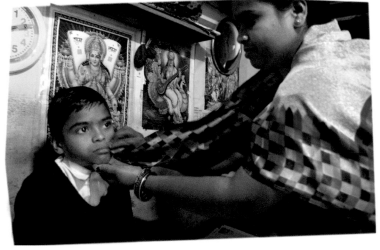

In one instance, Jaya's mother had intended to leave for the station once the child was asleep, and Jaya as usual fell asleep holding onto her pallu. Her mother did not wish to wake the child and then have to bear the tears of separation. So she carefully stood up and unwrapped the sari from her body, and asked her sister to wear the sari instead and lie down by the child. Her sister did this so carefully that she did not disturb the sleeping child or let her feel any movement in the pallu.

In a short story by Vishwapriya Iyengar, a girl in a boarding school pines for a letter from her mother who does not write to her. Her father does, but she thinks of his letters as 'starched serviettes'. She misses her mother's letters which she imagines will be like her 'soft voile pallav [pallu] which kissed lips as you wiped them'.[19]

nursing under the pallu

In contrast, a middle-aged man recalled for us his own far happier childhood, and did so precisely in terms of the constant availability of the pallu:

I had a very good childhood, I think of my mother and my grandmother, you know, showing their love, wiping the sweat off my forehead with the pallu, using it like a fan in the summer. My mother's mother – I would be lying with my head in her lap and she would just cover my head with the pallu. I would go to sleep in this way.

The pallu is, then, more than just a character actor representing a particular emotion or attitude. It is a critical component of the relationship between the individual self and the external world, and this is true as much for grown-ups as for children. The memories of the mother's pallu retain a powerful resonance through later life and relationships, continuing to reassure adults who have constantly to face up to their own anxieties of separation and loss.

For adults, the ambiguity of the pallu being simultaneously part of someone yet separate from them is extended by other ambiguities. Most important is the potential for beauty and eroticism that lies in a fabric which may appear transparent when in a single layer but is opaque when worn in several layers. This ambiguity of transparency is extended by a woman's manipulation of her pallu. Given the natural propensity of the pallu to slip down from the bosom, the action of constantly covering up one's chest can have the effect, if done well (and some do it *very* well), of constantly drawing attention to the area that is ostensibly being protected. So a man has no idea whether a woman is recovering herself because of what she does not want him to see, or is pointing out what she *does* want him to see. Another provocative form of manipulation deftly exploits the property of a sari as a draped garment, and consists of swiftly tightening it to accentuate the tautness of the bottom or the smallness of the waist.

The pallu is usually the most decorated part of the sari, often picking up and elaborating on the small motifs on the border or body of the sari. Much of the beauty of the sari thus lies in the pallu, and it is the part that designers agonise over and which shopkeepers use to clinch the sale. For their part, sari wearers hope that someone's gaze will be attracted to the pallu's sumptuousness and then led onward to appreciate the person behind it.

The same subtlety that applies to flirtation is even more commonly applied to the institution of modesty, in which the pallu plays a central role. Most Hindu women have to cover their heads in the presence of certain family members, while most Muslim women have to cover theirs before strangers. It is clear from Mina's story that this was a traumatic and difficult element of her experience of living as a young married woman in her husband's family home, and this echoes an extremely common shift in women's lives upon marriage. In Mina's case, the added unfamiliarity of the convention made it worse, because in her own South Indian traditions women do not cover their heads for the sake of modesty even after marriage. Once again, however, there are many subtleties to this act of veiling. Women have considerable scope to manipulate the precise way the pallu is held between the teeth or placed over their head, leaving the observing male quite uncertain as to the attitude that lies behind the action: it might be demure or respectful, tantalising or truculent. Again, these nuances of modesty and eroticism are used to great effect by those making films and soap operas.

Physical contact in public between men and women remains frowned upon. Even married couples promenading in parks will not, for example, hold hands. In this context, the pallu becomes an important point of playful contact between grown-up siblings or similarly aged friends. You can tug at it in order to encourage a sister or friend to 'get a move on'. Touching the pallu allows for intimacy in the absence of touching the body itself: 'It is as though by caressing a leaf one is able to touch the tree', as one woman put it. If someone gets too attached to another person, they are likely to be teased by having it said that they have 'attached themselves to the other's pallu' (as a television presenter said to a fan who kept phoning her show).

On the other hand, and for much the same reasons, in a sexual context touching the pallu can be a very intimate and personal act indeed. In Bengal, for instance, it is traditional for a bride on her wedding night to tie the end of her pallu to her husband's dhoti. This is movingly depicted in Satyajit Ray's famous film *The World of Apu*, and was also described to us by one woman who was recalling the morning after her wedding. When she had walked away from the bed, her sari had unravelled, its other end caught tight under her husband's sleeping form. Her surprise at being so attached, literally, to a man deepened when she saw him smile under sleepy hooded eyes as he watched her discomfort. It had been a tender moment which she still thought of fondly. These associations also help explain the comment of a sex worker in Kolkata, who told us that she did not like her clients to touch the pallu because she felt it should be reserved for her relationship with her husband.

The ambiguous 'semi-detached' quality of the pallu is just as evident in more mundane contexts. As a woman does her household chores, the pallu is in constant use as a kind of third arm, lifting hot vessels in the kitchen, wiping the seat she is about to sit on in a public place, cleaning her spectacles, collecting shopping or alms, gathering up rupee notes in a purse-like knot, or protecting her face from smoke and smog. The pallu's presence is so constant and available, so taken for granted, that it almost seems a part of the body itself.

The Animated Sari

The pallu may be used to

WIPE A TABLE

STORE

CARRY KEYS

LIFT A HOT VESSEL

PROTECT ONE'S MODESTY

Yet the same quality that extends the capacity of a person also gives the pallu the power to betray them. When something happens that represents the unwelcome intrusion of the external world upon the self, it may well have the pallu at the end of it. The pallu that protects from smog also gets jammed in a car door. It is the pallu that, when touched by the wrong hand, can make one vulnerable, or that flies in your face so that you cannot see, or that falls off your head when you are trying to be modest. The pallu may encourage an extraordinarily powerful sense of self in its wearer, but it is also liable to go off and do its own thing just when one wants to take its loyalty for granted. As Mina found with the stove, the pallu can connect the self to the external world with potentially disastrous results. The same pallu that is used to hold a hot *karhai* of food may actually catch fire when cooking. Such accidents are all too common, and can result in horrible injury and death. These are not always accidents. In many instances of bride burning, including 'dowry deaths', the groom's family claim that her pallu caught fire 'accidentally' while she was cooking. This is a plausible enough statement given the extremely flammable nature of synthetic saris, and it often proves an effective legal defence.[20] So, as the tool of another, the pallu can finally betray its wearer. On the other hand, desperately unhappy brides typically end their misery by hanging themselves from the ceiling by their pallu.

Thus the young wife finds that the pallu seems to have a life of its own. In a vivid trope for the way in which household burdens gradually weigh down her youthful spirits, she will generally seek before long to tame the pallu's natural wildness by tucking the end into her waist or by adding extra pins, or, most expressive of her new position, by weighting it down with a forbidding bunch of household keys.

In this chapter we have tried to show how wearing a sari is entirely different from wearing fitted stitched clothes. The sari is dynamic: unless you pin certain strategic points (and most women do not) it will be constantly on the move. As a result, its role in mediating the relationship between a person's sense of themselves and the outside world is not something that can be taken for granted and forgotten about during the course of the day.[21] Instead, the sari is like a

potential to betray

fellow actor, constantly on stage, whose presence must always be remembered. It can be extremely supportive when attended to, helping accomplish all manner of tasks, practical, social and emotional. But when neglected it can be quick to betray, causing others to judge you harshly for quirks of appearance you did not intend. Such varied and ambivalent experiences with the sari have a far-reaching bearing upon a woman's sense of herself, as an individual, as a woman and, as will be suggested in the final chapter, as an Indian.

tamed pallu

CHAPTER 3

Possession

the trunk as mirror

Most writing on women and clothing takes a single garment as its object of study. But if the aim is to convey an individual's experience of clothing, it would be better to begin with the wardrobe or trunk. In visual representations such as films, women are often portrayed trying on a garment and looking in the mirror. But in truth the most important mirror is the wardrobe itself, for the full range of a woman's clothes projects far more than merely a single image of her. It reflects both the various personae she has been and those she might hope to become. Each sari within an Indian woman's wardrobe evokes the memory of who had given it to her and in whose presence she had worn it, and embodies stories and anecdotes of triumphs and *faux pas*. Thus the wardrobe is an anthology and collection of memories, a multi-faceted, multi-layered mirror which reflects back the full complexity of an individual's identity and history.

In a city apartment, saris are likely to be stored in the all-important steel *almirah* wardrobe.[22] The village equivalent is the steel trunk or box. This is often the first major piece of furniture that a woman invests in. It is where she stores her most precious possessions, to be protected by a hardy exterior from termites and monsoon damp. In village conversations, the expectation is that new saris to fill the wardrobe or trunk will first arrive as gifts presented for either a relative's wedding or some annual festival. These gifts start life as 'best saris', to be worn for special occasions. Then, as other ordinary saris become worn and torn, these 'best saris' are downgraded to replace them, and the hope is that some new occasion will provide the required gift of a new 'best' sari. The trunk or wardrobe cannot however be assumed to come under the control of the individual whose saris are kept within it. The anthropologist Emma Tarlo tells a poignant story of a woman who, on leaving the village of her husband, had to acknowledge that her own clothing remained under the control of her mother-in-law, who carried the key.[23]

the wardrobe as mirror

A wealthy villager such as Meher might have up to twenty saris in her trunk. Predominant among these are handloom cotton saris which, because of their cost and fragility in comparison to mill-spun saris, are saved for special occasions such as festivals and weddings. Being the wife of an important man, she also has a larger than usual collection of gifted saris given to her by beholden relatives and friends. Meher's trunk, kept in her storeroom within a *pukka* (brick-built) wing of the house along with sacks of rice and grain, also has three new mill-produced saris of the kind village women wear on a daily basis. These she had collected over the year, to give away as charity during the festival of Id when poor folk come around asking for them. As a Muslim, she considers it a virtue to give away five or six saris in this manner. Meher also has two new saris for herself. Although purchased with the intention of wearing them during the previous Id, she had not done so. While she believed fervently, as a pious Muslim, that Id prayers required wearing new clothes, she had not been able to bring herself to do so because she was in mourning for the death of her co-wife's son (her husband was polygamous). She had worn a new blouse, but the new sari had lain there as a reminder of the dead boy, whose absence made it impossible to revel in the joy of new clothes.

Memdasi's trunk, on the other hand, was stored on the top of beams inside her tiny mud hut. Precious articles are often stored on a scaffolding of bamboo under the thatch, in order to keep them away from damp and dust and also to keep the floor clear of clutter. When the trunk was carefully lowered and opened (an operation which is now beyond her own strength) it revealed a collection of saris belonging to her daughter-in-law and daughters (who live nearby) as well as herself. There was even a spotless white *dhoti* belonging to her husband which he wore when visiting the temple. The saris in her trunk thus reflected a web of kin relationships and emotions. Each had a story illustrating its special quality: the first

handloom sari her daughter had bought, another given to her when her
first child was born, the 'silk' which Memdasi had bought her daughter-in-law in a fit of indulgence she
could ill afford. While urban cognoscenti pointed out unusual weaves and colours as the special quality
of their saris, Memdasi and her family named saris by the occasions they were linked to, since they were
fairly unremarkable as textiles. Given their poverty, it was the saris' very presence, acquired through hard
work and savings and stored like treasure in a box, that made them exquisite in their eyes.

The desire to hide saris out of sight and pollution is now fairly universal, and enclosed containers are
everywhere replacing open storage such as wooden racks (*alna*) or the use of bed frames and other
furniture. In Noori's house, a dressing table adorned one of the rooms, and this article of furniture was
widely accepted as a sign of her relative prosperity. But rather than the usual cosmetics (which she stored
in a plastic bag under her pillows and experimented with gingerly on lazy afternoons), the small cupboards of the dressing table were crammed with saris of different kinds. The ones from Noori's own
married days were in one, those for her sister's proposed wedding lay in another.

However, even the best of these village collections look small compared to the wonders found in the elaborate wardrobes of middle-class urban women. These may contain hundreds of saris, along with piles of petticoats and blouses. Typically, a woman with two hundred saris may have half that many blouses, including some generic black, white or beige ones that can suit several saris. In contrast, there will be relatively few petticoats, since these are not visible except through very thin saris and so rarely require an exact match. One woman describes her riches thus:

an alna

Fortunately or unfortunately I happen to have a very unwieldy collection of saris. Even there I have not hit a plateau! and the older they get, the more I love them and the more I preserve them. I have never done a count, never. Recently I moved to a farmhouse, and everyone suggested I have a walk-in wardrobe because there is no way that I can fit them into a cupboard of any sort. But instead of cataloguing them, I made separate cabinets for organza, chiffons, *chanderis*; this is the first time I have been a bit organised. Otherwise I used to keep everything in trunks and swap for the seasons. I don't forget any of my saris…it's just that I don't get a chance to wear them all.

Such a wardrobe can provide a much richer and varied portrait of a woman's personality than the villager's trunk. It is a visual 'memory box'[24] of how much she chose to spend, of what happened to her when she wore each garment, of whether she had felt lucky or sexy. The wardrobe also contains a memory of who she once was but now cannot be, perhaps because her job has changed, or simply because she has outgrown a certain colour. These saris may remain as the section of her wardrobe that she cannot wear, but cannot bear to dispense with either. Each sari is granted its own personality, and her bond with the saris reflects in a small way wider relationships with parents, cousins, even pets. In the corner or bottom shelf of many wardrobes lie saris carefully wrapped in muslin, never to be worn. These once belonged to a deceased mother or sister. There are other saris that have been inherited from close relatives or friends, which when draped, have the capacity to envelope one in the love and care that is still associated with those who first wore them. Many women claim to remember the history of every sari they possess.

saris
arranged
by colour

petticoats

best saris

Mediating between the individual woman and her sari lies the internal order of the wardrobe. Most incorporate a basic distinction between a wardrobe for summer or winter, wet or dry seasons. At any given time, for instance, a Delhi-based professional will have either her winter silks or her summer cottons in storage. Both may be found in large steel cupboards, arrayed on hangers either individually or in groups, or resting in folded piles on a shelf or in a suitcase. Most women also have a gradation from daily wear to special or evening wear, though formal occasions may sub-divide into saris for weddings (traditionally silks, but this is changing), concerts or parties, *puja* (Hindu rites) or formal evening gatherings associated with work. While some saris, such as those worn at weddings, may not be suitable for any other event, others can be worn equally well for a *puja* or dinner party.

Sometimes there is an evident aesthetic order to the wardrobe. As the owner of the wardrobe (shown on the facing page) notes: 'I just go according to the colour scheme. So if I have worn a whitish thing today, then I would go for green or whatever. In the mornings I would always wear a light colour sari, I would never wear a dark colour sari in the morning.' Less commonly, there are women who have a religious sensibility concerning the appropriate colour for particular occasions or even days: 'I usually wear saris according to the day of the week. Starting with Monday, I wear white saris because that is Siva's day. Tuesday is red because it is Mahavir's day and his colour is red. Today is Tuesday. I was to wear red but couldn't because I have sent that sari to be dry-cleaned. If I miss like this, I accept it, but I try and avoid getting it wrong. If you do this properly, then the day goes in your favour. Wednesday is blue, Thursday yellow, Friday green and Saturday is black. On Sunday any colour goes.'

Three layers in a villager's trunk:
A. The woman's own saris for special occasions
B. The wedding saris belonging to her two daughters who live nearby
C. Her daughter-in-law's special saris

But rather than following rules of auspiciousness, most women focus on personal aesthetic principles concerning what 'really suits them'. These generally relate to the relationship between the colour of the sari and the shade of her skin. As one woman put it: 'I have been told *ad nauseum* that golden yellow looks nice on me. Almost everyone who gifts me a sari gifts me a golden yellow sari. On the other hand, very sadly, I have come to accept that green doesn't suit me – especially a dark green. Musk green is still OK, but dark green, which I like, doesn't look nice on me at all.' Conversations of this kind tend to be dominated by both general and particular assertions as to what colour suits a particular skin complexion, with a very extensive and explicit discourse about what fair or dark women should or should not wear.

The personal aesthetic also extends to the choice of textiles. Certain professionals such as intellectuals, journalists, social workers and musicians almost always prefer natural fibres over synthetics. In contrast, women in the corporate sector, government office clerks, construction workers or policewomen often prefer synthetics. Such preferences have as much to do with style and ideology as with utility and cost.[25] Others meanwhile have clear views about narrow as against wide borders, or prints against monochromes. A wealthy woman in Kolkata explained: 'Some people like bright colours but I personally prefer a plain body with a narrow border. Other people like *butis* [small embroidered motifs] all over. The people who mostly buy me saris, like my mother or sisters or my husband, they know my taste, so they never give me saris with *butis* for instance.'

personal aesthetic in blue and white 1

Women further personalise their aesthetic by combining their choice of sari with accessories which may include the choice and the cut of the blouse, the style of draping, and the jewellery, hairstyle, *bindi*, and make-up that complement it. The style and cut of blouses are in fact more mutable than the saris themselves, and fashions can change from year to year. Sleeve lengths may change, puff sleeves make an appearance every now and then, embroidery on the back and sleeves in the colours of the sari may be sported, and there is a wide variety in shape of neck lines. Women may wear the same sari over a period of several years, but change its look from time to time by changing the blouse they wear with it.

Women generally discuss their preferences in terms of personal taste, but a market researcher or anthropologist would see many of these preferences as highly predictable given the women's social positions and educational backgrounds.[26] In rural areas in particular, there are many rules that continue to apply to sari wearing. For example, in a village in Madhya Pradesh[27] the women of one sub-caste are distinguished because they wear only printed saris, a variety forbidden to the other sub-caste. There are also many rules that dictate colours, patterns and materials of saris worn for ceremonial occasions such as weddings or prayers. Middle-class women also abide by conventions, however, and may have their own family traditions. For example, the young girls of a family may wear only striped saris, or may have given up bright colours relatively early on.[28]

The numerous levels and themes of discrimination between saris and the meanings ascribed to them can of course create acute problems of selection. The easiest thing in the world is to think of all the reasons why a particular sari would not suit a particular occasion: too thick, too dull, too recently worn, too 'last year', too cheap, too fancy. So while the observer sees abundance and diversity, a sari connoisseur will, just like a middle-class professional in London or New York, think of their wardrobe as the place they stand in front of during long periods of panic and despair, the only certainty being that 'I haven't a thing to wear.' The response of Indian men is equally predictable. As one put it: 'she asks me "what do you think

personal aesthetic in blue and white 2

I should wear?" and I am clueless. I turn to her and say "just pick up something and wear it". But for her it is like "oh I don't want to wear this, this doesn't look good, because this only matches with that", and all kinds of conditions and combinations are tried out.'[29]

What generates such a quantity of saris is often not so much the desire to buy them but the social unacceptability of being seen in the same one twice. For these women, such a thing would never happen in an ideal world.[30] In practice, of course, even owning two hundred saris implies some repetition. The wardrobe thus has to be managed so as to reduce the *perception* of repetition. Even if one wears one's saris two or three times before washing them, they would not be worn on sequential days; there would be a gap of a week or so between appearances. This is the case for work and for daily wear. For a special occasion, where people take more note of the sari, one worn for a dinner engagement would only be suitable thereafter for wearing at a wedding or puja, or to another dinner after several years had elapsed. This premium on unique appearances may also lead to regular swapping and borrowing between sisters, mothers, daughters and friends. The unfitted nature of the sari makes it ideal for this kind of exchange.

An impoverished villager who has only three saris in her trunk cannot see all the envisaged nuances of the self that a middle-class woman finds reflected in three hundred. But it would be quite wrong to assume that the sparse trunk does not function as a mirror for her as well. It was clear from conversations with poor village women that what they see when they look into their trunk is an integral part of their understanding of themselves. The narrow choice they see there reminds them that they are people who have no time or resource for thinking about styles or types of saris. It shows them their poverty, but perhaps also reveals their no-nonsense natures and shows how fully devoted they are to keeping their households going.

village women in working saris

The reflections can be still more bitter, however. The resigned acceptance of poverty is accompanied by a keen sense of respectability. When a woman needs to make a visit to a doctor, or to court to attend to a land dispute, she feels she simply must wear a different and better sari. It is understood by the villagers that even the barest trunk should contain a sari that is marked off from daily use, saved for these occasions when the dignity of all villagers is at stake. This is the very reason one has a trunk, to preserve from the dust and sun those better saris, so that one is never so badly dressed as to give village people a bad name in front of city folk. But when her trunk reveals that the sari she would have liked to preserve for this purpose has long since been sacrificed to daily use, she realises that all her pride and determination and hard work can do nothing to avoid the humiliation of having to make that journey in a torn and patched up workaday garment. This is precisely what makes for the searing hardship of poverty, and the gaps in the trunk reflect it back to her as unflinchingly as the threadbare contents.

village women in 'best' saris

Destitution

It is possible that the majority of women in India do not buy themselves a single sari in a given year and are dependent upon gifts for their clothing. Most live in villages, where gifting is associated with weddings or festivals. The most poignant expression of sari poverty we encountered in a village was Roshnara, a middle-aged Muslim woman. Her husband had abandoned her ten years earlier, leaving her to raise her three children alone. She earned money by doing odd jobs in the households of wealthier relatives. By caste she belonged to the elite, but in fact she was among the poorest people of the village. She reckoned that in twenty years she has never been able to buy a sari for herself. This was evident in her appearance, as she clearly displayed the signs of an ensemble put together by foraging through other people's clothes. She relied on people to give her their cast-offs. Some gave her their saris willingly, saying, 'You are like a sister. I have worn it so far, now you wear it. What is the difference?' Others presented her with a new sari during Muslim festivals as an expression of religious piety. However, as her kin are all among the better off people of the village, having to ask for a sari is humiliating.

Roshnara therefore communicates her need for a new sari by prominently displaying the tear in the sari she continues to wear, or by reminding everyone of her general misfortune. Her hesitation in requesting a sari can create problems. When she complained after the Id festival that she did not receive a new sari, one of her kinswomen retorted: 'Why didn't you say you wanted a new sari? We are

meant to give a new sari in charity during Id. Instead of giving it to an outsider I could have given it to my sister.' This was not meant to be hurtful, but it was so because she lives in constant hope that others will provide for her without taking pity on her – without her having to ask for a sari – acting as a husband would have. On the whole, though, while there are some uncharitable individuals, people around her are usually quick to respond to her needs and she does not have to wait long for a replacement.

But the receipt of a cast-off sari creates further dilemmas. In a village where everyone is constantly in the public eye and under close surveillance, women become associated with their saris, and especially if they only possess two working saris which they have to wear on alternative days for eight months or more until they wear out. So when Roshnara receives a sari from Sabera, she has to go to some lengths to make it her own. As she put it, 'However much I wash it with Surf or anything else, however much soap I use, Sabera's name always remains on it, and people in the village will say she is wearing Sabera's sari. The association always remains. Nuri's sari always remains Nuri's sari. Tell me, does anyone ever like to wear saris that belonged to someone else? Surely not. Somebody may have been ill, another may have been a widow's sari, there may have been mother's milk on one, but I have to wear them all. This is a big burden.'

Asserting her high-caste status, she reminds us: 'A lot of Muslims [meaning those of high caste] will not wear saris bought off the footpath [i.e. second hand] since you never know who has worn it before.

A cobbler's wife might have worn it or a *Dom* [an untouchable caste]. After all it is a sari, it is something you wipe your face with, your hands on. You don't feel like wearing it if a Christian has worn it or a *Dom*. These peddlers who sit on the footpaths go and buy saris from anyone who gives them. Then they go and wash them and iron them and sell them again, so you have no idea where they came from.' This fear of pollution through recycling is perhaps Roshnara's greatest fear. To clothe one's body in a torn sari which belonged to someone she knew is a better option for her than to buy a cheap and intact second-hand one from the anonymity of the market. Hence her reliance on the generosity of her relatives, even though this comes at a considerable cost in loss of pride. She constantly reiterates that, 'I don't ask for a sari, unless they are relatives of some sort, that is of my caste. I would never take it from a *Dom* who also live in the village. I always take from people who are my own. Usually people don't like to give their own things away. But they give it to me out of pity because I don't have a husband.'

Roshnara's case is poignant because she never gets to wear a sari that she has chosen herself. Even when she is gifted a new sari in charity, she is never asked what she would like. Rather, the sari is always the giver's choice. As she explains: 'This buying of a new sari is a very complicated matter because, for instance, Paru gives a sari in *dan* (charity) in the memory of her mother. So what sari she gets me is determined by what sari she would like to get in the memory of her mother. It depends on her will. If I say I want a handloom sari, will she give it to me? She will just say I am greedy. It is entirely dependent upon her will and her desire.' The destitute woman is thus deprived of each of the pleasures which other women can take in their saris. Roshnara's saris are rarely new, never to her taste, never in a colour of her choice, never bought with pride and savings.[31]

From destitution to excess

In stark contrast, several wealthy women told stories that began to follow a particular pattern. In conversations about their wardrobe, they referred back to a time when, almost on a whim, they suddenly gave away most of their saris, including gorgeous saris that had cost a small fortune. For these latter, they looked around for a suitable recipient such as a relative. Less costly saris were simply given away. These stories at first appeared shocking given these women's evident care and attention to sari purchasing and the connoisseurship they had developed. A sari wardrobe is always a visual accumulation of wealth, since an ordinary middle-class woman's cheapest saris would have cost three hundred rupees while the most expensive, those she expects to wear only two or three times to the most important occasions, will have cost many thousands. So it may well have taken perhaps Rs 200,000 ($4,000) to accumulate a fairly conventional professional woman's sari collection. Yet the women involved in these episodic give-aways were referring to collections worth considerably more.

No clear reason was given for these sudden outbursts of 'generosity', and after a while it became clear that these amounted to a kind of 'sari evacuation'. It seemed that for those dedicated to the pleasures of sari purchasing, there reached a point at which their wardrobes were simply too full. The discrepancy between the numbers of saris they possessed and their ability to actually wear them was becoming uncomfortable. So this was not really an act of charity or concern for others, but rather a 'spewing out' of the surplus that had engorged their wardrobes. Once they had completed their purge of saris they were able to return, like Romans to the feasting table, to the habitual pleasure of buying new saris for the now denuded wardrobe.

In most academic works and certainly most journalistic reporting of the relationship between poverty, wealth and possessions, such accounts would be followed by the assumption that sari purging was a sign of gross materiality, showing a concern for objects that was bound to be at the expense of an interest in other people. This materiality is seen as a kind of 'disease' of modern capitalist life, in complete opposition to the experience of destitution. But such assumptions are a projection of the way we ourselves wish to see the world and show a refusal to listen to the voices of those who actually suffer in poverty. Destitute women are in no way less obsessed by materialism than those who purge their sari collections. Nor is there any reason, as we have seen to suggest that impoverished women's concern with clothing is somehow less detrimental to their relationship with others.

We often romanticise poverty as though the people who suffer it were more authentic or sociable than the rich. But what the destitute woman is telling us is that she is forced to be constantly aware of material things such as her sari. She can never rest in a simple state of 'comfort' or identification with what she wears. Rather, she stands in a constant state of alienation from what she possesses and fear as to when and where she will obtain her next sari. Only an increase of wealth could free her from this enforced materialism and allow her to experience a relationship to other people which is no longer influenced by the constant gnawing knowledge of the absent saris that have come between them. Thus the destitute and the compulsive collectors alike can become oppressively absorbed in their sari possession.

CHAPTER 4

The Youthful Sari

CHAPTER 4 | *The Youthful Sari*

One of the most important factors to bear in mind when considering the relationship between the individual woman and her sari, as described in the last two chapters, is that no one in India is brought up wearing a sari. Children do not wear saris. In much of India, young girls wear the very different 'frock', usually knee-length and decorated with frills and buttons. Although it was introduced by British missionaries in the nineteenth century, the frock is no longer considered 'foreign' in the way that jeans or T-shirts are. It survives into adulthood in the form of the 'maxi', a simple long frock that is worn inside the home, (although increasingly it is also being worn as a semi-public garment in some regions such as Kerala).[32] In some areas girls moved directly from wearing a frock to wearing a sari, while in other regions there were special garments for older children such as the *ghagra* or *pavada* (half-sari).

a child's frock

The red frock was bought by the girl's parents. The white shirt with skirt on the right was chosen by the girl herself on an outing to the nearby town, the same day as she had her haircut.
Her friend in the middle has made her peace with having to wear her hair long and covering herself with a salwar kamiz. She is flanked by her married aunts.

maxi

half sari

girls in salwar kamiz in a train compartment

Traditionally, girls wore saris for the first time when being presented as potential brides during marriage negotiations. The move to wearing a sari was thus beset by anxieties and excitement because of its connotations of marriage and sexuality. Several women who had grown up in villages remembered hastily changing out of their borrowed saris the moment the prospective in-laws had left, desperate to savour the last days of childhood freedom. The growing expectation that girls should not be married immediately at puberty has created a new anomalous category of the 'post-pubescent but unmarried' girl. Young women in their mid and late teens (and their school authorities) are instead widely adopting the shalwar kamiz, even in regions where it was not a traditional garment. Often referred to as a 'suit', the shalwar kamiz is a three-piece garment, consisting of tunic (or *kurta*), trousers (*churidar* or *shalwar*)[33] and scarf (*dupatta* or *churni*). The scarf provides an extra layer of covering, which young girls often appreciate as it hides their newly developing breasts. This trend is described in more detail in the final chapter of this book.

The adoption of a distinctive garment for this post-pubescent period has allowed the sari to retain its association with marriage. The link between the sari and sexuality is thereby safely segregated from the sexual development of body. The sari retains a certain exotic appeal for children and teenagers alike, and it is common to see children playing and experimenting with pieces of cloth, draping them around their bodies and heads in a would-be sari way. Sometimes, children are drafted in by elder relatives to help smooth with their hands the puffed up starched pleats in the front of a sari. Our informants also recalled their fascination as they watched their mothers put on their saris:

She would do this in the bedroom. There was a cupboard that had her saris and on one door of the cupboard was a full-length mirror, very ornate, she had got it from her grandmother. And her dressing would happen in front of that cupboard. And my idea of my mother getting ready for some occasion, even for work, is linked to that door on the cupboard. And yes, it involved a lot of wrapping and it involved a lot of measurement. I was amazed by my mother's skill in doing it, to wear the sari. She could look the same in five minutes if she had to, as she would in half an hour.

Middle-class boys talked about the magical change in their mothers as they prepared to go out for an evening, transforming themselves from comfortable, domestic and maternal figures into elegant and glamorous ladies.

This fascination carries over into school, where teachers are expected to wear saris to work. The school system self-consciously presents the teacher *in loco parentis*, and the teacher's sari evokes that of the mother, caring but authoritative.[34] The

child drafted in to smooth starched pleats

majority of teachers regard being immaculately turned out as vital to maintaining the respect of their pupils. One teacher reported that whenever she saw a slovenly colleague who was letting the profession down, she would find some pins or *bindi* in her bag and insist that her colleague use these to change her appearance on the spot!

Retired schoolteachers told us of their relief now that they were no longer subject to the meticulous appraisal of their saris by female pupils. 'They notice everything, from the top of your hair to your toenails', said one with a shudder. By sizing up the teachers, the girls begin to acquire their own tastes. Village girls talked in great detail about their teachers' saris and how they themselves had adopted a certain style of walking or pinning the pallu in imitation. Maidservants recounted how their little daughters returned from school and told them they should learn to match their blouses or *bindis* with their saris, as teachers do. The mothers were embarrassed at these precocious rebukes, but also proud that their daughters were learning not only literacy but how to be fashionable according to urban and educated ways.

Coy adolescent

Although the linkage of the first sari to puberty may have faded, the first wearing has retained its significance as a ceremonial rite of passage. Nowadays in cities this takes place at the special 'school farewell' ceremony, which marks the end of the final school year, for girls aged around seventeen. As in the traditional meeting with prospective in-laws, the school farewell constitutes something of a test for the new sari wearer, at once exciting and nerve-wracking. The girls fumble around, scared stiff of the unfamiliar folds, dangerous-looking pins and sudden extrusions of loose cloth. They are continually worried about the risk of slippage, exposure and shame. One woman remembered that, 'When I started wearing saris I was so nervous of it coming off that I used to wear a belt over it!'

These worries about technicalities are exacerbated by the girls' anxieties over their maturing bodies. One woman recalled how she insisted on taking a taxi to and from her farewell, convinced her breasts were too clearly outlined and belly too exposed to be seen in the street. On the other hand, some found the sari a relief as it covered their legs in a way their frocks had not, a point made by women ranging from a seventy-year-old retired teacher from Cochin to a seventeen-year-old school girl in Kanpur.

And so, without even the luxury of a prior 'dress rehearsal', the girls must appear at their farewell before highly competitive peers, their parents and their teachers. If the girls are worried that any mishap with the garment will result in ridicule and comment from their classmates, they are quite correct: it will. Commenting with candour upon each other's clothes is common among Indian women, and the other girls' disdainful comments will draw inspiration from the long litany of sari critiques that they themselves will have heard from their mothers and aunts at a succession of weddings and social occasions. The girls' ability to tame and inhabit this fearsome flood of fabric will be taken as an indicator of their future ability to perform the social roles that will be expected of them. These anxieties heighten their sense of the farewell as the completion of their childhood and the beginning of their encounter with a wider, less protected world.

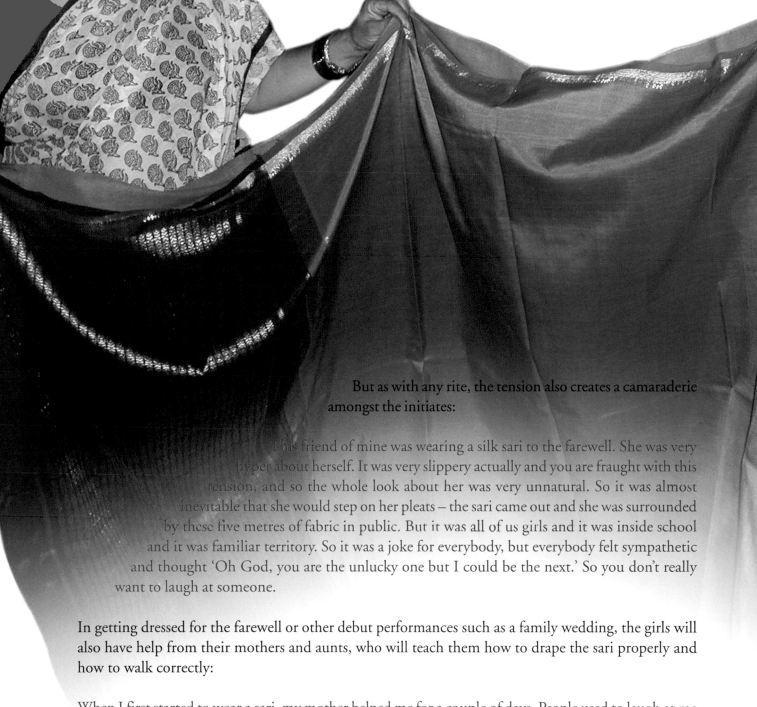

But as with any rite, the tension also creates a camaraderie amongst the initiates:

This friend of mine was wearing a silk sari to the farewell. She was very hyper about herself. It was very slippery actually and you are fraught with this tension, and so the whole look about her was very unnatural. So it was almost inevitable that she would step on her pleats – the sari came out and she was surrounded by these five metres of fabric in public. But it was all of us girls and it was inside school and it was familiar territory. So it was a joke for everybody, but everybody felt sympathetic and thought 'Oh God, you are the unlucky one but I could be the next.' So you don't really want to laugh at someone.

In getting dressed for the farewell or other debut performances such as a family wedding, the girls will also have help from their mothers and aunts, who will teach them how to drape the sari properly and how to walk correctly:

When I first started to wear a sari, my mother helped me for a couple of days. People used to laugh at me and say, 'look at her, she is going to fall down, the way she has worn her sari'. And I did fall down sometimes, because the sari used to get caught in my legs. I couldn't walk properly. The sari used to stick to my legs. So then other women also gave me advice and tips.

pinning sari to blouse to cover midriff

Another woman recalled her own difficulty when her mother seemed to lack the requisite skill and experience:

I did not even know how to wear a sari. I had to call my neighbour to help me put it on when I wanted to. I was living with my parents but I used to say to my mother that she wore her sari like an old woman, she did not know how to put it on for me fashionably. My neighbour was much younger. My mother, when she wears a sari, sort of just wraps it around herself. On her own body she does it OK, with safety pins and all, but not when it came to putting it on for me. The sari used to go all over the place – horrible. I was such a novice. I needed more help and more pins and my mother did not know where to place them strategically. So I used to put in one pin here and there. I used to feel odd in those days wearing a sari, because I used to be in shalwar kamiz most of the time. I felt awkward about showing my midriff. So I would want to use a pin after pulling the fabric up to cover it, but my mother never understood this. My mother always tied her sari above the navel. So did my neighbour, but she knew how to place the border smooth over the waist so it looked good. My mother used to just tuck it in any which way, scrunching it up. When my neighbour put a cotton sari on, she did it properly by making the sari sit properly, pressing it down so that it stayed the way she tied it.

pinning
pleats

Girls who started work as maids mention that their employers sometimes helped them work on their pleating.

As all these stories suggest, the new sari wearer has a very intimate sense of this long and complex garment. She sees herself as engaged in a constant battle to make a five-metre piece of rectangular cloth obedient to her will. At the level of safety and practicality, she must try to avoid the frequent injuries that arise from getting the sari caught in doors, machines or, worst of all, the stove. But to achieve social respectability, she must learn to move, drape, sit, fold, pleat and swirl the sari in an appropriate way. Eventually, such hard-won skills will give her a remarkable flexibility to hide or accentuate those features of her body which she wishes to expose,

pinning pallu to blouse

moderate or if she so desires, cover up completely. But this requires a constant, more or less unconscious responsiveness to the way the sari moves with every gesture that she makes. In striking contrast to most stitched clothing, which once put on in the morning can be largely taken for granted for the rest of the day, the sari forces a continued engagement and conversation with its wearer.

In order to understand the learning curve for an adolescent sari wearer, it is perhaps better to forget for a moment about clothing altogether, and consider instead all that is involved when a teenage girl learns to drive a car. Learning to drive and learning to wear a sari both mark a shift in one's own sense of age; there is a feeling of becoming an adult, with all the new freedoms, capacities, constraints and fears that growing up entails. Both are also very public events, and one's competence – or lack of it – are open for all to scrutinise and criticise. Both have the same involvement of the family, the same pride and fears of the parents, the common assistance of the neighbour, friend or relative who kindly gives the girl extra practice and helps her to hone her skills. Some girls turn out to be 'naturals'. Some, having had the misfortune to fail their test at driving or by tripping over at their school farewell, never achieve real mastery and acquire a new and unwelcome identity as 'poor woman driver/sari wearer' that will burden them for the rest of their lives. Most embark on the new task with difficulty, but through practice over the years gradually come to develop an automatic competence that allows them to proceed without much thought about the mechanics of what they are doing.

taking care while stepping into an auto-rickshaw

Men also have tasks and responsibilities to learn with respect to the sari. Traditionally, the first time a man buys a sari, choosing and paying for it himself, is an important rite in his own passage to adulthood. Many men reported that the very first thing they did when they started to earn money was to buy a sari as a gift for their mother:

At that time I started working part-time. I was in college. I could afford it. My mother was really happy about it. The other occasions I remember buying a sari would be when I got my first salary as a full-time employee. I thought it would be a nice thing to do if I bought some saris for everybody. For all the women in the family. There is my mum, there is her mum and there is my mum's brother's wife. So, three saris.

Men often remark that the sari is a perfect gift, meaning that they feel safe buying a garment that does not require any knowledge of the size or shape of the recipient. Certainly, when compared to Western clothing the sari is genuinely 'one size fits all'. What young men (and older ones too!) often miss, however, are the distinctions of feel and texture which are of considerable concern to women. The young man is also unlikely to be sensitive to the great variety of designs, colours and motifs, or to women's strong opinions about what best suits them.

Not surprisingly, therefore, this first choice of sari may not be entirely successful. In rural Bengal, Memdasi Dom showed us a sari that her son had bought her many years ago with his first wages. He had noticed that she did not own a sari to wear on special occasions, and so as soon as he had sufficient savings he bought her one. He had chosen a white sari with a red border, the iconic sari of motherhood in Bengal. However, his choice of 'modern' nylon material did not go down very well, as it was unbearably hot to wear and its shiny gloss against her wizened skin always invited teasing remarks from other villagers. The sari now lies unworn at the bottom of Memdasi's trunk: she does not wear it, but she could not bear to give it away because of the strong sentiment attached to it. Many elderly women have such a sari hidden away, an enduring proof of their son's love, but also of how much these boys had yet to learn about women.

After this first purchase, gifts of saris to female relatives tend to be associated with particular occasions such as Diwali and New Year. In north India, men also gift saris to their sisters when celebrating the sibling bond during the festival of Rakhi. Gifting to married sisters requires particular tact: the sari chosen must not be so frugal as to offend her, but not so generous as to irk her husband (who might never have given her one so fine). Not surprisingly, as young men become wiser they often take along a sister or friend to help guide them through this minefield.

There is great freedom in India for people to 'advise' their juniors, so a young woman wearing a sari on family occasions such as festivals and weddings will inevitably find an older relative adjusting her sari, a solicitous concern that also unwittingly and embarrassingly draws everyone's attention to her lack of skill with the garment. There is also no end of feedback from sarcastic aunts and cousins. The young woman will be subject to judgements that her sari's pattern makes her look too old, or that its colour makes her look even darker (for fair skin is highly prized) or that the material is too clingy (and so too sexy and immodest). These opinions are voiced through sham compliments and veiled jokes which only wound more deeply:

'Not this beautiful peach for you dear, it will probably be better for your sister, since with her fair skin she could carry it off better. Why don't you try the more dependable maroon?'

'Don't wear checks dear, you don't want people to think you are even older than you already are – they will never approach your parents with a wedding proposal!'

Many women found that such barbed remarks still rang in their ears while they put on their saris. The loud aunt who once noted, 'Piya, darling, why do you tie your sari so high, you might get mistaken for the maid!' still echoes in Piya's ears as she tucks her pleats in twenty years later, carefully checking their length in the mirror.

When the young woman goes to college, where there is a greater variety of social backgrounds, she finds there are many new forms of disparagement. One middle-class woman recalled that there were several groups whose saris occasioned comment. First there were those who tried to parade their family wealth by wearing their mother's expensive silks and jewellery: 'the whole combination was very incongruous in the college set-up and we would go hysterical because it just didn't work.' Then there were those who came from less affluent backgrounds but who were keen to wear their sari in a modern fashionable way: 'we disparaged them as *behenji*, "would-be sophisticates" who were not getting it right, the accessories wrong, the fabric unfashionable, and they pinned their pallus at a clumsy angle on their shoulders where the pin was visible from the front.' A third category were condemned as the 'artsy-fartsy' types: 'Their blouses were really low cut, the low neck and low back but long three-quarter sleeves, so it was an enticing kind of a thing in a sense. But the sari was worn low, below the naval and in a slightly careless fashion, it was never pinned and the *pallu* was always falling off.'

Some of these groups no doubt disparaged their critic in turn for her cheap cotton sari, pretensions or dowdiness. There is an acceptance in these judgements, too, that while different kinds of look are legitimate, they can be realised well or badly. The wealthy look may generally seem vulgar, but a woman who manages it with the right sense of cool and natural possession could actually appear quite glamorous and thus earn grudging respect. The problem with the *behenji* is not so much the cheap price of their garments but their inability to 'wear it right'. The artsy-fartsy look may be admired if carried off with a genuine bohemian conviction.

These judgments are cross-cut by other criteria. For example, irrespective of whether the sari was cheap or expensive, there were considerable differences in the ways in which girls used the sari to expose or cover their bodies. A college girl who wears a long-sleeved blouse which comes low over the midriff, where it meets a petticoat that has been tied above the navel, hopes thereby to look respectable and modest, but she is likely to overhear other girls describing her as a 'nun' (many of whom teach in schools and colleges). Another who comes to college with a blouse cut low at front and back and her navel very much to the fore will certainly attract attention from the boys, but risks being branded 'filmy' by her peers.

nun

filmy

Ideally the critical comments of this Greek chorus of peers, aunts and even complete strangers would gradually assist the new sari wearer's development of a more individualised and accomplished sense of fashion and self-presentation, which she seeks to express through her own purchases and deportment. But earlier, while this self-confidence is still emerging, a young woman will often turn for support to a group of professional advisors that are part of the modern urban landscape. Meet Auntie.

No one can tie a sari the way Auntie can

Auntie is a Punjabi woman with a formidable appearance that precisely matches her personality. She looks what she is, an expert on self-presentation. It is not just that the jewellery, nail polish and sari match, but also that they are large, bold and extremely confident. Her ability to wear striking glossy lipstick that remains unaffected by whatever and however she eats has become elevated by those who work with her to a thing of awe. She runs a successful beauty parlour, which has developed, between the facials and the manicures, a reputation as the place to have your sari tied. As she puts it, 'there are so many beauty parlours and some of them are very good. But I have a reputation for tying saris the best. Everyone agrees that no one can tie a sari the way Auntie can.'

Her daughter-in-law vouches for this. 'I never feel satisfied unless my mother-in-law ties my sari. For my brother's wedding, I was at my mother's house so I got ready there. I went to a local parlour and paid Rs 200 to have my sari tied properly. But I was still not satisfied. When I got to the wedding, I found my mother-in-law and so I took her aside and asked her to retie my sari for me. That is because the way she envisages the sari is also what I am most comfortable with and it suits me as well. She makes recommendations to her clients about the style of draping, for example, *seedha pallu* [pallu over the right shoulder], or in the Bengali style. I don't even know the different styles. But whatever she recommends is up to the mark always and it always suits the wearer. Recently she tied it for me Bengali style. There is currently a serial on TV, set in Bengal, where the characters wear it Bengali style. She tied it for me like that for a party I was going to and I got a lot of envious looks that evening from people wondering how I had tied my sari! She knows each and every style of wearing a sari.'

For Auntie, this skill is also part of her business success. As she tells it: 'People come to me and say "please tie my sari like so and so character in that TV serial". They come to me on their way to a party or a wedding to have their saris tied. I tie it for them just the way it is on the serials. I have been doing this for years.

Every parlour offers this service. Girls come all made up, their hair set and with their sari. I have so many staff, but when it comes to tying a sari it is always me who does it. I didn't really learn this skill anywhere. I have this talent that if I see a picture or a character in a serial, I can reproduce the drape immediately. It is the same for hair styles. However difficult the style, I can reproduce it. When my clients come to me they give me a hint of what they would like, the rest is up to me. They may mention the name of a serial like the Bengali style in *Kasauti*, like a character called Madhulika, and then I tie it like she does.

I decide where the petticoat should be tied, how long the pallu should be. It is different for every person. For instance if someone is very tall, I make her pallu shorter, otherwise a long pallu will make her look even taller. If someone is short then their pallu is longer. If someone is fat I suggest tying a *seedha* pallu. There is a technique to wearing saris. For everyday wear it doesn't matter that much. But for a party, one must wear heeled shoes to show off the sari properly. Your stomach is pushed in when you wear heels. And the petticoat should be tied tight. It should never be loose. Because if the petticoat is loose then the sari is too and then it won't be tight and won't drape the body properly. The petticoat should also be properly tailored and fitted properly, so that the sari fits properly. And it should be tied just below the navel. The girls always agree when I suggest it to them. If you don't tie it below the navel then the stomach sticks out too much and that also changes one's walk. When one ties a sari for someone one has to first decide whether they are fat or thin, then tie it according to that. If someone is thin, then one wants their sari to be slightly spread out around them. If it is winter then the sari should be silk, in summer chiffon or georgette or tissue. One can make the most ordinary sari look beautiful by draping it well.

The other evening I got a call from a girl while I was doing make-up for someone. She said she didn't know how to wear a sari and asked if I could tie it in the Mumtaz style. You know the heroine in the old film called Mumtaz? She wanted it in her style. I had seen this heroine but had never tied a sari like her before. She asked how much it would cost and I said Rs 250. So she showed up in 15 minutes in her car and I left my other jobs and tied her sari in 10 minutes. I did such a fantastic job that even she was ecstatic. Since then I have tied it like that for several other girls. From now on, when very thin girls come to me, I suggest the Mumtaz style to them because the pallu goes around twice in that style. You make fewer pleats too.

The rest of the make-up and hair should go with the sari. The hair-do depends on whether they want to leave their hair open or not. But if they are wearing a light-coloured sari then the make up too should be light. For a party the nail colour should match the sari. But if someone works in an office, it is not practical to have to change the shade everyday. If one wears white mostly, then a light colour, or red. Brown and black don't go very well together. With a green sari, maroon works. Orange with orange, and with a yellow sari a bit of magenta lipstick works very well. There was a fashion for net saris at one point. It works at parties. In fact what comes into fashion is usually reflected in party wear, rather than everyday wear'.

Auntie represents the commercial equivalent of precisely what she calls herself: an 'auntie'. As we have seen, most women tell of an individual who helped them learn to wear a sari, a neighbour, an older sister-in-law, or an auntie. Whether a relative or not, these are older and wiser women to whom one could turn for help. The emergence of the professional Auntie, whom one pays to tie one's sari, reflects the fact that urban residents can no longer assume they will have this traditional figure to hand. They may be living far from relatives, or not getting on well with their neighbours.

But just as important and evident in the way Auntie describes her work, is the increasing uncertainty about the nature of fashion itself, about how one is supposed to look. This involves knowing what is sophisticated or vulgar, which media personality to copy, and how to adapt such a style to oneself. Even if one's mother or auntie is to hand, an anxious young woman may view them as out of touch with current trends. By contrast, the professional Auntie is well aware of the latest styles, and her work and conversations with customers constantly refresh her knowledge.

So the more anxious an individual becomes about how she should look at a party, the more valuable is Auntie's knowledge and, above all, her sheer contagious confidence. Unlike a real auntie, she is unlikely to say anything critical or hurtful, and when she drapes a sari around you, she also wraps you in her overflowing conviction about what looks right for you. In a world where fashion and anxiety are increasingly synonymous, Auntie stands solid as a rock.

Under the gaze of men

A couple of days ago, I was in a small bus, which I prefer, since no one is allowed to stand up. I was sitting on the seats by the driver; he told me to shut the door properly in case I fell out. Then a man sitting next to me insisted on checking the door himself despite my protestations and his arm brushed against my bosom. There was such a crush, and his arm was against my side all the time. I thought initially that there was indeed so little space, he perhaps wasn't conscious of it, and I kept adjusting my sari trying to pull it from all sides. Then it got unbearable and he started speaking really dirty into my ear. I was furious and asked him what he was up to. He played innocent and insisted he did not know what I was making a fuss about. So I told him he would understand once he felt my shoe hitting his face. Initially I thought I did not want to say anything because I did not want to draw the attention of the whole bus. But when it got unbearable I opened my mouth. I told the driver to make him leave. He had been sitting on my right and while I was more covered on that side, I could feel him trying to touch me. It was horrible and I felt so cheap. Then the driver told me to sit

properly in the seat at the back.. But the whole bus was then staring at me. This might have happened to a girl in a shalwar kamiz too, but perhaps he would not have got such a ready opportunity. That day the fault was mine, I hadn't pulled my pallu around my shoulder, and it was still at the back. I had not had time before I sat down. So his hand could touch me more easily.

—Mina

Most city girls could tell of similar experiences. Out in public, where Indian men pursue the national sport of female harassment that goes under the undeservedly graceful name of 'Eve teasing', young women become seen as fair game.[35] As Mina's anecdote demonstrates, the sari exacerbates their vulnerability. Of course, most men have a very different attitude to their own womenfolk: Indian fathers and brothers still exert a close patriarchal control over women's sexuality and appearance, often combining it with a suffocating affection. Tarlo has documented intense arguments over appropriate clothing for young women in villages,[36] and these were replicated in our own observations of fathers whose primary concern was whether their daughter's clothing threatened the family's reputation by hinting at immodesty or wanton behaviour.

These concerns over shame and sexuality partly stem from the sari's capacity for revelation. This is not a simple measure of the amount of flesh exposed, however, but a more specific cultural notion. Underneath their saris most women now wear a blouse and petticoat (a legacy of the British missionaries). So if a European or American man was to see an Indian woman without her sari, he would hardly think it shocking, since he sees a bodice on top, with a full-length skirt tied at the waist. He would see little flesh, save some of the belly. Furthermore, he would see very little additional flesh being covered by the act of putting on a sari, and might assume the sari was largely decorative rather than an addition to modesty. But, even within her own home, an Indian woman would never stand around in the presence of others wearing only a blouse and petticoat, as she would feel thoroughly *naked*.

The crucial covering of nakedness is thus perceived to lie in the layers of the sari itself. The blouse, being a tightly fitted garment which potentially exposes some cleavage, is considered modest only if the pallu passes over and conceals it. The petticoat, though long and opaque, is not considered modest unless covered by the sari's pleats, even if the sari is so sheer as to be transparent. To be decently attired depends on the overall integrity and coherence of the sari. Indian women who are entirely comfortable wearing skirts, shorts or even bikinis, still stand in horror of losing their sari or having its drapes seriously disrupted. The writer Nabanita Dev Sen told us the following illustrative story:

There was once an embarrassing incident. When we were younger, in 1964, we were in Berkeley, California. We had a car and offered to drive our friend Deepak to look at second-hand cars. One such day I was wearing a nylon sari I had just bought. I remember the sari very well, it was a mauve sari with blue flowers. I was driving a station wagon. We got off and he and my husband went off to look at cars. As I stepped out I suddenly noticed that my sari was spilling out of the car and trailing along the ground. My breasts were very nicely covered by the pallu, but the rest was totally not! I was horrified and quickly started pulling it and gradually re-formed it around myself backwards. I was very pleased that I had managed to do this without anyone noticing. When I finished wrapping it, Deepak came back and asked me if I was done. He had, in fact, needed to step on my sari on his way out of the car and walked away so as not to embarrass me. The two men were not looking at cars at all, they were just trying not to look at the six yards of love and loveliness and embarrassment!

As the politely averted eyes attest, the unfortunate Nabanita was regarded as re-duced to partial nakedness and exposed to the public gaze. For the same reason, less well-mannered boys dream of such car-door fiascos, or tread on the ends of saris in the streets. The hazard of such an exposure is fully exploited in Indian popular cinema, where endless sequences tease the audience or the hero with the possibility of the heroine's sari unravelling. In most cases it is merely that the blouse becomes more or less exposed for romantic effect, to the embarrassment of the 'naked' woman. But sometimes – and they are still quite rare occasions, despite the now frequent on-screen kissing and 'dirty dancing' in Indian cinema – the sari may be totally unravelled, to depict either the sexual wantonness of the woman or the serious threat to her of potential rape.[37]

These last two scenarios are, of course, the ultimate nightmares of male relatives, who insist that their daughters and sisters dress as modestly as possible with multiple layers and pleats providing coverage and de-fence. The maturing young woman is torn, however. In pleasing her father, she runs the risk of looking like her mother, or worse still, her teachers; and she wants to be admired by her peers, not least by boys. Young men told us of the dramatic effect sari wearing could have on them at college. They said that when dressed in their day-to-day wear, a shalwar kamiz or trousers, female students were just their friends, the people they studied and played with. But when the same girls turn up in saris they suddenly appear as attractive mature women, with a disorient-ing potential for relationships:

At this point those wet sari scenes in films that you had thought about 'long and hard' and that made your parents uncomfortable watching in your presence, were suddenly brought into perspective with people you actually knew.

Compelled to admire, the boys hide their confusion with jokes about bra cup sizes or offer to send out a photograph of their friend in the sari with a CV so she could get married straight away. Among them-selves later, they would quickly divide the girls and their saris into those who looked dull and modest, and those who looked 'filmy'.

a completely 'naked' Indian woman

The sari's greatest moment (from the male point of view...)

For uncountable numbers of Indian men, there is an abiding image of the sari with a particular shape and hue. The colour is blue, a blue that shifts and shimmers from electric to translucent to ultramarine as the sheer chiffon catches the light. The shape in question is that of a large and almost impossibly perfect breast. It belongs to the actress Sridevi. Since the memory of this breast is now shared with much of the male population of India, it is entirely appropriate that the image in question comes from the film *Mr India*. The same breast with a similar chiffon sari takes an encore in the equally memorable film *Chandni*, helpfully supplemented by a particularly tantalising wet sari sequence.

Most men report that, 'I can't really remember any details of the sari she was wearing at the time'. Actually, there were no details. Unlike the gorgeous and elaborate saris that festoon films actresses and woo the female audience, these breast-wrapping saris of Sridevi and the countless copies that followed were simply featureless flows of monochrome chiffon. They had no borders, no embroidery, no pallu, no design, no butis, nothing except the shifting play of light as they embraced the shape of the breast.

The critical sequence consists of the actress slowly climbing a spiral staircase, filmed from an angle which seems to show the breast coming up the stairs, with the rest of the body merely following in its wake. Sridevi achieved this iconic status because she managed to perfectly express the potential of the sari to cover, caress and outline the body, simultaneously concealing and revealing. As a seamless simple cloth, here reduced to a thin and sheer silken chiffon, it fulfilled what seems to be the ultimate destiny of such chiffon, to surrender itself to the task of accentuating this pure sensual image in a way that the viewer passionately believes no other garment, or indeed no lack of garment, could ever achieve to the same degree.

Of course, such imagery long pre-dates the movies. Even the iconic images of goddesses within celestial settings found in art were 'never emptied of sensuous content. The seeming injunction against nudity did not preclude the desire for the voluptuous, hour glass figures of goddesses. Nor did the transgressions of academic realism deprive these figures of their fullness of contours and curves. Wholly or partially clothed, these divine faces and bodies remained steeped in sexual allure.'[38] The sari was integral to this allure, being the perfect garment to accentuate the classical female form of small waist and full breasts and hips that was celebrated in temple sculpture and then calendar art. The sari's drape draws attention to the acceptable erotic zones of the breasts, waist and hips, even while covering them.[39] Dwyer argues that the eroticism found in much of Bollywood cinema is 'not based on pornographic genital excitement but rather in a totalising sensual experience of lover, mutual pleasure, and desire enacted within a strict code of language and conduct. The sari has a special place within this code of eroticism.'[40]

Goddess Lakshmi

Outside of the movies, many women gradually become more confident and adept at exploiting the sexual potential of the sari for their own purposes and amusement. As one college student said when we asked her whether you can flirt with the sari: 'No problem, sir! Just let it slip! But not too often…' There is much scope for such erotic playfulness around the inherent ambiguity and uncertainty of whether the sari is *actually* covering the woman's body, and this can be far more tantalising than plain exposure. Many saris are made of relatively thin material such as fine cottons and chiffons. While the lower body's petticoat is safely wrapped in several layers of the sari, the blouse may be only partly concealed by a single layer that a man can 'sort of see through', enticingly and exasperatingly, to the flesh underneath.

This playing around with the ideas of coyness and modesty, at once demure and erotic, is reinforced by exposure to films and television which treat the manipulation of the sari as a dominant *leitmotif*. When every film has a dozen songs accompanied in most cases by women playing with these ambiguities, it is hardly surprising that one becomes constantly aware of them in everyday life. In Britain the expression 'navel gazing' is used to describe an act of introspection, but in India it better refers to the devoted appraisal of others!

This ability to play with the sari and exploit its ambiguities is not restricted to the media, or even to women. One of the most common images of such play remains that of the sari as central to the performance of the *hijras* who enliven Indian weddings.[41] *Hijras* are for the most part hermaphrodites, who traditionally have banded together to survive, and they often dress as women in saris. They make their living through music and dancing, especially at weddings and births, where they arrive uninvited but expected. Their entertainment value is accompanied by an element of intimidation, however, for if they are not rewarded adequately they threaten in loud camp terms to raise their saris and reveal their unusual equipage to the assembled guests and so spoil the dignity of the occasion. This leads to elaborate and conventional negotiation and abuse, as uncles and fathers from the wedding party haggle with the *hijras* over the price of continuing modesty. This often amounts to many hundreds of rupees.

A sex worker in Kolkata told of how she was once paid Rs 300 by a famous actor, not for sex but simply to wear a particular white sari with a red border which he brought her, with nothing on underneath. The cotton was very thin, so her body was clearly visible underneath. He then talked to her, and made up a number of fantasy situations in which they went rowing on a lake and visited a temple.

There are striking parallels between the visual imagery created by this woman's client and motifs found in Kalighat painting, a popular genre of art developed among the mass population of nineteenth century Calcutta which satirised the emerging genteel Anglicised elite culture. Courtesans were an important part of these images, and foppish men were 'sometimes depicted as careless husbands deserting their wives, sometimes as sheep taken around by their collar-straps by educated wives or mistresses'.[42] By the later nineteenth century, as Kalighat paintings were reproduced in new coloured prints, the satirical purpose had faded and the women had replaced the fops in centre stage. The women were now 'posed on carpets [or] made to preen before a mirror in a middle-class boudoir',[43] and the images were consumed enthusiastically by bourgeois men. In these portraits, as in the sex worker's client's fantasies, the modest, respectable and iconic image of a woman in a red bordered sari is transformed into something illicit, subversive and tempting.

Sex, the sari and the solution

For a man growing up in an urban middle-class milieu with the usual set of fantasies and expectations, the sari can represent something rather intimidating. An Indian man may become increasingly anxious about how he is going to assist a woman in taking off her sari for the first time, far more so than his European counterpart will be about how to undo a bra. In India he has to deal with all this pleating, all those pins, all the clasps of the blouse – before he even gets to the bra! But as one man found out, perhaps he needn't have spent quite so much time worrying.

'I used to always wonder how the hell women are gonna have sex, you know. If they feel really horny what are they going to do? How are they going to get rid of the sari? And I used to always have these visions of the *Mahabharata* in which we have this character Draupadi, and she just keeps turning around and round. We were seeing this on television around the time when our own fantasies were bearing fruit, and you know the sari never ended. [In this story the Gods protect Draupadi from dishonour by gifting her an endless sari that prevents her being disrobed.[44]] And I looked at them and I said, well you know, if I ever have a wife or somebody I love, what the hell am I going to do with the sari? I see all that paraphernalia and stuff,

---

and think 'By the time I get it off…' Actually there was a point up to which I was constantly thinking this. At that time there was somebody I was seeing and she was wearing a sari and I was really excited, and she was excited as well. We were both pretty excited, you know, and we wanted to make love. I was just looking at her. How do I do this? But this woman had all the answers. She just bent over and picked her sari up. And she didn't have to take any-thing off! She just slipped out of her blouse. All right, the only problem was that she looked like she had a quilt on her middle, but it was accessible, very accessible. People, I think they tend to forget this, you know, because they see all this cloth. You don't have to unwrap it at all, you know. It stays in place. So you don't have to worry – unless she is wearing something that is easily crushed!'

In other anecdotes, sex workers recalled being asked by customers to accompany them to pilgrimage sites out of town. They would insist that she take a dip in the tank before entering the temple, ostensibly for the sake of ritual purity, but really so that they could walk slightly behind a woman in a wet sari. All the sex workers we interviewed recalled being asked to accompany their clients to parties and weddings of distant friends, where the client would usually spend the entire evening making sure that her sari remained in the exact provocative manner in which he had first arranged it. They sometimes asked the women to drape their sari in an unusual style, and once it was on they would make fine adjustments to reveal more, according to their taste. As one of them noted, laughing, 'I don't know if anyone else noticed me, but my client certainly spent the whole evening staring at me.' These are just a few examples of cases where clients used the sex workers to play out fantasies which are otherwise taboo.

The same sex workers also provide evidence that the erotic charge associated with the essential modesty of the sari may be changing. They noted that it used to be unthinkable that they would wear anything but a sari: 'We looked decent, some of us even covered our heads.' This was partly to avoid the notice of the police, especially if they were under age, but it also worked well in attracting clients. Now, however, they had to expose much more of their bodies when touting for business, for instance by revealing their legs or cleavage through their sari. Some were even turning to shorts and miniskirts. They felt this change reflected wider trends in society, where women in general were covering less and the film stars who fuel clients' sexual fantasies were revealing ever more of themselves on screen.

This chapter has been concerned with both sex and shame. The various ways in which the sari may be used to flirt and its deeper association with sexuality is entirely compatible with its portrayal and main-tenance of modesty and its role as a form of veiling. Indeed, the ambiguity of the sari becomes an integral part of its effectiveness. Thus many of the woman's movements achieve their power and nuance as an act of covering up while still betraying a possible hint of desire, or an exposure that is eroticised precisely because it is so subtle and discrete, confirming the allure of modesty. This simultaneity is perhaps most fully expressed in the subject of the next chapter, the bride who must be at the same time both as desirable as possible and as protected as possible.

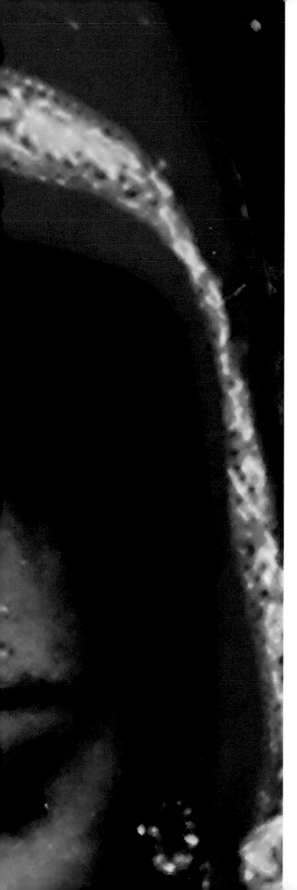

CHAPTER 5

The Married Sari

The Married Sari

My husband's sister gave me a suit and two saris, all cotton, for wearing at home. They knew I didn't have anything, not even my slippers. So on my wedding day I had six saris. Now I have about eighteen or twenty saris for outside wear and several cottons to wear at home. My husband is the youngest in his family, so I received a lot when I went to visit them in Bengal. People came to see his bride and gifted me saris. Before I visited them there, I had the six saris from the wedding and perhaps six more gifted by neighbours...but once I went to Bengal it increased. At that time we were living in a different part of Delhi, my landlord gifted two, as did a cousin. My husband also bought me two saris because he could see I had nothing.

— Mina

Traditionally, Indian marriage is an alliance not so much between two individuals as between two families, and this alliance is marked by a mutual exchange of many gifts. The bride herself is conventionally regarded as the precious climax of these exchanges, but cloth, which is held in great esteem in India more generally,[45] is also a vital part of the exchange. Weddings, then, are engulfed in a cascade of sari giving and receiving.[46]

In the years before the potential wedding, a bridal trousseau will be gathered together by mothers (and, increasingly, by daughters themselves). Urban women, including scientists and other professionals, stressed the importance of this period of sari buying. Typically, these unmarried young women would own between ten and forty saris, most of which they kept unworn at their parents' home. They regarded these saris as the core of their potential 'wardrobe', to be supplemented later by saris received as gifts at their wedding. That wardrobe would accompany them throughout their marriage. This was true even for those women who did not intend to wear saris on a day-to-day basis.

In the weeks before the wedding, saris are bought as gifts for others. In much of India, the parents of the bride and groom are expected to present saris to significant female relatives in both the groom's and the bride's families:

I did the buying over several visits. One for my sister-in-law and three for my sisters. In all I would have bought about fifteen saris, six for the bride and the rest to gift. For the reception I bought her a red South Indian temple sari in red and gold. For her wedding her mother had given her a Benarasi. One was a Baluchari, a Kanjivaram and a Gadwal. I prefer South Indian saris, the silk is superior, traditional handloom

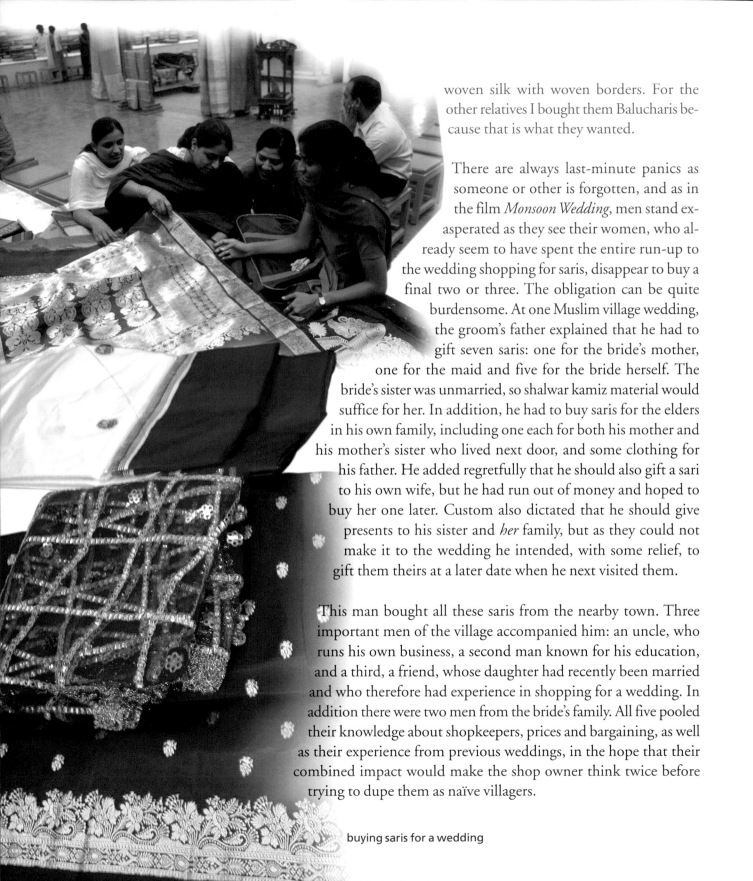

woven silk with woven borders. For the other relatives I bought them Balucharis because that is what they wanted.

There are always last-minute panics as someone or other is forgotten, and as in the film *Monsoon Wedding*, men stand exasperated as they see their women, who already seem to have spent the entire run-up to the wedding shopping for saris, disappear to buy a final two or three. The obligation can be quite burdensome. At one Muslim village wedding, the groom's father explained that he had to gift seven saris: one for the bride's mother, one for the maid and five for the bride herself. The bride's sister was unmarried, so shalwar kamiz material would suffice for her. In addition, he had to buy saris for the elders in his own family, including one each for both his mother and his mother's sister who lived next door, and some clothing for his father. He added regretfully that he should also gift a sari to his own wife, but he had run out of money and hoped to buy her one later. Custom also dictated that he should give presents to his sister and *her* family, but as they could not make it to the wedding he intended, with some relief, to gift them theirs at a later date when he next visited them.

This man bought all these saris from the nearby town. Three important men of the village accompanied him: an uncle, who runs his own business, a second man known for his education, and a third, a friend, whose daughter had recently been married and who therefore had experience in shopping for a wedding. In addition there were two men from the bride's family. All five pooled their knowledge about shopkeepers, prices and bargaining, as well as their experience from previous weddings, in the hope that their combined impact would make the shop owner think twice before trying to dupe them as naïve villagers.

buying saris for a wedding

Since this was the first wedding in the family, they were extravagant with the bride's sari, spending Rs 1,350 on what, all agreed, was a beautiful double-toned textile showing different shades of red in different light. By contrast, the sari purchased for the maidservant was an ordinary printed voile costing Rs 200. Other saris for the bride included various simpler ones for everyday wear. The sari for the actual Islamic ritual was a traditional white, that for the ritual bath an ordinary floral print with a bit of yellow, and there was a red sari for the *sindur* ceremony which cost Rs 350. The sari for the bride's mother was a coveted Tangail handloom in pale yellow. This sari was intended for the traditional exchange between the two mothers at the moment when the daughter finally leaves her parents' home.[47]

Choices have to be made carefully, bearing in mind the status of the giver and recipient, the significance of the ritual at which they are exchanged and, of course, the overall budget. Things frequently go wrong, especially given the touchiness of grooms' families who, in India, conventionally regard themselves as having the higher status. In this case, they had already demanded a dowry of a bicycle, a pair of gold earrings and Rs 24,000 in cash (which they said they had spent on the wedding itself) and a gold necklace worth Rs 2,000.

At the wedding, the predictable happened: the groom's mother did not like the red sari given to her by the bride's family. To make her displeasure clear, she offered her new daughter-in-law the offending sari on the first morning after the wedding, saying, with heavy irony, that *she* might appreciate wearing a light comfortable cotton sari, having spent the previous few days in the heavy silk wedding ones. On the face of it she was generously giving her new sari to her daughter-in-law, whose bridal status suited its redness. But she admitted in private that she gave it away because it was too short in length and because the colour would run, as she suspected the sari had been bought from the village peddler at a cheap price rather than from a shop in town. The next day, she offered to soak the sari before washing it and the colour duly ran as expected. She dried it and packed it into the bride's trunk with the words, 'you might like to give it to your mother'. The real message was, of course, 'how dare your parents present me with such a sub-standard sari'. When we asked if she expected a replacement, she answered haughtily, 'it's up to them, if they do, they do – if not, I don't care.'

In addition to the saris one buys for oneself and as gifts for others, there is a third set of wedding saris, namely those bought for the new bride by relatives and friends, who generally still consider a sari to be the most appropriate wedding gift. In one government office, colleagues present each other with saris if one of them gets married. Often they pool their funds in order to make the gift together. The decision about the type of sari to gift a bride, especially when the relationship is a distant one, is arrived at in various ways. One lady explained her strategy:

We first decide the budget, give or take Rs 50. There are occasions when one has to buy within Rs 500, Rs 200 or Rs 1,500 depending on whose wedding it is. Within the budget, one first decides silk or cotton. Then I have some favourite shops, which I always buy from. I prefer to give cotton rather than synthetic, because I think they are more elegant, especially for Bengalis with their handlooms, and you can buy a good cotton sari with 500. But for a non-Bengali wedding gift, I would rather give a cash gift of Rs 501 [it is always auspicious to give an odd sum]. They don't understand the value of a cotton sari, so I would rather they bought something of their own choice. The colour I decide by age. If it is a young person, then a pretty bright colour. If the bride is someone I don't know very well, say if she is my husband's colleague's daughter, then I try and give according to her lifestyle. For a professional woman, I would give her something other than a Bengali handloom, something easier to maintain.

All this gifting of saris to new brides can be a problem for those urban women who intend to remain in shalwar kamiz after marriage. As the mother-in-law of one such bride put it:

The new bride was given loads and loads of saris, thirty or forty. We had to literally pack them up and give them away to whoever would have them. She told me that she would never need them, so why hang on to them? These were mostly saris that came from people who we don't know. People have this idea associated in their mind, that for a wedding you gift a sari. The close relatives knew that giving a sari would not be appropriate so they didn't. Our new daughter-in-law doesn't wear saris and had expressed her emphatic request not to be given any. It was different when I got married, when I got saris as gifts I was thrilled. But now with these wedding gifts, I have no guilt about giving them away. What am I going to keep them for? Where would I store them? Even though I knew my daughter-in-law wouldn't wear saris, I gifted her some for the wedding. How can you have a wedding without saris? Maybe she has kept those ones and not given them away? She just stuck them in a cupboard and left for Delhi. She only took one token one. But I had felt compelled to buy them because everyone said, how can you not give saris at your son's wedding?

Though weddings are the most extensive occasion for such sari giving, smaller flows of gifts will continue throughout the couples' later life, along with the accompanying tensions and room for error, as

Mina recounts:

For Durga Puja[48] I get saris from everyone, including all the sisters-in-law. Because I am the youngest I have to give less than I get. I have to buy one for my mother-in-law because she is a widow, and one for my sister-in-law or a dress for her daughter. On Diwali, my son's birthday, or my birthday, my mother gives me a sari. I also had a 'shaad' ceremony during my pregnancy, held in the fourth month, to bless the health of mother and baby, but my sister-in-law wasn't here so I didn't get any saris then. We have a similar custom in Kerala too and then my mother gave me a sari and lots of bangles as is the custom. In Bengal we also give gifts when we go to visit.

If I receive saris which I don't like then I gift those to people in my natal home. Like the ones I got from Bengal, one was pitch yellow with a zari border. I gave that to a cousin who is fair-complexioned. Yellow doesn't suit me because I am dark-skinned. Two others my sister took and had shalwar kamiz made out of them. They were from my mother-in-law's relatives in Bengal. But I can never give away the ones my sister-in-law gives me, because she sometimes insists that I wear one particular sari she has given me. If I want to convey my taste in saris I do it through my niece. Before any occasions I tell my niece which saris I like. She is the only daughter in the family so she always goes along on shopping trips. I know she understands why I am saying this and she tries to make sure that they buy what I want – though this has only really worked on two occasions so far...

The wedding, its prelude and aftermath, can be a very stressful and emotional time for the families involved, not least because it can involve, and challenge, many of their assumptions and beliefs about life. A son's parents who have long professed liberalism and support of women's rights suddenly have to decide whether they will in practice forgo the personal benefits of demanding a dowry. Or, they may have accepted a lower-caste bride, or a very well-educated one, but how now will they actually deal with her? Any discrepancy in their views may be obscured during the period of the wedding, but can emerge destructively thereafter. The most dramatic and tragic example of this is 'dowry deaths', where disappointment and anger at the actual value of the dowry which arrives with the bride leads the groom's family to murder her, typically by burning.

Such tensions can simmer away at a lower intensity, and bring other changes to the young bride's life. In most of India outside the urban middle class, the new bride moves into the groom's parents' home, where she is expected to submit to the dominating influence of her mother-in-law (and sisters-in-law). In the increasingly frequent marriages across communities or regions, castes or socio-economic levels, this may well entail quite different expectations concerning suitable dress and behaviour. Many young women, when asked whether and how they would wear saris once married, replied with something along the lines of, 'I will just have to wait and see what his family expect of me.' Mina was a case in point:

My sister-in-law insists. Where we live there are lots of other Bengalis. So perhaps my sister-in-law did not want the others to say that the new bride wore suits because she is from a different caste or community. The rules may have been more relaxed if I was Bengali. So I agreed because I thought – what the hell, one has to adjust in any new household. In any case I had a craze for saris then, I was newly married. Now I have got used to wearing saris so much that even if someone gave me a suit, I wouldn't like to wear it, I would feel odd. These days when I am at home I wear my cotton saris.

Whenever I go out with my sister-in-law somewhere I am always nervous about doing something wrong. I can cook anything, but don't ask me to serve. There are so many little rules about what should be where on the plate and how exactly one should cook things. So when I go out with her I try and wear one of my lucky saris so I don't get into trouble with her. There is always some problem or other. If I am going out with her, I try and wear something that makes me look like a good Bengali bride, like the lemon yellow sari, a patchwork sari, a sky blue.

Here, as in Chapter 1, Mina has to adapt to the different expectations of a different community in a different region. Indeed, as her comments make clear, she was expected to be even more orthodox in her dress to make up for the fact that she was not Bengali. What makes this especially complicated for her is that there is clearly no real consensus among her in-laws as to what is expected. Her mother-in-law and husband's younger sister are relaxed on the subject of the sari and sympathetic to her youth. But her husband's older brother's wife is not, and since in the absence of the mother-in-law she is the senior woman in the household, she has the decisive say.

serving the in-laws

As Tarlo's village study similarly shows, even without such inter-regional distinctions the new bride often faces the extremely difficult task of learning to wear saris in new ways, while at the same time being expected to be both at her peak of beauty and attractiveness and the epitome of modesty and control.[49] Within most rural areas, the possibility of not wearing saris remains largely hypothetical, and it is still only a very small urban elite that would allow a daughter-in-law to avoid saris altogether after marriage. As a result many urban women, often used to wearing shalwar kamiz day-to-day, have to carefully plot their wardrobe when making visits around India (there is a broad pattern in which saris are worn least commonly in Mumbai and most commonly in Kolkata, with Delhi and Chennai in between), so as to match the specific expectations of each relative or friend.

Where it is taken for granted that a sari will be worn, the new bride will still find that the *way* she wears it is under close scrutiny. Bindu, an attendant in a hospital, remembered the first time she had covered her head with her pallu as a new bride. The pallu was so long and was pulled so low over her face that she could barely see her feet. If her aunts and cousins hadn't been holding her, she would have fallen down several times. She had to keep her head covered all the time in the village, when cooking, working in the fields or collecting firewood. Even when she thought she was alone, she never really was; there was always someone who would report back to her mother-in-law. She was sometimes a bit careless, hitching up her sari to wash clothes at the tubewell in the courtyard and then forgetting to lower it again before stepping into the room where the elders were sitting; or she would tuck it high into her waist when working in the fields but forget to leave the petticoat hanging underneath to hide her legs. Unless she was careful, there would be scoldings every day.

Style can also be used as a sign of independence and resistance to such pressures. In many rural areas, pinning a sari is seen as rather a 'modern' and urban thing to do. In a village household, one of the young daughters-in-law had her studies at school interrupted against her wishes when her parents married her off. She determinedly and conspicuously continued to wear her saris in the pleated Nivi style even after marriage, although the other village women, particularly older ones, considered such pleating as 'dressing up'. They felt too shy to wear such a style for everyday wear, reserving it for when they ventured outside the village. They claimed the traditional drape was better suited to housework ('the pleats get between your legs' or 'the pallu needs to be tucked in'). But the young woman insisted that she had no trouble at all doing her household chores in the Nivi style, and added that her teachers at school had told her that this was the way to wear a sari. In this way she asserted her distance from the illiterate previous generation and established her own modernity. The other villagers, however, saw her careful pleats as a sign that she had got above herself: 'look at her, sitting like a queen with her pleats and pins, not willing to help with the housework at all'.[50]

The new bride may also encounter new and unfamiliar religious or symbolic ideas, which influence the execution of her domestic tasks. As Mina noted:

> I always change my sari when I get home; my sister-in-law will throw me out of the kitchen and the house if I don't change my sari before starting my household jobs. They also have this other curious custom, I don't know if other Bengali families have this, but every time you go to the toilet you have to change all the clothes you were wearing.

In many areas and for many castes, the prospect of the hanging drapes of the sari touching food or plates, or dirt or latrines, gives rise to fears of pollution. Consequently, once one has eaten a meal or been to the bathroom while wearing a particular sari, one has to change into a fresh one before cooking the next meal.[51]

Time and experience may ease the wife's practical difficulties and increase her domestic authority. But in many households, she will long remain subject to a level of formality and an expectation of modesty that prevents her feeling truly comfortable at home. This is not always due to pressures imposed by relatives; instead, her own internal sense of decorum and what represents inappropriate behavior will put pressure on her. An account by an elderly woman from Puri, talking about her daily regime, shows how such internal sensitivities about shame and self-presentation are common to women of all ages:

I wake up every morning at six and get into my sari. I wear saris during the day and morning when I am cooking. I have a different sari for cooking because it gets turmeric stains. I have four saris for cooking. I have two on the go, wear them for a week then send them off to the laundry and use the other two in the meanwhile. These get washed by the *dhobi*. He can get rid of turmeric stains. The maid washes them daily. Early in the morning the sweeper comes to clean the bathrooms. Then the newspaper man comes, then the maid. I can't wear anything but a sari in front of them! But after they have left I take off the sari and do all my jobs in my blouse and petticoat. I wear my shalwar kamiz when I go out in the evening to shop for my vegetables and fish. I have a young man who helps me. When I get back from that, I have a wash and then change into my blouse and petticoat and housecoat, which I wear at home in the evening.

This woman was brought up wearing only saris, and worked in a government job where they were compulsory. It was only after 1993, when her daughter married and moved away to Mumbai, that she was persuaded to try a shalwar kamiz on her visits there. At first she was uncomfortable, but then found the garments were actually quite easy to move around in. So she has partially adopted shalwar kamiz, wearing it when she goes out shopping in the evening. This makes it easier to walk among the potholes, and she does not mind being seen in one amid the anonymity of the market and the fading light of dusk. But saris remain required in front of tradesmen, and only when she is totally alone does she allow herself the informality of a blouse and petticoat with a housecoat over them, the psychological equivalent to a Western woman walking around her flat in only a T-shirt.

The perils of patriarchy

Strictures regarding Hindu women's clothing – often created by men – have been around for a long time.[52] Examples of texts discussing the cosmological rules governing an individual's life, including their dress, are found in the *Gautamadharmasutra*, composed between 600 and 400 BC. One eighteenth-century text, the *Stridharmapaddhati* (Guide to the Religious Status and Duties of Women), contained detailed rules ranging from prescriptions to cover the upper body during the day to a prohibition on wearing heavy earrings during love-making. The historian Julia Leslie argues that the guide is meant to both censure what women commonly wore and provide a utopian ideal of the Hindu woman.[53] The rules presuppose that a woman's appearance is a symbol of her relationship with her husband and of her duties as wife and mother. The guide portrays the woman's very existence as justified only by her relationship with her husband, who is her lord and master. Women are thus warned that transgression of the rules will result in the loss of a child or, worst of all, in widowhood.

These texts demonstrate the presence of an ideal based upon a close societal control over women and their sexuality. In an average Hindu household in contemporary India, many more rules are enforced for daughters and married women than are applied to men. And men continue to take women's clothing and self-presentation as the critical signifiers of their inner virtue. For example, one woman explained rules about modesty and covering by saying: 'we must be well covered because after all, God has created this body to be seen only by one man'. However, such guides are evidence of the development of formal codes rather than an indication of how people actually acted. To the extent that they were ever followed, the women's movement in modern India has campaigned vigorously to reveal the hypocrisies of patriarchal traditions within all of India's religions. Feminist periodicals like *Manushi* have provided an active forum for debate and discussion about issues of clothing and behaviour, and women from many different social backgrounds take part in these. Yet it is striking that the robust women's movement in India has rarely treated the sari itself as a garment of patriarchal oppression; it was never assumed that the sari was intrinsically conservative, and its potential for being part of emancipation was understood.

While such ideas embody patriarchal influence and power, on a day-to-day basis most of these rules are enforced by women upon other women. Women's stories reveal many quarrels over appropriate and inappropriate dress, with mutual accusations between mothers and daughters-in-law of being old-fashioned or immoral. Such arguments may not at first glance reflect well on the women concerned. But as the anthropologist Patricia Jeffery showed in her book *Frogs in a Well*,[54] much of the atmosphere of such competition and disdain reflects women's internalisation of the tensions and rivalries which male heads of family pursue among themselves, for instance through disputes over dowry and bride price. The men do not acknowledge this, however, remaining aloof from what they view as the trivial squabbles over dress among their womenfolk, and blaming women for being divisive. Meanwhile, women complain again and again that their men very rarely comment positively upon the appearance of their saris or notice the effort or concern that has gone into it. When they do notice the sari, it is too often the father's wrath at perceived immodesty, or a male's frankly predatory gaze.

CHAPTER 6

The Working Sari

Lecturer :   Respectable saris, the smell of chalk...
Receptionist : A one-inch wide smile, perfumed sari held with a pin...
Artist :   Handspun saris in ethnic colours, quantities of kohl...

(a young woman assesses her future career options in a short story by Mrinal Pande)[55]

working women: farmers at a conference, flower sellers, musician, village woman carrying fodder, construction worker, vendor

As we saw in the previous chapter, it may take years for a woman to learn and fully conform to the expectations of her in-laws and the wider demands concerning her new role as wife and mother. However, growing numbers of urban women are also working outside the home (rural women have, of course, long been working in the fields), and this can require a different approach to dress and appearance. Here, profession and career are often more important influences than age, religion or caste. This other 'look' may in turn upset mothers-in-law or husbands, and so part of the dilemma of being a working woman in India is juggling the expectations of the workplace with the sensibilities of those at home.

Satyajit Ray's 1963 film *Mahanagar* (The Big City) brilliantly captures the tensions of this transition. In Calcutta, a bank manager loses his job and his wife Lila, hitherto a housewife and mother, finds work as a sales representative for a firm selling mechanical knitting machines. She finds to her surprise that she has an aptitude for business and is soon promoted to be supervisor of the other sales girls. Her husband and parents-in-laws watch her metamorphosis with growing bemusement and anxiety. She starts to drape her sari in the modern and fashionable Nivi style, rather than the more homely and traditional Bengali one. She starts to carry a handbag, dons sunglasses before stepping into the sun and experiments with lipstick. Her conversations are no longer about the details of domestic life but concern her boss's likes and dislikes, her colleagues and their chatter, and her encounters with strangers as she sells door to door. Lila, like millions of Indian women over recent decades, had to learn to dress differently; but as the film shows, this transformation was part of a more fundamental change during which she became more self-assured and confident in dealing with men inside and outside of the family, and with life in the big city more generally.

For me the main thing about work saris is whether I am comfortable in the bus. I live very far away. The long commute, running for the bus, etc. should all be comfortable. I used to have this thing that I should wear my sari low so that the feet don't show. The neighbour who taught me to wear a sari had taught me this. She always said put on your sandals before you wear a sari, feet showing doesn't look good, it looks awkward. So to look good I wear it low. But since I have started commuting, I have started to wear it higher to be able to run for the bus easily.

It is a pain to wear cotton saris first thing in the morning, you need an extra person to make the sari sit properly. I have to report to work by 8.00, so I have to leave by 6.45. I just prefer to wear synthetics. But it is a fact that a good cotton looks beautiful. If I wore a cotton to work then I would either take an auto-rickshaw, or ask my husband to drop me, or take only a direct bus. Cotton saris look very good but once you sit down the whole thing gets crushed. So for work I prefer a sari that will look and stay the same way all day regardless of what I do and the commute by bus. Delhi is too horrible. Before I started this job I always wore only cottons. But it is commuting in buses that has made me wear chiffons. Earlier I did not even own any and if I wore them, it was only if I felt like it, but now I wear nothing else.

— Mina

In the big Indian cities, public transport is usually extremely crowded and frenetic, and journeys can last well over an hour. As Mina's comments indicate, the mere fact of having to commute influences her choice of fabric and the way she wears it. As another woman commented wryly: 'The day I wear a sari I become the most generous person on the bus, offering an empty seat to someone else, because you see, I prefer to stand in the bus to avoid getting creases in my ironed sari!' Cotton also needs to be starched with rice water and

ironed, tasks which the hard-pressed woman chasing the early morning bus can well do without. Synthetics do not require this however, they dry overnight and do not require ironing. For women of modest means, another critical advantage of synthetic saris is that they last longer than cotton ones, which, if worn and washed every day, wear out quickly.

Most people wearing stitched garments, as in the West, focus upon design, shape and fitting. The precise fabric is usually of less significance, and rarely defines the essence of the garment (exceptions, such as the fur coat, rather prove the general rule). Similarly, for the stitched shalwar kamiz, the design or decoration usually attracts more immediate interest than the fabric. As noted in Chapter 1 however, the sensual nature of the sari and its presence as a 'second skin' means that for the women who wear it, the sari is as much a textile and texture as it is a finished garment. Thus a sari is constantly referred to as 'a cotton', 'a silk' or 'a synthetic' (or 'chiffon'), each with different implications for the way it feels and is worn.

Such comparisons and preferences are a frequent topic of conversation between working women:

'I prefer silk, it feels softer. Silk is better because it moulds the body better.'

'I prefer cotton because it sticks to the body better, I feel very hot in silk and it feels rough.'

'I don't like wearing nylon saris at home, they are very uncomfortable and dangerous. But to go on the bus, I wear it.'

'If you get wet, a cotton sari clings to you and it looks crushed. Silk is very uncomfortable in humid conditions. So the best thing to wear are synthetic saris.'

'You can't cover your head properly in synthetic saris. They constantly slip off.'

'A rough and tumble life is no good for silk chiffons. It is a very demanding kind of fabric. It has got to be worn very flowingly. You can't have a kitchen-duster-over-your-shoulder attitude with a chiffon pallu. A lot of women end up doing that when they wear synthetic saris. But chiffons take a personal touch and skill. Also, during the monsoons chiffons can be obscene.'

Such assessments blend notions of comfort and function with social and aesthetic ideals, and incorporate a sensual engagement with the sari. There is the ostentation of a shiny chiffon versus the quiet elegance of a handloom cotton; the static the former creates and the way it rubs the skin, softly or coarsely; the way a synthetic sari smells or the pleats of a silk sari rustle. Finally it is worth noting that these conversations about the relative merits of various sari textiles are often only loosely related to the actual composition of the saris, concerning which there is increasing confusion. For example, a high percentage of what are called 'silks', may be at least partially synthetic, while the term 'chiffon' may refer to silk or synthetic, depending on the knowledge and taste of the speaker.

working saris (left to right): synthetic, cotton, silk

Banno thought to herself that perhaps it was time she swapped some of her saris around. The ones in the cupboard at work had been there for nearly two years. But they were just right: light, old and comfortable, and perfect to work in. She didn't really want to wear them at home anyway. Those were 'work' saris, for cleaning toilets and sweeping paths. They were polluted by sprays from cleaning the sinks and floors, and stained from the red dust of the pathways around the Centre's buildings. They were clean, of course, washed at the end of every week when she brought them home. But she couldn't bring herself to play with her grandchildren or cook a meal while wearing one of those saris. It was unthinkable. Soap could clean the dirt, but it could never remove the association of the work she did in those saris and who she was when she wore them. At the Centre she was the faithful old sweeper whom people barely noticed, covered as she was almost entirely by her sari. She minded her own business, made a modest attempt at keeping the place clean and spoke when she was spoken to. At

home she was the proud widow who had managed to own a room despite all hardships, a grandmother of three, living with a difficult but well-meaning son and affectionate daughter-in-law.

To be that person, Banno felt she had to change into one of her two 'home' saris when she returned from work. Her grandmother had taught her about germs, and said it was unhygienic to stay in clothes which have been worn in public because bus seats, pillars and handles all carry the germs of thousands of people who touched them. It was the women of the house who fed and looked after others, and everyone's health was in their hands. For all these reasons, it was important to change saris.

Banno decided she would continue her present system of sari-changing, which worked well. The outdoor bathroom at the Centre was perfect. In the morning she could use it to change out of her 'bus' sari into her 'work' one, and then again at the end of the day back into her 'bus' sari – of course,

from the back and over her right shoulder, so that she could pull both sides of the sari shut if she wanted to close herself in. Banno really needed to do this, especially for the long two-hour bus ride to work. Travelling with all those strangers, one never knew where their eyes were going, especially those young men hiding behind their sunglasses. Banno knew that ever since she had started carrying a small handbag and making the pleats in her sari carefully, people at the bus stop treated her with more respect. Perhaps it was her age, but Banno wasn't sure. Other women, especially the labourers with their crumpled saris hitched high and their pallus tied like ropes around their waist, never got a seat on the bus. Banno was sure that her neat appearance, white saris and glasses gave her some quality which made the young men call her 'amma' and help her off the bus, rather than shrink away as they normally did from other sweepers and poor and low-caste women.

only after a proper bath. The bathroom was too wet and cramped to put on her fresh sari properly, so Banno did this in front of her cupboard. A long time ago the Director, a lovely old man who had now retired, had agreed she could have a cupboard in the corridor at the back of the building to keep her saris and towels. Over the years the cupboard had become hers, and by opening both its doors Banno could make a little room around her to re-tie her sari in with complete privacy. Not that she needed to, of course! Everyone knew her regime and stayed away from the area around the cupboard during her bath and going-home time. Now, Banno even kept some good saris there in case there was a special function in the Centre, so that she could change into one after finishing her cleaning work. Not that anyone came to meet her of course, but still Banno felt loyal to the place and thought it would make a nice impression if visitors could see that even the sweepers were well-dressed here.

Banno loved to wear her sari as her mother used to. The pallu draped around

Pollution in the home and the world

A particularly important aspect of many working women's lives is the way they must maintain separation between the saris they wear at work and those they wear in the home. This is usually less a matter of fashion than one of hygiene and ritual purity. The strict regime which Banno the sweeper maintains, changing her sari up to five times a day, may seem excessive, but reflects the profoundly important distinction between pure and impure in Hindu cosmology. Dirt is not just dirt, but at a simple level, pollution is heightened by the presence of bodily fluids such as saliva, semen or blood. In the occupational hierarchy, castes are ranked according to the contact each occupation has with these substances. Thus according to these cosmological principles, a Brahmin is placed at the top because the nature of his work – priestly duties and learning – brings him into contact only with sacred objects. At the bottom end are washermen, sweepers and tanners because their work involves handling bodily fluids.[56]

The advantage of urban life for a woman like Banno lies precisely in the anonymity which it brings and the control she can exercise in manipulating her appearance in order not to betray her low-caste identity and role. As her identity at work is that of an old sweeper woman, she is less concerned about looking presentable and so changes into her old saris once she arrives at work. But she feels she has to change out of her work sari into her bus sari before and after work because she does not want to be instantly classified as a lower-caste woman in the crowds of a public bus. When she arrives at home however, she shares with all Indians the notion of the outside as being more polluted than the inside, and therefore she changes once again, taking off her bus sari and putting on her home sari.[57]

Sex workers also followed rules about pollution. They preferred not to be wearing their sari when having sex, but clients often insisted that they did, and thus the sari became polluted. To respect the sanctity of the home, the sex workers kept their work and home saris separate:

We had to explain that we may be in this trade, but we too have gods and goddesses, we too have children and households, and so we cannot go straight from being with a client and then touch the domestic shrine or light the evening lamp or nurse our baby or touch food. But some customers are so insistent on having sex while we are still wearing our saris that they offer extra money to have it cleaned, however expensive that might be.

It is also for reasons of pollution that press wallahs often refuse to re-iron starched cotton saris after they have been crushed from a single wearing and have not been laundered again. Their fastidiousness, however, will tend to depend upon who has been wearing the sari. In practice, a respectable middle-class woman can often prevail upon him to press an unwashed sari. But he would not do this for lower-caste women and certainly not for sex workers; instead, he would insist that they wash their saris before bringing them for ironing. The press wallah justifies this by saying, 'this iron is my Lakshmi [i.e. it is sacred]', and indicating that he is unwilling to pollute his iron by bringing it into contact with a sari which is likely to contain polluting substances. However lowly his profession may be in the caste pecking order, he still seeks to assert his superiority over those beneath him.

The capacity of the sari to absorb pollution is addressed in various ways in the domestic sphere too. Mina was required by her Bengali in-laws to change out of her sari if she had worn it in the toilet. Similarly, village women have to change out of the sari they have worn while eating before cooking again, in order to avoid polluting the hearth.

washing and drying saris on the ghats of Benares

Uniform saris

While conformity with the rules associated with cosmology and pollution may be one way of policing the sari, these rules work at an invisible level. To an observer, all of Banno's saris may look identical: only she knows whether her sari is polluted from work, the bus journey or because of her sleeping in it. By contrast, other spheres of work impose a more visible uniformity through the wearing of uniforms. Unlike the rules of cosmology, which are internalised as moral concerns, uniforms are usually imposed by an external authority. In either case, rules both invisible and visible have implications for daily management. What you are seen to wear, and what you yourself know about what you are wearing, are equally important.[58]

hotel receptionist

The most extreme example of control over the visibility of the sari comes in those sectors of employment that require 'uniform-saris'. Worn by airline crew, hotel staff, nurses and policewomen all over India, these saris are regimented and disciplined. Like any uniform, they are intended to remove the scope for individual expression or will.[59]

the distinctive uniform-saris of the 'Sisters of Charity' founded by Mother Teresa

uniform-saris of a caste association at a picnic on Juhu beach, Mumbai

At gate no. 2 on the southern exit of the government buildings complex in Pune, two women are at work among their colleagues. In the late afternoon sun, their khaki uniforms look golden, firmly in place, the strains of a day's work invisible except for a few stray hairs which have escaped from their neat chignons. Among the phalanx of police forces who look over the visitors leaving the building at this time of day, Seema and Lata stand out because they are the only women. Though Seema is dressed in trousers just like her male colleagues, the presence of Lata in her sari changes everything. Rather than the nondescript appearance of their colleagues, these two women are conspicuous despite the dullness of their khaki. Lata and Seema are best friends, which is why they are often put on duty together. Its good for their morale during the long hours of standing around, chairs having been sacrificed to create an aura of ever-ready alertness.

Seema is thin, with fine features and pretty eyes, and has continued to wear trousers since training college. Her friend Lata is taller, fuller in figure, and has a thick chignon at the nape of her neck. She can't bring herself to wear anything but a sari. But she hates the standard issue thick cottons which have to be starched and ironed each time of wearing, making them expensive and time-consuming to maintain. Besides, one has to wear these uniforms according to the precise rules taught during training: five pleats, pallu the length of an arm passed through the shoulder epaulets, and three pins, one at the shoulder, one underneath the left breast and one to keep the pleats together. Controlling those thick cotton saris was hell. They crushed the moment you went to the loo, and they shrank after their first wash. So Lata started to wear khaki-coloured polyester saris instead. At least these stayed the same all day and felt softer to touch... No one has objected so far. In any case she has paid for them herself, all Rs 450 of the cost. By washing the saris herself and drying them by stretching them out on the clothesline, she could recover the cost within two months through the saving on her laundry bills. The saris she wore now had been bought nearly a year ago and still looked pristine.

Seema was always after her to at least have one pair of trousers made because she insisted Lata would also look good in trousers. She insisted that one could run better in trousers. But Lata was happy to pass up that pleasure and in any case, the men did the running after illicit visitors! Seema looked good in trousers because she was thin and her hair was shorter. With Lata's big hips and small waist, she felt she looked her best when they were covered by the elegant layers of the sari. It wasn't that she was fat, it was just that her figure was better suited to the sari. It was the older policewomen, who had had their babies, who used the sari to cover their bulges. Lata knew from the looks she got on the train that she looked really good in her uniform, unlike her older colleagues.

There had been much opposition in the family the day an excited Seema and her father had come over to tell her the good news of their acceptance into the Police Training College. No one in her family thought it was at all the right career for a beautiful young woman and Lata knew her mother was worried about whether any man would ever marry her policewoman daughter. Now that she was back living at home, she could at least dress according to her parents' taste, and more importantly meet the approval of the neighbours. They probably even secretly admired the fact that her blouse was long with sleeves below her elbows, rather than the skimpy sleeveless blouses worn by film stars and copied by young girls. As policewomen, they were constantly told that they needed to stand out in a public place and their appearance should evince respect and admiration. The uniform-sari was a good compromise. Wearing her uniform-sari did not at all feel like wearing an ordinary sari; it felt much more regimented and at one with the uniforms of her colleagues.

Seema thought wearing a sari was a bit silly. Having finally made it into the police, why would you want to dress like ordinary women? The training had been hard, having to rise at dawn and those endless changes of uniform in the course of each day. Why couldn't they just stay in their trousers? Instead they had to first wear a T-shirt and track bottoms for PT, then change into khaki trousers before parade, then into saris after breakfast. At lunchtime it was back to the more casual PT dress, which of course they could not wear if they had a law class in the afternoon, for those they had to remain in the sari. Perhaps adopting the shalwar kamiz for everything might have solved the problem, but it wasn't yet officially allowed as uniform in Maharashtra. Seema was glad about that. Unlike her mother and aunts, she wasn't shy to go out in trousers, just as she wasn't shy to be a policewoman. One felt so smart and proud on Monday morning when everyone could see the hard work you had put in over the weekend: those bright shining buckles and shoes offset with the jaunty angle of the beret. The sari wearers missed out on all these pleasures.

She wished Lata would see her point of view. Lata was not even allowed to salute in a sari, as that was reserved for those who wore a beret with trousers. But Seema also knew that Lata could not afford the extra cost. Lata's saris cost only Rs 450 whereas her own ensemble cost more than Rs 1000. Seema did not mind the extra expense. She was still single and living at home, and had her own disposable income. She was pleased that at least she spent it on her work uniform. They were always told to stand out from the crowd and not look like other women on the street, so what better way was there to achieve this than to wear trousers with the shirt tucked in and a belt over it? Very few women ever dressed like that in India!

Seema always believed that it wasn't enough to just wear a uniform, but one must strive to look good in it. Lata believed this too, of course, but then she always looked good in a sari. Unlike Seema, Lata never seemed to mind that her curves were accentuated, or that her belly showed a bit. Seema felt none of those anxieties when wearing trousers, except when she first started wearing them and was always anxious about forgetting to do up the zip. It was fun that they worked together, and there was never any competition between them. Perhaps if they both wore saris there might have been. But this way, they looked like a good team.[60]

Each institution has its own colour or design of saris so that staff are easily identifiable with a 'signature look'. All drape their saris in the modern Nivi style kept in place by numerous pins and tucks, which leaves the arms free and reveals very little flesh. Part of the initiation and training in these jobs involves learning to wear the sari in the exact prescribed fashion, which may be very different from the woman's usual style. This has the effect of eliminating the particularity of body shape, skin colour or hair. The sari as uniform creates a statement about neatness, efficiency and the new working woman. Above all, it stands as an emblem of India's distinctive embrace of both tradition and modernity.

an Indian Administrative Service officer at work in a sari

It is not surprising therefore that even in areas where there is not a uniform as such, for instance in the vast ranks of the bureaucracy, the Indian state has firmly encouraged its employees to wear the sari to work. Several senior bureaucrats recalled being given the *Handbook for Officers* as trainees and an accompanying pamphlet called *Shishtachar* (Propriety) which discussed dress codes. While for men the regulations clearly state the type of clothing to be worn for different occasions (Nehru suits for flag-raising ceremonies, lounge suits for formal dinners), for women the emphasis was on sober colours and narrow borders. That the women would wear saris was taken completely for granted. To this day, the State and its employees would find it unthinkable that any of its female staff would even consider wearing 'non-Indian' clothes, though junior staff have managed to make alternative Indian clothing such as the shalwar kamiz acceptable. Both male and female officials felt that the government did not feel it necessary to specify the wearing of saris because the expectations and criticisms of husbands, mothers-in-laws and colleagues would be sufficient to ensure that female colleagues wore them.

One retired bureaucrat remarked that in thirty years of service he had never met a female colleague dressed in anything but a sari. He did recall one occasion when one of them had worn a loud red sari to work. According to his rule book he was required, as her boss, to discipline her for this transgression of the 'dress code'. But he felt that subtle censure from her colleagues would be far more effective, and he held his tongue. He judged rightly, for she never infringed again. This continuing confidence in peer pressure reflects the public sector's self-conscious perception of itself as being more worthy, more middle class and more genuinely Indian than the supposedly more glamorous private sector.

an Indian Administrative Service officer at work in a shalwar kamiz

In recalling their working life as teachers or lecturers, many women could offer specific instances of being censured about their clothes. This was often through sharp but subtle put-downs, more rapier than bludgeon. Several recalled the apparently innocuous expression 'Oh, are you going somewhere special tonight?' when someone wore a particularly nice or showy sari to work. What was this supposed to mean? The beauty of such refined disdain of course lies in its ambiguity. The comment could be taken as a compliment, an appreciation of the effort and care that went into wearing a particular fine sari. But as both speaker and target will know, the remark may well mean something quite different, such as: 'For the first time in several years she is wearing a vaguely presentable sari. Why on earth can't she choose something half reasonable on all the other days?' Or: 'The stuck up little madam, who the hell does she think she is? Wearing this kind of expensive silk to school, when anyone with the remotest sense of decency would know that this is the sort of thing one wears only to a party in the evening.'

How the remark is received depends on the self-confidence of the target. Some take it to heart and still flush when recalling the conversation years later. Others dismiss it as a jealous taunt from those who feel threatened by an ability to look special in a sari on an ordinary working day.

Comments are not always even this subtle: 'In my school, for instance, where I have been teaching nearly four decades, there is a very controlled section of ladies who are fairly well dressed, their saris comfortable, bright, appropriate. But what's truly offensive is sometimes people forget they are at work. During the daytime you don't wear certain colours, certain fabrics or certain styles, like gold, intricate weaves. I have seen some of these ladies coming to work in them, they are so inappropriate for our institution…people snigger, talk behind their backs, that's the only weapon. Reactions are really candid. And sometimes one hears very "unparliamentary language". Totally vulgar! We end up saying, she's looking like a tart, or when some-one wears a certain shade of pink, we call it the "bordello look". To say she is a "pain in the what-ever" is a very normal kind of reaction. I have seen some people being told this. There is a time and a place for everything and you should be appropri-ately dressed otherwise you are bound to invite a bit of censure. Women are the best critics of one another. This is a woman's world and a very un-sparing one!'

The power sari

The sheer level of disdain experienced by many women may paradoxically become a positive contribu-tion to women developing a nuanced sensibility about socially appropriate dress. Even those women who start as Mina did, with fear and lack of confidence, may over the years develop a sense of authority and self-confidence based on both their increasing mastery of the sari and these constant jibes about what not to wear. Precisely because everyone knows the difficulties and problems, a person who shows accom-plished skill in making the sari serve their will and express their purpose is much appreciated. This is especially the case where this authority appears to be effortless, with the garment worn with complete confidence and lack of anxiety. This is what one woman described to us as the 'carefully casual' look:

For example they might wear a chiffon, but with only a single pin. This is quite different from the carefully pinned pallu associated with hotel receptionists that is intended to be smart, controlled and in place. A pin on a single layer of a chiffon pallu keeps a smart base line but allows much of it to cascade over the arm, exploiting the slippery potential of the fabric.

Skilfully deployed, this carefully casual look can be extraordinarily powerful in a work situation:

The first glance a senior woman in a sari would throw in my direction for instance is to say: O.K. you are trying to look comfortable, let us see how effortless you can be in a sari. That is the first thing that comes across to me. I am someone who has over the years pinned my pallu. But I have now come to a stage that I don't pin it anymore. Women are usually circumspect because they know that now it is going to drop, that she is going to lose it. But if they see I have an effortless way of putting the pallu in its place, not bothering about it as I do it, it immediately establishes that I am in more control of things than anyone else in this place.

This woman exploits what to others is precisely the weakness of the sari – that when left unpinned the pallu will tend to fall off the shoulder and appear to be out of control. In contrast, she asserts herself by half hinting that she can control the pallu by sheer will power, and by showing that she is confident enough not to care even if it does slip down her arm in the middle of a conversation. She returns it to its place only if and when she chooses to, refusing to be intimidated by either the garment or the worried looks of others. Her studied casualness gives her both freedom and control.

It might be thought that such mastery is not something particular to the sari. As one woman put it: 'If you are not at ease with yourself it doesn't matter whether you are wearing a suit, a skirt or a sari, because at the end of the day if you can't carry yourself, whatever else you drape around you, it is going to look awkward.' But most women did not share this perspective. They felt that with Western clothes or the shalwar kamiz, the garments largely take their shape from the tailoring. As a result, they do not communicate anxiety or inability as easily, even if you are not fully comfortable in them. Wearing the sari was far more demanding, risky and vulnerable, a high-wire act where nervousness was transparent. But for the same reason, a successful performance could give you an aura and authority that tailored garments could not. A confident sari wearer notes that her colleagues try to disparage her, suggesting her sari is archaic. But she responds that this is testimony to its power:

the power sari

For them it has to be a big deal about getting into a sari – it unnerves them that here is someone who doesn't need an occasion to wear one. Personally, when I go to meetings and I know that I am going to meet someone senior for the first time and that I have to make it work the first time to establish myself, lay down the rules, show them how it works – then most often I am in a sari because then I know that I can clinch it.

The best evidence in support of the 'power sari' was the number of men who complained that in the politics of the office they were at a distinct disadvantage, because they could not compete with the power the women conveyed through their saris. As one man said of his professional wife: 'When she is in a shalwar, she looks like a housewife. I am always scared of her, but when she is in a sari, I am even more so!'

A male lawyer confirmed this effect in more detail:

If a woman carries her sari particularly well and with ease then everybody is trying to figure out what this person is about. The impression is that she wears a sari and she looks good and looks confident, and then when you see the careless move of putting her pallu back on her shoulder, you know exactly what kind of effect it has on the people. And when she sort of shakes her hair and puts it back, you can immediately see everybody and especially the men who are almost saying, 'Oh God, if only she wouldn't do this kind of thing.' It is magical to see the effect it has on people ... no matter how hard the men try to look good, all she needs to do is to get into a traditional sari, and everybody's attention will be focused on her.

A further advantage of the power sari is that its traditional associations create a smoke screen for the woman's own manoeuvres, as one man recalled:

Hindi movies are littered with examples of the woman who wears Western clothes being the bad scheming one and the woman who wears the sari as the homely one, the innocent gullible who ends up winning through virtue. But eventually I have realised that the ones wearing the saris are just as scheming, just as manipulative, but in fact they are even cleverer, in that they are using that skill from behind a garb.

However, unlike a stitched Western 'power suit',[61] which can be forceful but unequivocal, the power sari can be handled dynamically and ambiguously, as two women described to us:

The sari can be used as a strategic weapon in a place of work to either sexualise your working context or bring in some kind of maternal or sisterly light – and you can do it in an instant. It's not that you have to put on a whole new sari, it's just that the way you wear it can suddenly sexualise the work context –

so a flick of the wrist, and suddenly it's: 'lets work together, but I am also a sexual entity who's trying to deal with you. I don't know how we do it but that's what happens!

What is achieved, whether the pallu is half controlled or not pinned at all, is the sense that the wearer can switch at will between creating a more attractive and alluring style, or a more ordered and businesslike style. The key is to strike the right balance between casually playing with something and appearing to be anxious about it or fidgety. The same goes for the relationship to one's hair. Are you pushing it back as a means of altering your look and to distract men according to your will? Or is it coming forward of its own accord and distracting you.

Of course such strategies can be overplayed. A women who played around with the sensual possibilities of her sari too much, constantly letting her hair cascade, might achieve a certain power with respect to men. But she would do so at the expense of her reputation with other women, who would feel that the truly accomplished sari wearer does not need such vulgar tricks to achieve authority.[62] The quality they hope to achieve is an imperious elegance by virtue of wearing the sari well, so that, as a woman from Jaipur described it, 'she makes a graceful silhouette as part of the sari floats behind like a queen's train'.[63]

Politicians

Indira Gandhi on a campaign tour in India

The most high-profile and powerful working women in India are the growing number of female politicians. The various messages that they convey through their saris, and how these encode their larger political message, is a topic much discussed by the public but which Indian political analysis usually ignores.

For most of the twentieth century, Indian politicians were drawn from among the social elite. They were patricians doing good for the masses, and their dress was that of the class they belonged to, not those they represented. Mrs Gandhi, as Nehru's daughter, was in some ways the epitome of the elite politician, and her unfailingly exquisite saris conveyed an almost regal sense of her own divine right to rule.[64] On the other hand, she also contributed to an unprecedented populism in Indian politics, bypassing the institutions of the State and her own party to appeal to the people directly with her own slogans and programmes. Her saris managed to convey this approach too, as she always carefully wore the sari of the local region she was visiting, and used it to cover her head when canvassing in a more conservative area. Just as Mahatma Gandhi had spent years trying to find the right 'look' for a leader of a poor country bonded in political and economic oppression,[65] so Indira Gandhi adroitly positioned herself in the status of Mother India, recognisable and familiar, yet transcendent and perfect.

While Indira Gandhi made sure she kept the limelight to herself, since her death[66] several women have risen to prominent ministerial positions in the national and state governments, though without achieving the same exclusivity. The former film star Jayalalitha became Chief Minister of Tamil Nadu in the 1990s. A screen siren and very public mistress of M.G. Ramchandran, himself a superstar of Tamil cinema who had gone on to become Chief Minister, she always emphasised her glamour, charisma and mystique by wearing one and a half fabulously expensive Kanjivaram silk saris (the half covering her bullet proof vest), an opulence which Mrs Gandhi would never have touched. In her second term, however, from May 2001, she resolutely sported anonymous printed synthetic saris, the ordinary garb of millions of other women. As the change followed the charges of massive corruption which the federal authorities brought against her, albeit unsuccessfully, in the wake of her first term, the new saris could only be interpreted as a message of self-chastisement and contrition to her public. (Ironically, she was then condemned by the Tamil Nadu State Handloom Board for setting a bad example by promoting synthetic saris!)[67]

Jayalalitha in her second term as Chief Minister of Tamil Nadu

A contrasting case is that of Mayawati, the leader of a Dalit party (representing the lower castes). She had always worn low-key clothes not dissimilar to those of her rank-and-file followers, mostly old cotton shalwar kamiz, which emphasised that she was of them and among them. However, when she won an election and became Chief Minister of Uttar Pradesh, the most populous state of India, her wardrobe underwent a sea-change. She now appeared in shalwar kamiz of glittering material, cut in the latest fashion. The *dupatta* scarf was worn as a decorative accessory around the neck, rather than as a garment of modesty covering the bosom. The change appeared to be popular with her supporters, and she seems to have been responding to her, and their, expectations about the need to mark success and upward social mobility by a move from cotton to synthetic, and from modesty to fashion.

Another major female figure, Mamata Banerjee, has successfully led a new party, the Trinamul Congress, in Communist-dominated West Bengal, and served as the national minister for railways in a BJP coalition government. Kolkata is a city which prides itself on appreciating the higher things in life, such as music and education, rather than the superficial consumption of fashion and food which Kolkatans believe characterises Delhi and Mumbai. Kolkatans know their city is poor, and they are not ashamed of it. Coming from a modest bourgeois background there, Mamata always wears inexpensive handloom saris in nondescript colours which are almost never starched and thus look slightly crumpled, sometimes even torn. Her 'look' is quite typical of a certain category of lower middle-class Bengali woman in their fifties in Kolkata. For her opponents, the saris are a cheap populist gimmick, the tears self-inflicted, a ruse to endear herself to the ordinary voter in the absence of properly worked-out policies. They complain she looks like a maidservant

Mamata Banerjee at a sit-in

rather than a leader of the people, in contrast to patrician Communist leaders such as Jyoti Basu with their immaculately ironed clothes and shining shoes. For her supporters however, her crumpled simplicity is seen as a visual challenge to the crisp folds of her Communist opponents, and as evidence of her humility, incorruptibility and commitment to the ordinary person.[68]

There are few similarly popular women politicians on the right in contemporary Indian politics. The eccentric Uma Bharati dresses as a female Hindu 'monk' garbed in the saffron robes of an ascetic. More typical, however, is Sushma Swaraj who wears her 'traditional Indian woman' look like a badge, with conservative (but not 'ethnic') saris worn with careful pleating and pinning, a big *bindi*, and vermilion prominently worn in her neatly combed and oiled hair. This is accompanied by frequent mentions of her duties as wife and mother within the home, and as a cabinet minister in public life. Her statements and looks seem intended to represent the sort of Indian woman that the right-wing BJP, with its religious nationalism and free market capitalism, needs: a woman who aims to have a career but who does not neglect her primary duties in the home.

The title of this chapter refers to the working sari, not just the working woman, as again and again the sari appears as an active agent. The various examples we have seen show this capacity of the sari in two quite contrasting ways. On the one hand, it is the sari that stands for the world of work: people who hold office show their conformity to their station in life by wearing their sari appropriately and well. At the same time, the carefully casual businesswoman and the politician seem to collude with the possibilities of their clothing in order to make an impact upon the world. This tension between the static and the dynamic, the conformist and the leader is precisely what involvement in work brings to the sari and the sari brings to work, and becomes one more facet of the dynamism and ambiguity that seem to define the sari as clothing in action, both at work and within the home.

Growing Old Together

The relationship between a woman and her sari is a bond one cannot break – you wear it when you give birth, when you get married, to your funeral pyre – it is an indestructible bond.

— A sex worker in Kolkata

CHAPTER 7 | *Growing Old Together*

During the first few weeks after her wedding, a bride is on show to her new relatives and to outsiders. During this period, she tends to wear the saris from her trousseau and those gifted to her for her wedding. She is considered a novice, who needs to be guided and chosen for, so that she may wear what is appropriate for a daughter-in-law of the family. Her wardrobe thus consists mainly of saris which she has not chosen herself, in colours which others want her to wear.

But after a period of time her novelty will wear off, and following the birth of her first child or the arrival of another bride in her husband's family, she will gain some sartorial independence. Whether she works in a field or an office, she may now have a little money, saved after household expenses have been met, with which to buy her own clothes. If she has the financial resources (many women never earn enough money to fully participate), she is able to make choices, experiment with colours and materials, and learn to spot a bargain. In other words, she becomes an active consumer of saris.

It is during this period that the woman really develops her individual style, making decisions about which colours suit her, which designs she prefers and what kinds of material she is able to best manage and enjoy. This is also the period of her life when she has to juggle the demands of children, husband, relatives, neighbours, friends and workplace. These may all constrain her choices, but where she is able she dresses herself accordingly for these different audiences, occasions and moods.

As Mina noted:

I like cotton saris. I have got used to them, also chiffon. What I don't like are too many flowers, and yellow. I like all Bengal saris as long as they don't have too many flowers and print on them. I like handloom, patchwork... I like South Indian ones too, I guess, but they are too bright. All the saris I got from my mother's side were all bright. Also they have too much zari, not at all suitable for work. The other day I was wearing a bright blue sari with gold work. I wore it because I was going to my mother's house after work. I wanted her to see me in it. My neighbour had liked it so my mother bought it for me as she knows I like the neighbour's taste. But I did not like it too much. It is too bright for work. It is OK if you wear it to parties and weddings. It's too heavy and difficult to handle in a bus and feels heavy all day.

This period of relative freedom of choice does not last very long, however, for there are strong cultural expectations concerning what is appropriate dress for a woman as she enters the later stages of her life, as mother, grandmother, elder and widow. The sari of the bride is marked by an exuberance of colour and an emphasis upon design. In the early years of her marriage, she remains able to wear bright and vivid colours. With advancing maturity, however, she is expected to move to cooler, paler colours, with narrower borders and less elaborate designs. Finally, should she become widowed, she is expected to wear only white or some other prescribed colour. Indira Gandhi did this for three years following the death of her husband Firoz in 1961, saying that all the colour had drained out of her life.[69]

These expectations have strong cosmological associations. The Sanskrit word *maya* means both 'materiality' and 'illusion', and is the core term for a philosophy which sees all materiality as illusion. We can free ourselves from illusion only gradually, through greater maturity and understanding and by renouncing our links to the material world, turning instead to prayer and spiritual pursuits.[70] As with many normative ideals that reflect a wider cosmology, some women – for example, those from higher castes or particular regions – will experience more pressure to conform to these ideals than others who only pay lip-service to them.

It would be a mistake to consider these rules and norms as simply religious injunctions. Many of these beliefs about the appropriate wearing of the sari have much more resonance among Muslim Bengalis for example, who have worn the sari for generations, than for Hindus from the North-West who have adopted the sari only recently. Going beyond religion, we find in these beliefs common fundamental views about the world, including shared views of purity and pollution, attitudes to hierarchy and the role of caste and class in organising society, beliefs about gender and social position, astrology, fate and luck, or even about eating a meal or greeting a friend. These beliefs are typically experienced as 'customary', and the people involved usually cannot give very clear accounts of the reasons why things are done the way they are (though they generally think there must be a priest somewhere who can give explanations). Nonetheless, such ideas command the landscape of the imagination within which the sari is visualised and lived.

The bride, in her youth and fecundity, represented by the red of her sari, is allowed to revel in such illusion, being fully connected to the world by her desire for people (her sexuality) and for things (her jewellery and beautiful saris). She herself is a beautiful illusion, a kind of living doll, with colours that dazzle and *zari* work that shimmers, brilliant in her individual-ism. With increasing age, however, a woman is expected to dis-tance herself from such desires. Her transition away from red to cooler colours marks the waning of her sexuality and fertility and presents her as having diminishing appetite for worldly things, as she no longer yearns for ever more beautiful saris.

An older village woman complained that it is hard for her to make herself look beautiful given these constraints. Even though she is still married, she cannot dress well or wear jewellery or tie her hair nicely because then people would think she had 'gone mad'. Another villager in her fifties was persuaded by her young niece to buy a sari with red flow-ers on it, but simply could not bring herself to wear it in front of her sons and son-in-law. After it had lain in her trunk for a few weeks, she exchanged it with the peddler for a more sober one. Some men also express their regret at the gradual fading of the saris, and even insist that their wives continue to wear bright colours as they did when they were young brides. In these cases, women are anxious to make it clear to their peers that they are only wearing such colours in deference to their husband's wishes.

In widowhood the woman is expected to abandon colour completely, embracing a white that she shares with *sanyasis* (religious ascetics) and nuns. As one informant put it, 'white is associated with everything that is good and simple'.[71] Wearing white every day, deprived of any distinguishing features, languishing in a social death, she begins to blend with her surroundings. 'While a wife is her husband's "half-body" (*adhangani*), one can almost say that on his death she becomes half-corpse. She must henceforth dress in a white shroud-like sari and is excluded from any significant ritual role on auspicious occasions like marriage.'[72]

That it is her relationship to her husband which determines what the woman wears is confirmed by considering what happens when a high-caste woman dies before her husband. 'Her corpse is elaborately adorned and dressed in bridal red, or in an auspicious *chunri* sari (with yellow speckles on a red ground). Her feet are decorated as a bride's, with henna: she is decked in ornaments, made up with cosmetics and presented with a comb and mirror.'[73] This celebratory air reflects the traditional Hindu belief that it is a woman's great good fortune to die while still married. Symbolically, the married corpse is considered almost more alive than the living widow.

The colour of the widow's sari varies across India. White is the prescribed colour for widows mainly in the north and east, and pilgrimage centres such as Vrindavan and Benares have a high concentration of white sari-clad widows among the population. In other parts of India, however, white is the colour for brides, and a different colour is specified for widows. There are also other restrictions, such as widows in many northern and eastern villages being proscribed from wearing printed saris. 'Women belonging to the low Dom caste are given a specific 'sari of widowhood' which they have to wear at the cremation of their husband, at the ritual bath that follows, and then for a year after. These are gifted to her by close relatives, and she is required to put them on immediately, one on top of the other.'[74]

Everywhere in India, however, there is some specific colour which is pre-scribed for a widow, and she is barred from wearing all other colours. Fur-ther, she is denied all means of adorning herself with jewellery or make-up or any accessories which could make her look attractive. In a poignant short story called 'Twilight', by Manju Kak, an old and ill widow con-fined to her bed reflects on the drastic change in her life: 'I, Shanta, who took such pride in my housekeeping, who never wore a saree unless it was crisp with starch … and now I wrap them around, limp like yesterday's rotis!'[75]

It was that familiar smell again. It woke Reshma up. The wind must have picked up overnight, blowing the putrid odour from the huge open drain towards their neighbourhood. A mixed blessing that drain. At least it provided some drainage for all those new communal toilets provided by that local organisation. But when the wind blew, the smell was everywhere. Here in Kanpur it was a far cry from the birdsong and cockerels which used to wake her up as a child in her village in Punjab. But there it was a long walk to the train tracks for the daily ablutions. She had to get up now. Everyone was still asleep, the children in a jumble all around her, her son and daughter-in-law on the other side of the sacking. Removing a small knee from her arm, Reshma pulled her sari down from where it invariably rode up during the night, and stood up. She was always grateful to her mother for teaching her to wear knickers. But now that she was up, she took them off as they would only get in the way in a cramped toilet, and collected her toiletries. Slipping into her toilet slippers and covering her head and chest with the pallu which she had wrapped loosely around her waist during the night, Reshma stepped into the lane, hitching up her sari slightly to avoid the puddles. It was a bit of a walk, but at least these toilets had water and were clean.

Once back, it was time for a cup of tea. While the water boiled, Reshma stacked the dirty dishes from last night's meal in the corner for her daughter-in-law to do later, and prepared to sweep out the little yard outside their room. In the middle of June, the dust was dry and got everywhere. Reshma un-hitched the pallu from her waist and covered her nose and mouth with the end of her pallu, barely breathing to avoid that gritty taste in the mouth she hated. That done, she could savour her cup of tea in peace, the only time in the day when she could enjoy total solitude.

The sun was already high in the sky but the family still slept, so Reshma decided to do the dishes too before her bath. Her friends chided her for pampering her daughter-in-law by continuing to do housework and holding down a job, but Reshma did not mind. The children, the shopping, the rest of the day was all the young girl's responsibility and this was the least she could do to help in return for their agreeing to live with her in her old age and widowhood. Reshma looked at the indistinguishable pile of white and nearly white saris on the clothes line which were hers, and picked one. It was one she had had a long time, gifted to her by a sweet young receptionist at work. At first she wore it only to neighbourhood weddings and to visits to her village twice a year. But there had been comment about the tiny pink flowers on it which the young woman had not been able to resist, so Reshma decided it was best to avoid talk and wear it only to work. There the young activists always encouraged her to wear brighter colours, and some had even gifted her some brighter saris at the last Divali. Reshma thought their enthusiasm was kind but could not bring herself to wear them. The image of her grandmother in her widow's white sari was too vivid, too important to ignore. Reshma accepted the presents, but put them aside for her daughter-in-law.

In practice, things are not always as strict as these descriptions might suggest. Even though widows are reduced to wearing white saris, as a concession they often display subtle but elaborately decorated borders. And while there may be social pressure on older women to wear light-coloured saris, it is tacitly accepted as impractical to wear them to work in a dusty, muddy village. So, while making sure they wear the right colours in public, in private widows will wear dark-coloured saris which do not show up stains. In urban areas the emphasis on widows wearing only white is becoming less stringent, and a range of lighter coloured saris are tolerated. But there remains a strict avoidance of red, the colour traditionally associated with fertility and fecundity in north and east India (and of black among Tamils, for the same reason).

Some couples (for example, academic couples) have sought to break the association of white with widows:

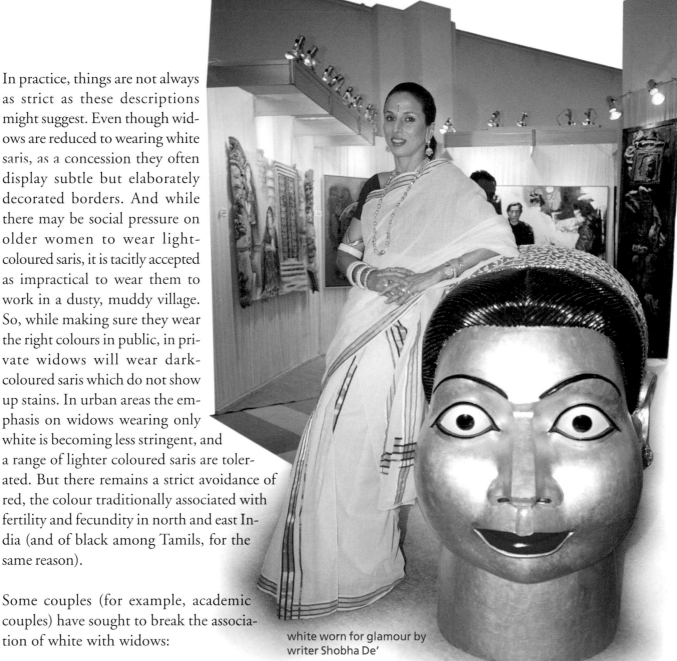

white worn for glamour by writer Shobha De'

After I got married, my husband pointed out to me (he was the first person to do so) that cream and white actually do look nice on me. That is particularly significant because in the traditional Hindu norm, a young or a newly married woman would not wear white or cream. But I mean, don't we all protest that we don't want our widows in white? So one way of making that statement is to wear it while you are still married, especially if your husband likes that colour. Thankfully, though I am quite traditional in many ways, this was something which didn't bother me at all.

Mina also told of a white sari:

I had a beautiful white sari. It was a special sari which my husband had bought for me after the wedding. It had little pink flowers on it. When my sister-in-law saw it she threw a fit. She was appalled that he had bought it for his new wife and to my obvious delight. I told her I liked the colour and she said it wasn't the colour for me. It is true that after my marriage for a whole year I did not wear black or white, not even a blouse. That day I had left the house surreptitiously so my sister-in-law would not see me in the white sari. My husband said why wear it when there may be trouble. But I wanted to wear it for him at least one day and have him see me in it. It took me ages that day to wear the sari because it was a new cotton. When I wore it, everyone at work complimented me. But on the way back I got grease on it. Even after dry cleaning it the mark hasn't gone. When my husband saw that he said it was retribution, but I dismissed it saying it was blind superstition. But I agreed with him. I started crying when I saw him. It was an expensive sari for Rs 1600. I felt terrible. Then my husband consoled me by saying that it had happened only because I had attracted someone's evil eye, as I was looking so beautiful in it.

This sense of tempting fate is not unusual. Other women also felt compelled to acknowledge their wearing of white or off-white saris as significant departures from the norm. Such judgments still acknowledge an underlying anxiety about what is morally sanctioned.[76] There is a common saying in Hindi, *aap ruchi khana, par ruchi pahanna* – that is, you can eat food which is to your individual taste, but what you wear must please others. As our discussion of saris through the life cycle has demonstrated, such implicit and explicit control over clothing is a critical dimension of social life in India.[77] The numerous rules with regard to comportment and colour, design and decorum, cleanliness and comfort, veiling and vanity are all created to ensure that what one wears is acceptable. Although as many of the previous examples have shown, creative or recalcitrant individuals find ways to defy such norms, as exceptions they may be used by the larger social group to confirm the existence of the norms themselves. Individuals construct their own trajectories and interpretations with extraordinary creativity. Indeed, in the following case of Chandra, such norms have been extended and pre-empted in a way one might never have predicted, through her deep immersion in religious and cosmological sensibilities.

Chandra suffers from a condition experienced by many women in India. She works within a government sector where the hierarchy of jobs is completely fossilised. Within this petrified establishment, it is clear that a woman aged forty-seven is not going to gain promotion — now or ever. The work is not well paid. She and her husband have had to take jobs several hundred miles apart. Her son, her only child, is being brought up by his father, whose conditions of employment are much better than hers. She sees them only on those weekends when she can afford to make the trip. Compared to most villagers, she is affluent and middle class. Once twenty years before, the couple had even enjoyed a year's posting in Dubai.

But what she is lacking in her life today is any sense of hope. She wears her saris in a manner that envelops her. There is no exposed midriff: even her blouse is hidden by its folds. For her the sari is a support, a cocoon. She quotes a story by Tagore about a little girl whose candle is blown out at the top of the stairs and suddenly confronts the dark and the loneliness. She uses this to introduce her own sense of feeling alone even in the crowds of Kolkata or sitting in her work cafeteria. She goes on immediately to note how she is a junior staff member and is not supposed to speak in meetings, endless meetings full of men talking and her sitting in silence.

In all this she feels her sari to be a comfort, a friend, part of her but also a companion. She quotes a poem by Pablo Neruda about this ambiguity between a person and their clothes, and a Hindi riddle about 'is the woman in the sari or is the sari in the woman? Sari is the woman and woman is the sari'. 'But that is why I think the sari is a wonderful dress in a sense because it is an extension of me, my personality.'

Chandra is aware that the sari also represents the social pressure that stops her rebelling against her condition. The very formality and respectability associated with it constantly keeps her in place, socially and physically. 'Maybe I want to laugh loudly and I want to whistle, but I am wearing a sari and I know that I can't. So the sari is preventing me from whistling. You can't whistle in front of your colleagues and if you feel like doing this and if the sari prevents you from doing this, then the sari is your helpful friend.' The sari creates order for her, and she wants this order to be perfect: 'Let me tell you about my dream. You know, what happens is I have got my saris then the matching blouses. What happens every morning is first I take out a blouse, then I match it with the sari. Though I know that nobody can see my blouse because it is really covered up, but it happens every day. So my dream cupboard is that each sari will have one blouse for that sari and ideally one petticoat. But so far it hasn't happened.' For her, only the perfectly ordered sari cupboard could bring the perfect order she is looking for in her life.

Chandra has a strong sense of lucky and unlucky saris. If wearing a sari results in her 'head of section or whoever just blasted me or something happened, something bad', then she will discard it. But she also has her lucky saris that she wears when she thinks she is going to need extra support. She can secretly appeal through her sari in such circumstances: 'you know there is a belief that if you are in a tight corner you can tie a knot to Hanuman Ji's [the monkey god's] tail. So it is a symbolic tail and suppose I am in a tight corner and I am going to meet my immediate boss and I know something has gone wrong then I will tie a knot here (in her pallu) and say – Oh Hanumaanji, please save me this time and I will meet you there in the temple with *prasad* (offering of sweets). It

is a promise and then when things are OK, I will say it is over now, and then I will open the knot.'

She can also feel supported by the mere possession of a sari infused with memory, 'like there is one special sari which was given to me. You know in Bengali marriages one sari is kept to be worn for the first night after the marriage. So that is a very special auspicious sari. That I haven't worn afterwards but I have kept it very lovingly. Happy memories.' Her relationship is personal partly because it is not acknowledged by others. 'My husband never notices when I am wearing a good sari or not. Whenever I ask he will look in a very abstract way and say you always look all right, I mean what is the difference. My son is too busy with his computers and stuff. My mother criticises me a lot. She says, oh you should have longer pallu. Or what have you done and she just pulls it up, puts it

down. Always criticising and correcting me.'

The young men at work worry her. She always checks the seat of a chair before sitting down because she heard a story about them putting chewing gum on chairs. The looks of the young females intimidate her: 'saris – this six yard thing – covers all the deficiencies in your figure, but these young things have a nice figure, so they want to show all that.' But in compensation she feels the sari gives her the cover of a conventional and respected role: 'they call you aunty ji and if you are in a shop then you can say *beta zara jaldi saaman dedo* (please serve me quickly, my dear). You can show that you are a different kind of a person and could command some respect.'

But ultimately, the sari is viewed as giving her the peace that comes from being cocooned inside it, protected from the gaze of the world. 'I like to wear a sari because I don't want to be noticed. I just vanish and disappear, invisible, that is why I like it. My husband is staying far away, so I don't want to attract any attention. So a sari is very safe. It is like a *burkha* (a full body veil), you just cover yourself and you are not there.'

Her identification with saris provides many images of them as living beings with their own life cycle. 'After wearing them for many years, what happens is that a sari grows old, like a dress grows old. Maybe today I am feeling that this is a good sari and I can wear it to the office. So after wearing it for say one more summer this will become a sari that I will wear only at home, when I am cooking or when I am going shopping buying vegetables

and all. And then one day comes when you feel really it is no more, it has died a natural death.'

The sari that has been her comfort in her life ('sometimes I feel nostalgic about some of my saris that I remember that my mother bought, a mustard yellow sari with black border') is also an important part of her looking forward. A remark that crops up again and again in her conversation is how she wishes that she were much older than she is. She likes to think of herself as aged, 'I don't know why I want to be older – most of the people I meet are so immature. But I have my own concept of old age, being matured. I think I am fossilised. I think I am ninety-two'. She feels she was always fixated with the image of old age; even as a child she used to seize the white saris from her mother's collection, not the young colourful ones. Her conversation carries images from the Sufi poetry which she loves to read. It is poetry that helps her think about fate and suffering with a poignancy that is tragic and sentimental, but for her, also undeniably beautiful. The same sari that confines and defines her, will become the site of her ultimate release. She speaks of 'a trunk full of old saris in the crumbling attic waiting for their rebirth. How comforting it is to know that at the end of your journey bound in a sari – your soul will be unbound for the next journey.'

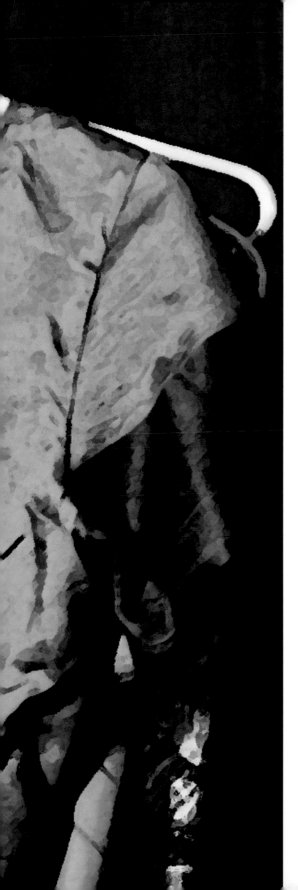

The Problem of What to Wear

CHAPTER 8 | *The Problem of What to Wear*

The mistress

Compared to the general noise and bustle of the public side of Delhi life, the city's many middle-class residential areas can be relatively quiet. Indeed, at 5.45 in the morning Shona might have been able to hear birdsong from the trees that grow outside her second-floor flat. Her husband lies asleep still, beneath the fan. Sleepily, she catches sight of the low table, (though in its original village context it was used for sitting on) that she had rescued when the family had wanted to leave it in the village as antiquated and useless. She had seen that it would make a fine setting for her jute shaded lamp that matched the jute shaded light fitting, both of which she had bought from a Bengali cooperative at Dilli Haat. Against the far walls, which are all painted a light terracotta shade, is the heavy metal cupboard where her clothes are stored, and next to that is a smaller and rather beaten wooden cupboard that serves for her husband's clothing. As her eyes become used to the low light she can finally make out the most prominent feature of her room, the collection of small ornaments such as the 'lost wax' metal figures with their characteristic look of being wrapped in filaments. These figures are evidence of her current employment by an enterprise selling craft and staging events in Delhi on behalf of artisans and artists from Eastern and North-eastern India.

For sleeping, Shona wears an old black and brown *kurta* that is too worn for daywear but has developed a soft cotton feel from use over many years. She continues to wear this as she begins the tasks of the day. After washing she spends half an hour in exercises that serve the dual function of trying to fend off a gradual growth in girth since her marriage and, as they are performed in front of the small shrine next to the cupboards, are also important to her spiritual well-being. While making her first cup of tea she prepares the rice and fish for the cat. At the same time she makes the rice water ready for the maid to starch her saris, which were washed on the previous day. Mentally she is already thinking ahead towards an important meeting in the afternoon that will be instrumental in determining next year's budget. She appreciates that her choice of clothing could have a significant impact on the meeting.

There is no doubt in her mind that she will be wearing a sari. Most days she wears a shalwar kamiz, but for any important occasion or meeting she prefers a sari, which these days means once or twice a week; and this meeting is particularly important. By the same token, although she usually performs many of her household tasks before taking her bath and changing, today she will make sure that putting on her clothes is the very last thing she does before leaving home, since she wants to avoid having them spoiled by housework. By this time the maid will have arrived, and so she can avoid any of those final demands that inevitably crop up after you think everything is ready.

By the time the maid arrives, Shona has finished her chores. She bathes and puts on her bra and panties. She is a senior and confident manager, a pragmatist who is clear about her priorities and most especially her ethical priorities (her friends see her as a bit preachy on occasion). She is offended by the vulgarity of wealth and commercial dictate, and does not want to be deflected from the business of the day by the business of selecting what to wear.. Her long and hard-fought feminism does not wish to be reduced to some parody of 'I haven't a thing to wear', especially given that she takes considerable pride in the slightly embarrassing richness of choice that confronts her: there are over 200 saris in her collection. In a confident expression of her abilities, she goes straight over to the wardrobe and takes out her newest acquisition, a cream and olive green *Dhaka* Bengal handloom. She had recently been persuaded by one of her friends who helped organise an exhibition of saris in the school for the blind to buy one of these 'to die for' pieces, well beyond her usual price range. Now, if this sari could serve such an important meeting she could justify the purchase. She knows just the blouse to go with it, and extracted it from the pile of creams and white blouses on the wardrobe shelf. She gives it a quick iron, having not worn it for a while, and proceeds to put it on. But then she suffers a shock. The sleeves are too tight: the excesses of recent festivities have clearly left an unfortunate legacy. Since any other shade of cream would be a disaster with this sari, an alternative will have to be found.

After trying something new, she now turns back to the safe core of her collection, what used to be termed her 'ethnic collection'. The term 'ethnic' has now gone out of fashion but nothing has replaced it, leaving one of those aesthetics of fashion that is too self-conscious to name itself. In any case, this is the part of her wardrobe with which she most fully associates herself. Some of these saris are more exotic and distinctive, representing very particular regional traditions, but most of them have centred around a series of browns, terracottas, deep reds and vegetable dyes.

Yet even this area of maximum choice presents a problem. First, there is her over-reliance upon this group. These saris are now very familiar, not just to her but also to her colleagues, and frankly she is pretty tired of several of them. She doesn't like to admit to herself that she is bound by conventions. Still, she knows wearing the same sari two days in a row would clearly be a source of disdain. Indeed, she prides herself on her ability to manage her appearance, which is a source of authority at work. It is not the visiting dignitary at the meeting that matters: she has plenty of saris that will delight and dazzle and give her a platform from which to show her mastery of her brief. It is more her own colleagues who have high expectations of her, and her management of her wardrobe must show originality and creativity that leaven the control and appropriateness that she exhibits through her clothing.

Not only do these expectations affect her choice, but there is also the matter of that most central question, that of being appropriate. Many of her ethnic saris are from the North-eastern area represented by her work, including some fine and lavish Assamese garments and also the more unusual products of Manipur. But her sense is that these should be avoided. They are simply too blatant an expression of the position she has to take in today's meeting. Such a lack of nuance would be read as vulgar and would probably diminish her effectiveness. The paper she has prepared is carefully constructed so as not to appear to be based on parochial or regional interests. Rather, she is trying to push for the cosmopolitan nature of modern India and the necessity for the equal representation of all localities within this. So the North-eastern material will not do.

The second major contribution to her 'ethnic collection' is that which comes from her own birthplace of Orissa. Not surprisingly, since this is the region she knows best, it includes some of her choice and unique items. But the danger of appearing as merely the embodied representation of her birthplace is that this too takes away from her message of the commonality of cosmopolitan representation. This then suggests one of her interesting saris from south, such as those from Kerala that are souvenirs of several workshops and conferences to which she has been invited over the years. But the problem here is that this same logic has led her to wear these saris in several of the pre-meeting briefings of recent weeks, and so these saris have already been deployed. This thinking through of her options has only taken a minute or two, and a similar time is spent coming to the familiar conclusion that she really needs to have some new and 'more realistic' blouses tailored, but this is not something she can do right now.

A few minutes is also quite long enough for her to become entirely fed up with such indecision. So she strides to the wardrobe and picks out a much favoured *Kota* sari from Rajasthan. The fine pattern of tiny and empty squares of beige cotton fibre characteristic of *Kota* cloth makes the garment light and airy, and she wants to be comfortable. It has enough starch to keep its pleats and appear elegant, but not so much as to prevent the aura of casual comfort that she will achieve by a certain looseness and relaxed feel that will emerge by the time of the meeting. There are no fussy embroidered elements, and this sari has authentic hand block printing rather than the machine printing found in cheaper imitations. The border is thin and simple, a two-colour mix of dull ochre and maroon that both here and dotted throughout the garment echoes a well-known

traditional Rajastani floral motif. The empty squares of a *Kota* sari also give it a quality of transparency and thereby potentially an allure she may or may not seek to cultivate at the meeting in question. It completely avoids the sheen of synthetic or the sheer of chiffon. Instead, the combination of starch and the texture gives it a firmness and crispness, but also as with all cottons, an underlying softness and possibility of movement that makes a fine balance.

But it is not just the ability to select the precise garment that leads to a knowing smile as Shona takes out this sari. She has suddenly thought how to achieve her sartorial goal in one deft stroke. While she has worn this particular sari on several previous occasions it has always been with the same beige blouse, picked simply because the beige is identical to that found on the sari even though it was originally made for a completely different beige sari. But as she visually browsed through the contents of her wardrobe, her eye had fallen upon a strikingly different blouse, one that will serve perfectly for her act of self-presentation today. The *Kota* sari, while appropriate and correct, does not draw particular attention to itself and indeed has a potential for a softer more romantic appeal: she can never choose it without remembering one evening when a man had drawn it gradually over an otherwise naked breast, part of a very memorable experience that had had rather appalling consequences. But the subtle appeal of the plain beige blouse didn't really serve her need to keep all eyes on her at the meeting. This alternative blouse, mustard with an intricate woven maroon border, would do precisely that. She knows that while it does not exactly match any of the colours of the sari, it augments all three. In addition, the cut is extremely clever. It is not immodest, but it is so well-fitted that it gives her breasts a firmer, younger look, and the extra length of the blouse has a slight corset effect, making her stomach more shapely. The ensemble is sufficiently unusual so as to draw attention to itself and stand for the desired sense of originality and individuality.

Now the difficult task is accomplished, she puts on a simple off-white cotton petticoat. This is just a sewn tube of cloth, tied at the waist with a drawstring that comes down to her ankles. A key decision is where precisely to position this string. In the past she had always tied it just above her navel. Somewhat to the surprise of her husband and mother – her husband has never mentioned it, but her mother has on several occasions – around a year ago she began to tie it lower on her hip, below her navel. She couldn't say herself exactly why this is the case. Perhaps there is a quiet refusal to be seen simply as middle-aged and having lost her allure as a woman; certainly those meaningful glances at work have declined, though they have not disappeared altogether. Or perhaps it is actually a middle-aged refusal to be dictated to by concerns over modesty and propriety, strictures that can now be relaxed as more important things are attended to. Sometimes she is convinced it is one, sometimes the other. Either way, her navel is now clearly visible above the petticoat line that sits a bit more comfortably on what remains of her waist.

The petticoat string is done up in a simple bow, balancing comfort and security. The blouse is secured with four clasps at the front. Then comes the task of putting on the sari, which still brings back memories of gawky uncertainty when first attempting the same task twenty years before; now it is accomplished in a few deft movements. First tucking one end into her petticoat at the navel and then wrapping the rest around her waist, she takes out a length of cloth to make pleats with later while passing the remainder around her upper body to rest on the left shoulder. Returning to the business of pleating, using one outstretched hand, each pleat is folded sequentially between her thumb and little finger to create six pleats. The pleats easily take and keep their shape thanks to the prior starching of the cloth. Looking into the mirror Shona checks that the set of pleats are level and that their bottom edge covers her ankles, and then tucks them carefully into her petticoat string to keep them secure for the day. Even in those early days she never resorted to using pins to keep these in place, but trusted to this operation alone.

All that remains is the arrangement of the pallu draped over bosom and falling over her left shoulder. As she passes the pallu over her shoulder she recalls that this actually was one place she did originally use a pin to stop the pallu falling off. Indeed, although after a few years such assistance was no longer needed, she had continued pinning for some years further, sporting small brooches as an accessory rather than the usual discreet safety pin. Today, however, any kind of pinning would take away from the necessary and intended effect of demonstrating her effortless mastery over this garment. In fact, she now has her signature style. Instead of letting the last pleat of her pallu flap on her arm, she folds it back loosely, exposing the underside of the border, and pushes the loose cotton in at the waist. Just to emphasise I still have one! she thinks.

For jewellery, she feels she can display one of the items for which she is directly responsible: an unusual necklace with a bamboo and terracotta disc that goes with any of her core earth-coloured saris, and helps to keep in production a craft of the North-east. Her ensemble is now complete, though she is well aware that its effect will have just as much to do with the way she manipulates and shifts her clothing during the meeting as with the actions she has so far performed. But the foundations have been well laid.

The maid

Bimla woke up with a start. She did not want to be late for work today. That was her mistress's special request last evening. She had some big meeting to go to, and wanted the housework done, breakfast ready and lunch packed all before 8 o'clock. This would take at least two hours, and then there was the half an hour walk to the house. Bimla wanted to have this job on a permanent basis, and so didn't want to be late. She wished she could take the bus, but to spend three rupees each way on the fare was too extravagant. That sum would buy her daughter a hair clip with flowers, or an egg for her next meal.

Bimla had to hurry. Careful not to wake her parents, who were asleep nearby, she rewrapped her sari quickly from the loosened folds which lay about her. It was too hot to sleep with it round her, but she would have to make do until she could afford the kind of nightie her neighbours now wore. Bimla looked quickly away from her sleeping baby on the tangle of little quilts made from old saris. If she lingered she would be tempted to stay and play with the child's hair, which lay around her face in damp curls, telling her stories of the women who had worn the saris which now formed the sheets on her

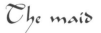

bed. Bimla hoped her
daughter would find a man who would
love her, and not be abandoned the way she had by
her alcoholic husband. She would insist her daughter study
for as long as she wanted. And learn computers. And have a
proper job, not like her, washing other people's dirty dishes. She could work in an
office and travel in a bus without worrying about the money. Bimla remembered a conversation she
had heard between the woman next door and her daughter last night. The little girl was describing her
teacher, going into great detail about the colour of her sari, the matching hair clips and bangles. The girl
wanted to dress like that when she was older. Bimla hoped her daughter would learn these things too,
and hoped also that she wouldn't be embarrassed by her mother.

Having washed in the communal toilets, Bimla changed into the sari she had worn the evening
before, tied her hair quickly and found her sandals. It took longer to get ready with this new sari style.
On top of that, one can't leave the house without at least a *bindi* and some fresh *sindoor* in one's
parting. A basic tidiness was called for when dressing for work. But it was worth the extra effort. She
could sense that her mistress approved her wearing her sari in the 'modern' style. Her previous maid
used to wear it in the traditional village style, but she had been older and set in her ways. Bimla felt
as if she fitted in more easily in Delhi ,and noted that her mistress wasn't embarrassed by her in
front of guests when she brought in the tea. It took a little longer to drape it this way, as she
was still getting used to the new technique, but it was a matter of habit.

But the first day had been traumatic, and it had taken forever. If the woman next door hadn't
helped her, she would have been late for her interview. It was a bit nerve-wracking through
the day, as she had missed her pallu being in the front. Even now she groped for it at the
back, and often preferred to tuck it in front into her waist so at least she knew it was
there! This way also it did not keep slipping off her shoulder. Through experience, she
has also learned that tying it high made it easier to sweep the floor and wash clothes.
Bimla was pleased that these days it took no time at all to put on her sari.

As she crossed the railway tracks, Bimla noticed the sun was already climbing. It rose quickly in these summer mornings. She was glad she had
worn the sari from last evening. Cotton was so much easier in the

heat. Her back was already drenched in perspiration and the sweat was running between her legs. Hopefully it would not show, especially as she was nearing the tea stall. The men seemed to be parked there mainly to ogle at the sight of a woman with her clothes clinging to her. She wasn't afraid of men staring anymore, now that she was at least notionally a married woman. But there is no way you can stop men looking. Perhaps those long blouses that they wore in the village would be more suited to city buses. When her mother and aunts told her about when they used to wear blouses long enough to cover their waists, Bimla had thought that was excessive modesty. But now she could understand why. Men would be men. It was up to the women to not show too much to tempt them. Unless one wanted to, of course!

Wrapping the pallu closer around herself, Bimla was glad that the worn thin cotton dried quickly. At least her blouse was thick. These new velvety ones which seemed to have invaded all the shops were very comfortable. All the girls were wearing them. They cost Rs 25, no more than before, but one could just slip these over one's head without having to deal with fussy buttons. And the stretch fabric was good for feeding the baby, too. She wondered why her mistress did not wear these instead of sticking to the old-fashioned ones in cotton with the thin borders on the sleeves. She should do, Bimla thought, given how much she cared about looking good. These blouses were a little hot, but their durability made them a clear winner. The earlier ones were so thin that they ripped easily at the armpits. Perhaps her mistress did not need the durability. Her blouses lasted much longer, but then she did not have to dust the ceiling fans!

Bimla hated having to wear synthetic saris because they would never stay on her head and the pallu always slid off, though she admitted they were quite good for visiting aunts and cousins, since one is always expected to make the tea or do the dishes on such occasions. Her mother told a story of the first time she had worn a synthetic sari. It had been given to her by her husband's cousin for her wedding. She had been the envy of the village, where everyone else had only cotton saris. The mother-in-law had insisted she wore the synthetic every time anyone dropped in to see her new daughter-in-law. But she had found it incredibly hot and hard to keep it in place. She didn't know then about safety pins. After they moved to the city and Bimla was born, the rules about veiling had become less strict. But even now when relatives from the village come visiting, Bimla's mother's first response is to change into her cotton sari so her pallu will stay in place and no one can gossip that the city has corrupted the modesty of a village woman.

Bimla wished this sari wasn't so small. There wasn't enough material for more than a pleat and a half, and it made walking quickly difficult. It kept sticking to her damp legs. No wonder her aunt had given it away to her so readily! When her aunt was gifted it by her employer last Diwali, Bimla had remarked to her how nice the muted colours were. Then, after wearing it a few times, her aunt passed it on to her to replace a sari that Bimla had torn on a nail. Bimla was relieved when she got it. She was tired of all the bright saris her own previous employers gave her, deciding for her that as a newly married woman these were what she should wear. In the summer they themselves wore saris of thin cotton fabrics in those wonderfully pale shades of blue and cardamom green. But the ones they gave her were invariably of that silky new fabric which was in the shops everywhere. Bimla knew it was a sensible fabric. For poor people, synthetics were a godsend. You could wash them every day and they never faded. However, Bimla noticed that while her aunt always agreed with the others, she herself mostly wore cotton. She had worked in the same house for over twenty years, so by now she felt free to let her mistress know what she liked. Bimla admired her courage for doing that.

Bimla had nearly arrived for work; there was just a final walk across the park. Her mistress must have had her tea by now, so she could start with last night's dishes in the kitchen and then knead the dough for the *chapatis*. She must remember to keep out of her way this morning or she would be scolded. But at least this mistress was better than the previous one, who was mean. Even though both she and her aunt had worked for her, she had given them only one sari between them for Divali. Her aunt had given it back protesting that there was only one, and none for her niece. The mistress then gave the same sari to Bimla two days later. It was a dark maroon sari in a silky fabric with yellow and green flowers. It was a thicker synthetic, of better quality than the ones she had already, and would shrink less quickly. It must have cost closer to Rs 250 than the Rs 100 or 150 ones she had. So it had become Bimla's special sari, which she kept in her trunk to be worn when she went visiting.

Hopefully she would have better luck with her new employer. This one had more than three wardrobes full of clothes, and she wanted them washed and starched just so. Most of her saris were in pleasing light colours with narrow borders, and she might give the same kind to Bimla. These would be totally inappropriate for village wear, where only old women wore saris with woven borders. On the other hand, who was there in the city to see or comment? There was also a wedding coming up. Her mistress's husband's brother, who lived in America, was coming to get married in Delhi. As they had no other relatives in Delhi, everyone would stay in their house and Bimla would be the main servant. There would be a lot of work to do, as her mistress had warned her when she gave her the job. Bimla would love a bit of gold as a reward for the work, to save for her daughter, but she doubted she would get any. But perhaps it would be another bright synthetic sari…

Mistress and the Maid and mutual misunderstandings in the language of the sari

The formal gifting of saris, especially on the occasion of festivals such as Divali and Dussera, is an integral part of family life. The traditional inclusion of maids and other retainers in this cycle of gifting has the effect of incorporating them within quasi-family relationships. Often these gifts take the form of 'hand-me-downs' of worn saris,[78] as the mistress takes the opportunity to tidy and edit her own collection. For example, an elderly woman in Indore was being gifted too many expensive saris by her daughter, who had married a wealthy man. While she couldn't refuse these, she felt as an elderly person that they were unsuitable for her. She preferred soft worn thinner cottons over these heavy and bulky new items, which she therefore passed on to her long-serving maid.

This process of gifting is not without tensions, however, due to frequent misunderstandings and incompatibilities of taste. Not one of the maids we spoke to had ever been asked by their mistresses about what kind of sari they would like for themselves!

Frequently, a mistress will tend to assume that while her relationship to her own collection of saris is highly nuanced and discriminating, her maid lacks such sophisticated sensibilities and will be happy to wear anything. So she will simply go to a shop and ask for a 'maid's sari', and spend what she thinks is an appropriate sum. She will take for granted that the maid prefers synthetic rather than cotton. And she will not stop to think that synthetics actually vary considerably in thickness or opacity, which may be a very important consideration for an especially modest maid, or one keeping *purdah*. She will assume the maid is largely indifferent to differences of style or fashion.

In reality, few of these assumptions are justified. Many maids, like Bimla, doubtless concede the practical advantages of a synthetic, but that does not mean they would not be delighted to receive the more delicate (and not necessarily more expensive) cotton to keep as a special, non-working sari. Equally, while the maid may not share her mistress's interests in the detailed differences between regional saris and ethnic styles, she does watch the television soap operas and is very aware of how the clothes of the stars affect fashions in saris and in other elements of material and design.

In addition, the maid's tastes and wish lists are influenced by her delicately balanced position between the world of the village from which she comes and that of the town in which she works. Commonly, maids go back home for major life-cycle events or crop harvests when extra labour is required, and these visits are also occasions for fulfilling elaborate obligations of gifting and sharing. As a presumably 'affluent city worker', she is expected to both wear and gift a better class of sari than those the villagers already possess

Most mistresses are quite unaware of how important their gifts of saris to the maid are to the maid's own gift-giving in her native village. Indeed, a modern-day maid who might work in several urban households may be regarded as an indispensable source of saris by an impoverished village. Most maids said that at least half of their saris were handed on to sisters-in-law and other female relatives.[79] Given that they know the mistress has usually given little thought to the gift in the first place, they have little compunction about doing this. So what the mistress often sees as greed or excessive interest in clothes by the maid actually reflects the burden of incessant demands upon the maid from her village. In addition she has to negotiate her own appearance, both as the individual who introduces urban styles to curious villagers, such as pinning the sari or wearing matching blouses, and as someone who is able to return to a more 'homely' rural appearance. Her dilemma is that she needs to appear simultaneously as modern, the conduit to city style, and as someone who has not 'lost touch' with her roots and does not consider herself superior to her peers.

As a result, if the saris given to her by her mistress are considered either too crude or cheap, or too immodest or vibrant, they are likely to be a source of embarrassment to the maid. A kindly employer had given her maid, Lakshmi, an expensive off-white Bengal handloom sari with a woven *zari* border. The maid's experience in the city allowed her to appreciate its quality, and she treasured having it in her trunk. After some time she travelled to the countryside to visit first her in-laws and then her mother. She decided to wear her exquisite new sari to see her mother. But her disapproving mother-in-law and sister-in-law made her change it. They felt there would be talk in the village because it looked like an old garment, the colours pallid and seemingly faded. Lakshmi felt they didn't like it because even though the sari had green, yellow and white stripes on a cream base with a yellow and *zari* border, it did not have any 'designs' or 'flowers' on it. Lakshmi felt contempt at the way a much cheaper and older sari, with loud flowers, met with more approval. She passed on the expensive sari to her mother who, being a widow, was unlikely to encounter such censure for its gentle colours.

While in many cases such misunderstandings may occur even with well-intentioned mistresses, in other cases they manifest a conscious exertion and expression of the mistress's power and position. A mistress may dress with considerable care and attention when going out in the evening or to work, but many treat the home as a place of relaxation where she can go about in an unstarched, relatively unkempt sari. Her maid, however, who sees this home as a place of work, is likely to be much more carefully dressed and 'groomed'. Some mistresses become sensitive to this and feel threatened by the greater smartness of the maid. One mistress told us adamantly that she did not want her maid walking around in clothing than might be confused with her own. Therefore she did not give hand-me-downs, and quite deliberately gifted the maid clothing that she regarded as clearly representing a maid's aesthetic rather than her own. By contrast, several others, with a rather different sensibility, were more concerned that their maids should be an asset in showing off the style and respectability of the house, and assuming that left to their own devices the maid would choose something dreadful, selected saris to match the style of the home, thereby reducing the maid to being just another part of the interior design.

the mistress's muted handlooms

These misunderstandings are a contributory factor to a larger shift in the exchange relationships between employers and employees. Traditionally the gifting of saris to the maid during festivals was seen as an auspicious act, quite separate from wage labour. Gradually, however, the gifts have become the subject of more explicit negotiations, with maids making demands for either better quality or more numerous saris. This process has been taken further in some households, where mistresses agree to give money for the express purpose of allowing the maid to buy her own saris. Finally, for some, the money has just became a bonus with no pretence that it should be spent on saris at all.

As a wealthy Mumbai woman noted:

I would like to give my maid a sari for Pongal. But they all have their individual tastes. So they say give us the money and we will buy it ourselves. Maybe they want to buy it for themselves or for their daughter, or mother, or sister. I wouldn't be offended if they used the money for something else. It is theirs, after all. This has become more and more popular practice. Earlier at Pongal it was standard that we gave the maid a sari, blouse and petticoat. This was the case up to ten years ago. Now a lot of the girls who work in the house, are younger and they won't take a sari. They wear shalwar kamiz.

This shift is a significant one, for it shows that mistresses are increasingly unable and unwilling to impose their choices on their maids. This in turn reflects both the decreasing extent of traditional social hierarchy and submission in modern India, and the increasing complexity and unpredictability of the fashion tastes of Indian people.

This chapter began with an account of a mistress and a maid getting dressed and ready for their work. It revealed how their very different resources and expectations are expressed in their choice of clothing. When we then turned to the relationship between them, we found, rather than a simple case of patronage, a surprisingly convoluted and contradictory series of projections. Often despite good intentions, what happens tends to reflect ignorance as much as knowledge. Although these two figures share such intimate domestic space and indeed much of their lives, a focus upon the sari demonstrates just how far apart they remain.

the maid's bright synthetics

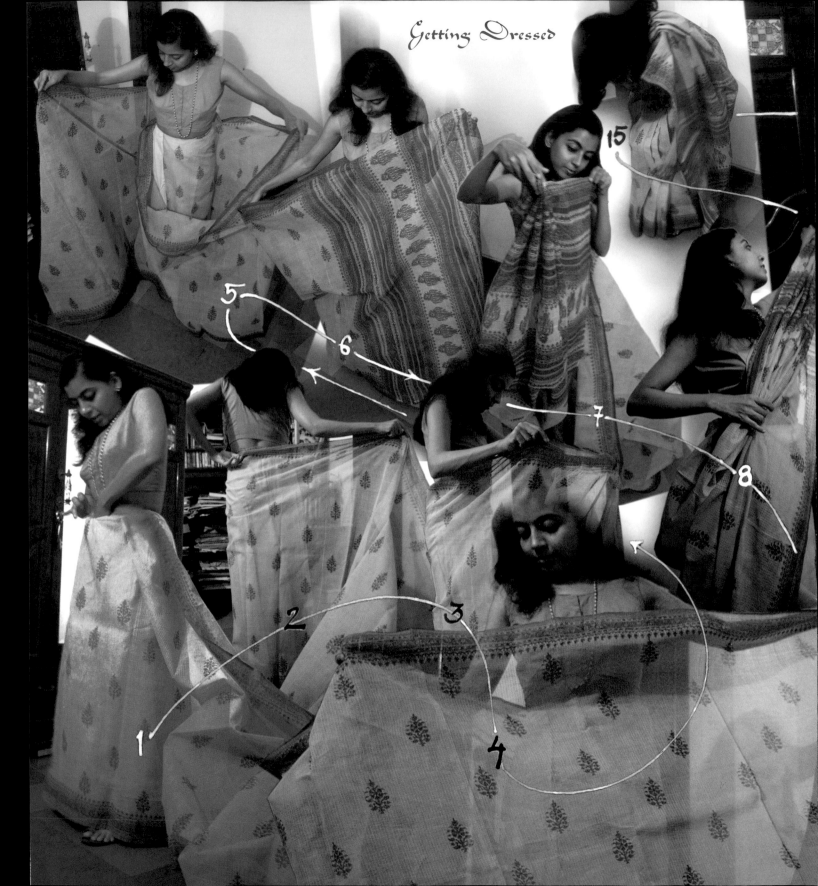

Getting Dressed

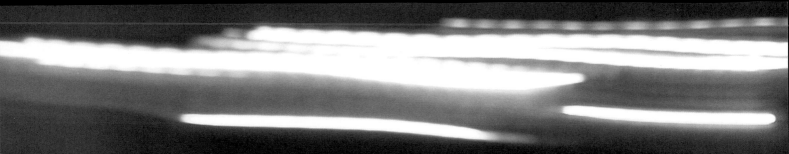

The Pleasure of What to Buy

The Pleasure of What to Buy

When do I buy saris? There are a few occasions. When I buy saris I do so from a Bengali shop in my neighbourhood. They have lots of variety and are within my range. Whether you are going for a Rs 200 sari...or a Rs 1,600 you can get both. I am not influenced by TV soaps in buying saris. My main criterion is that I should like the colour, it should suit me and it should be simple and not too bright. I learnt this by what my husband said to me. He would say "this looks good on you".
                                                                                              -Mina

Most women such as Mina who have the resources to do it, view purchasing a new sari as a significant event that involves skill, negotiation, anxiety and, hopefully, in the end, decisiveness. In most cases this is a social rather than just an individual activity, with relatives or other companions providing support and, sometimes, opposition. In turn these experiences depend upon the different kinds of retail outlets which exist in India, and the customs and expectations of those who make a living selling saris. In this chapter, we present three common shopping scenarios in order to show something of the diversity that emerges out of the possible combinations of buyers and sellers.

SHOPPING SCENARIO 1

The village and the itinerant peddler

He rang his cycle bell, as he always did, just as he went past the first pond and while he was approaching the big *neem* tree. It was a distinctive bell, not rung with the lengthy abandon of novice young boys, nor the cautious sharp bursts which came from middle-aged peasants returning with jerrycans of kerosene balanced on their baskets. His was a business-like bell, three short rings, not too peremptory, creating just enough of a presence to announce his arrival as a source of pleasure and business.

For the women of the village, the sound of the peddler's bell signalled indulgence and trepidation, just as the ice-cream man's loud film songs did for the children. Though few could afford to buy, looking through the tempting displays of new saris was free. From the bend in the village lane, he peddler knew that most households could hear him clearly and the children would spread the word further. He had decided to make an unscheduled stop in Madanpur today. He had been the previous Thursday as usual

and the women would not expect him until Thursday this week. But he knew their big Muslim festival was approaching, and not all the women had managed to buy their saris yet. He reckoned that dropping in early in the week, after they had bought their food on Sunday, might be a good time to coax them to spend some money on themselves. And it was a good time of the day to come. Everyone would have finished their baths and mid-day meal, the men were back in the fields or dozing in their courtyards, and the children were napping or playing out by the road where the traffic was less at this time of day. It meant he had to skip his own meal to cycle over from the other cluster of villages about twelve kilometres away, but he didn't mind. The extra sales would compensate.

Alighting near his favourite bamboo grove, the peddler heaved his heavy bundle to the ground. As he was doing so the first women were already approaching, crisp in their freshly wrapped saris, the vermilion bright in their hair and their skins glistening with oil. One of them was unfamiliar. Perhaps a new bride or a visiting relative? That was always good for sales. He could point out the superiority of his stock compared to what she would have seen in her own village. The women squatted down waiting for him to produce his wares, and he spread out a large torn bedsheet on the dusty ground. Untying his bundle, he first took out some of his best handloom saris. Not many people bought these anymore as they complained they were impractical, but the peddler knew that the women still coveted them. First impressions lasted, so allowing a glimpse of their complicated weaves and starched folds was a good ploy. He pulled them out nonchalantly and let them settle in a mosaic of coloured squares. The women shifted uneasily, but no one said anything. Then came the mill saris, his biggest sellers, dozens of brightly printed saris, in plastic wrappers with the names of the companies who made them in luminous white painted letters. They were mostly in English letters which he couldn't read, but that didn't matter. The women couldn't either, and in any case they did not select according to the name. Their constant demand was for new designs, new colours.

The peddler wished more women would show up. They would be pleased with what they saw. He had worked hard to get hold of this consignment. His supplier just did not understand the importance of new saris in Muslim festivals. But the peddler knew how every woman used this occasion to replenish her old saris which were falling apart. After twenty years in this business, he could see instantly that this consignment had some new designs. The colours were more or less the same, but the combinations were different.

One of the women picked up a pink sari with yellow dots and asked to see it properly. The peddler pulled it out of the wrapping and spread it out over the others, being careful not to let it touch the ground and get dirty. Soon more arms reached out and more saris were unfolded. Suddenly the bamboo grove was buzzing. More women had arrived, rushing now so as not to miss the best designs.

Asma came late. The peddler could see that she clearly liked a purple and green sari that Paru was already inspecting, but did not know how to get it from her. Asma was not quick like the others; she was careful to take everyone's opinion into account rather than impetuously choosing something she found. She turned her attention to the ones still lying on the bed sheet. He pointed out a green sari with big blue flowers which he thought would suit her. She had been buying red ones for ages now because that was what her in-laws wanted her to wear, but she seemed to like the green. Naseeba was inspecting a pale mustard one with brown flowers, but her grand-daughter was trying to talk her into a bright maroon and blue one. Naseeba was protesting loudly, but was clearly tempted. Would she dare wear such a bright colour at her age he wondered? He doubted it, but one never knew with women!

Paru was still inspecting the purple sari with the pink and green design, which reminded him of tyre marks, and was shaking it out to look at the design on the pallu. He thought the colours might be a bit inappropriate given her usual pretensions to sober colours, but held his tongue. It was too early to say anything yet. They were all immersed in their own perusals, seeking opinions from others, checking out the quality of the fabric, some even putting it against their skin to see if the colour suited them. They must have seen women do this in the shops in town, he thought to himself with amusement. The shopkeepers there did a hard sell, offering their opinions constantly, taunting the village women for their lack of knowledge about variety or prices, and the peddler wondered whether these women bought saris in those shops out of fear and embarrassment rather than choice. He preferred to do things differently. He knew they would ask him for his opinion eventually, so it was best to wait and watch.

The two sisters Noori and Meena gazed from the sidelines, offering their opinions but without any intention of buying. They were wealthier than the others and preferred to buy their saris from town. Meena was a good bargainer, and why wouldn't she be? She went to the bank and the shops on her own, travelling easily, dressed in her shalwar kamiz. They only showed up when the peddler came so as to offer their opinions, pass sarcastic remarks and keep an eye on who bought what, to gossip about later.

Naseeba asked if she could exchange the sari for a different one in case she changed her mind. It was evident that she needed reassurance today, because he always had an exchange policy for unworn goods. He could see that today she had to give in to her grand-daughter, so he told her not to worry. He put the money into his belt. Naseeba stood clutching her purchase, which looked even brighter next to the drab green sari she was wearing, waiting to see what the others would buy. Bina asked if she could see one of the handlooms he had taken out first. He unearthed them from the bottom, and Bina and her daughter-in-law looked over a striped orange and green piece. The young daughter-in-law asked everyone from her family what they thought. They all liked it and looked at it longingly. Bina offered to buy it for her. She asked the peddler if she could pay Rs 30 today and pay the balance over the next few weeks. He had to agree. The peddler knew that none of these women would have the Rs 200 all at once, and this was the only way he could sell the saris. He made a note of the balance in his little notebook, which he then carefully replaced in his breast pocket.

Paru looked at him for assurance. He held out a grey and purple one instead, and asked her whether it wouldn't suit her taste more? She agreed, relieved to be helped in her decision and paid for it in full. She had no children, and so had enough money to produce the Rs 150. The peddler pushed the purple and green sari rejected by Paru in Asma's direction. She looked up with a grateful smile, but the peddler was careful to keep his eyes downcast. It wouldn't do to let on that he knew these women like he did his own family. They trusted him to not take sides and give impartial advice, and this reputation was the key to his success. Asma skipped off happily to confer with the others and even disappeared from view when she went home to ask her invalid mother for an opinion. The peddler knew she would be back, and turned his attention to wrapping up the other sales. Meher and her daughter had shown up to exchange a blouse she had bought last week. It was too small, she said. She had worn it once and washed it but the peddler took it back nevertheless; he could sell it for a reduced price to a poorer woman. He would incur a loss, but in the long term it was better to keep the good will of the village big man's wife.

The women who had selected their saris now wanted blouses. This was easier. He knew who would want a contrasting blouse and who a matching one. The older women did not like the new designs with the puffed sleeves, so he didn't even bother giving them a choice and just handed them the conventional straight-sleeved ones. It had taken him a while to learn to guess their blouse sizes by just looking at them, but now he did it without even looking too hard. He just knew, and the women were grateful that he did.

While he gathered his bundle together, the peddler did a quick calculation and realised that he had sold twelve printed saris and one handloom one. A good haul, as he had hoped. And there was still another stop to be made at the other end of this village, and two more in the village across the main road. Not bad. But suddenly he felt adventurous. He knew that Sabera was planning her daughter's wedding because the women had been discussing it for weeks now. So he asked her if she wanted a special sari for her only daughter's trousseau. Sabera was wealthy, her husband was a primary school teacher and had a salary, and so he did not feel guilty about tempting her. He pulled out one of the very special saris that he kept wrapped in an old sari from the bottom of his bundle, a beautiful red and pink with lots of shiny *zari* on it. Everyone gasped at the sheer opulence of the sari as it lay there glinting in the afternoon sun, putting all their own purchases to shame. Sabera was embarrassed because everyone knew she could afford to purchase it right then and there. She covered it up by asking him to bring it again after the festival was over so she could think about it and confer with her husband in the meantime. The peddler nodded obligingly. The groundwork was done. The prospects were good for a further sale.

He pedalled off, ringing his signature tune on his bell.

SCENARIO II

*Third time lucky**

DRAMATIS PERSONAE

The Husband: In an off-white shirt, the brown belt over grey brown polyester trousers just about managing to contain the belly, well-oiled hair and moustache, a model of the contemporary middle-aged Indian male.

The Wife: A sweet 'homely' face with prominent matching *bindi* and lips, wearing a mauve shalwar kamiz and a gold necklace.

The Shop Assistant: As the husband, but ten years younger.

*This scenario is based mainly on a conversation we recorded, with speculative unspoken thoughts in parenthesis.

THE SCENE:

It is about 5 o'clock on a hot Friday afternoon. 'Sari Palace' is a windowless shop on a busy street. Endless saris drape the shop front, the inside walls and much of the ceiling like exuberant bunting, the array broken only by occasional tilted signs giving the fixed price, piles of boxes and a kind of hanger with hips used as a mannequin.

The Husband: See, I told you, this shop has all sorts of saris, the rate is good, the quality is also good, it is a very good shop. Much better than those fancy show rooms. Here they are all displayed so clearly. If there is something wrong with the sari you can bring it back and take another in the same price range.

The Wife: I need two new saris for my brother's wedding. One for the *tilak* ceremony and one for the wedding proper.

Husband: This shop is very very good. Most of the shops around here are selling off stock they have had for five or even ten years. They will take a sari which costs 200 and sell it to you for 1,000. You know those well-lit showrooms, they hardly sell three saris a day. They can cover their costs only by overcharging. But here on the main street the stock is fresh and the designs are always new.

Wife: Hmm. Here we will find designs that the relatives in Kanpur will never have seen. Latest styles. (To the shop assistant) Bhaiya! I want to see something nice for a function. Show me some cheaper ones as well.

Several saris slither across the counter and come to a halt with their zari borders glinting through plastic covers.

Wife: Oh this pink is perfect, it's wonderful, it may be the first thing we have seen but I am sure it is right. (Then quickly upon seeing her husband grimace and move to pick out a light blue sari) Of course, I will buy a sari of your choice. After all, when I wear such a special sari I will be going out with you and you must feel happy. Last time I came here with Sarla Auntie. She found two lovely saris for her daughter-in-law.

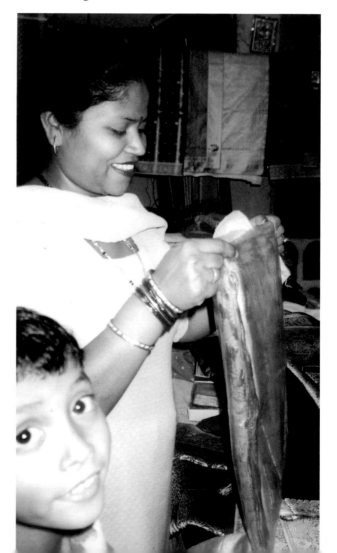

Husband: Oh you mean Sarla Auntie next door? You two women must have looked at a hundred saris at least, but today I am here. I can help make a swift decision. After all, I know something about the cloth business from my father.

Wife: Do you like this mauve one, it's not quite as good a colour but is still very nice?

Husband: What's the point of this sari, it's the same as the pink one before. It's just a lighter shade, too light. Do you really want that? Besides they have overcompensated with the design – they think if you don't wear a bright colour at a wedding, you need to flood a lighter colour with *zari* to make it look showy. Simple is best, not too much tinsel. I like this blue one, you can wear it to a wedding or for visiting. Rs 250 is about right.

Wife: Then is this purple one better?

Husband: It's a good fabric, it's heavy, it has gravitas. And it won't tear easily. Look out for the *zari* border on this though. You complain that this kind of embroidery snags in your jewellery.

Wife: (realising that her husband will keep the blue and reject her choice, decides on a compromise). You know I was also looking for a sort of greenish one, I saw it the last time I was here.

Husband: So take it, there is a greenish one over there.

Assistant: (handing her a greenish sari with a net effect). This is a good piece.

Wife: Have a look at this sari, what do you think? It's nothing like that green one I saw last time I was here but it's not bad. When you see a colour once which you like and don't have, it's hard to get it out of your mind. (To the assistant) Does the whole sari have this net effect, or is it only on the pallu? (Turning it towards the light) Don't you think perhaps it's a bit dull, though? I don't want my sari to look dull at a wedding. At a wedding one should wear bright colours. It looks like it is an old sari. It doesn't look shiny enough. It looks too dull. Very very dull.

Assistant: It's a new design.

Wife: It will look even duller in natural light.

Assistant: It will look very good, once you drape it, you will see what I mean. The colour suits you.

Wife (sharply): And if I don't like it will you also reimburse my rickshaw fare when I come to exchange it?

Husband: (trying to compromise in turn) This cloth is good. It can even be washed at home. (To the shopkeeper) This won't shrink will it? You see this won't catch easily either because the *zari* on it is not superficial, it is well embedded. It is solid work by a machine. Go on, take this one, and don't worry about 100 or 50 Rs here or there. Get something of your choice.

Wife: It's so hot.

Husband: Ah, but it's the lack of fans that keeps the prices down!

Wife: OK, which ones shall I take then? This one or that one? Which one did you like?

Husband: Leave that purple, take this green one and the light blue I found in the beginning. Don't worry about the price, the all-over *zari* on the green

sari has pushed up the price but if you like it, the extra 50 rupees is worth it.

Wife: Unfold the blue sari and show it to me. We should check it for flaws inside. What about a blouse piece, will there be enough fabric?

Assistant: You can always tell the tailor to cut out a bit of the sari itself for the blouse piece, and add some other cloth in its place. As that bit will be on the inside, it won't show.

They pay and leave with the two selected saris, the

blue and the green. But just outside the shop she inspects the saris again, this time checking their colour in the natural light. At this point the wife weighs up the pros and cons in her head. She thinks: *I agreed to the green sari because perhaps the all-over zari work compensated for the light colour and combined with the net effect makes it unusual, more like an expensive benarasi, and it comes with an extra blouse piece. The assistant has said the colour would suit me once I wore it. On the other hand it's not really the green I was looking for, that net effect will make it more prone to snagging, and now I look at it in natural light it really does seem light-weight.*

Wife: You know I really think perhaps this greenish one looks too lightweight with this net effect.

Husband (resignedly): Would you have preferred that pink one you were looking at?

The husband sighs. The wife returns to the shop and with a broad grin exchanges the greenish sari for her first love, the pink sari. She even gets Rs 50 back as the pink sari is cheaper than the green. But on going out she first peers into the two bags and then pulls them out of the bag for a final inspection. She thinks: What I really detest is that blue sari, but if he is going to give up on that, maybe I should give up on the pink. After all, I already have a pink sari. True, the purple doesn't have a blouse piece and the zari border isn't great, but it's much better than the blue. It is a heavier 'silk', which will last, and would seem to reflect well on his prosperity, which is why he might relinquish the blue for it. The green wasn't that bad and so a compromise might be best ...

Wife: You know maybe you were right about quality. That greenish sari was first class, perhaps I should get it after all, you liked it didn't you? Why not exchange this blue one for the green. And at the same time, I don't have to have this pink one, I already have a sari of this shade anyway, so why don't I exchange it for the purple one whose quality you also said was very good.

Husband: (to shop assistant) Please give me that green one again, and I want to exchange this pink one for that purple one we looked at earlier.

Assistant: But she just said she found that green one a bit light?

Husband: No, yes, well, I had one of my choice and this one is hers.

(Turning to his wife he says with a smile) Third time lucky!

SCENARIO III

Going to town

The final illustration is an establishment which, while smaller than more famous shops, still makes its own claim to be a 'name' in Kolkata. The centre of the shop is decorated with photographs of famous Bengali celebrities and politicians who have used it over the last century. Most of the people in the shop, however, would see themselves as quite ordinary. Unlike smaller shops where customers sit on soft mattresses, here the male assistants, many of whom have worked in this shop for more than ten years, are separated by white desks from their customers. There is a subtle hierarchy present, and an unspoken assumption that the most experienced man, with cultivated tact and charm, will take charge of selling the most expensive wedding Benarasi saris. These usually involve whole families in purchasing decisions. 'It takes longer to sell one. You have to convince the customer. People will buy a cotton handloom in five minutes, but a Benarasi takes over half an hour because there are so many opinions. So we have to play off people against each other. We have to eavesdrop on their discussions.' To sell an expensive sari, the salesman has to be sensitive to hierarchies of age, status and experience within the party and provide counter-arguments to their reservations without hurting sensitive egos.

At one end of the shop, two elderly gentlemen look simultaneously hapless and excited in front of a huge pile of slithering silks, desperately trying to make a choice. Their anxiety is only increased by the evident discrepancy between their lack of expertise and the sheer dexterity and speed of the assistants who seize saris from the shelves behind them and cast them over the desks. These gentlemen are in the city for a business trip, and one of them has been asked by his wife to pick up a sari for a niece's forthcoming wedding. Having purchased saris on a regular basis from this shop over ten years, he trusts the quality and reliable prices. Rather than traditional Bengal handloom (which he explained were readily available in Bhuvaneshwar) he intended to buy a printed silk, since the range of designs and colours was vast in Kolkata. Being the bride's mother's brother, he shouldered the bulk of the responsibility for gifting in the family. He had three criteria in making a selection: to avoid a sari without a border (as that was associated with widows), to buy a pale colour which he thought would suit his dark-skinned niece, and to choose a modern rather than a traditional design. The shopkeepers were eager to help an old customer, producing only around sixty saris rather than the hundreds they might have done. After long discussions the two men left happy with their purchase of an olive green sari with an abstract all-over design.

By contrast, another customer exhibited a common scenario in male sari shopping, a defiant self-confidence, in denial of their lack of any specialist knowledge. 'I like to shop for saris. I do not know very much technicality: the weave and the warp and the weft etc. but I do know a good sari when I see one. I like colours a lot. I like texture and design. Those are the three things that I look for. I mean, if I buy a sari I may not be able to tell you whether it is a *Kanjivaram* or *tanchoi* or something like this, but I could say that it is a nice sari. Even if there is something that I don't know about the technical things about saris or art for that matter, if I like a sari, I just buy it. If I like it I buy it. I don't really know if I should bargain, that is why I go to a store where I know it will be priced at the price you have to pay. I just go and choose'. The wife of one such man told us later, 'I wear what my husband buys for me. Even if I don't like it I am too scared to say anything. Now that I have two children I may say something once in a while, but even then he refuses to take it back and exchange it. He says, "if you don't like it then give it away to someone". So I land up wearing it myself.'

At the other end of this same shop we spent several hours observing the kind of scenario that both fascinated and in some ways threatened this traditional male shopping. A couple had come to the city from their village to shop for their son's wedding. Their two married daughters accompanied the elderly parents. The father carried a list, which he nervously consulted from time to time, of clothing he had to give as gifts. His entire budget was Rs 15,000. We encountered them as they had just finished buying the *dhotis* for the groom's male relatives. As the daughters were present, they then turned their attention to the bride's saris. They bought a wedding Benarasi and a veil to go with it from one section of the shop. They then went across the shop to buy the bride a white sari with red border for the ritual bath, and a printed cotton to wear afterwards, as well as one for her last meal as an unmarried woman and finally an ordinary sari to sleep in. Each was bought with a matching blouse and petticoat. These saris were chosen largely according to the tastes of the three women, but they were careful to avoid any with black and most of them were in shades of red or yellow. Additional purchases were made for other rituals associated with the wedding such as a red handloom *lojja bostro* to cover her face when the groom puts the vermilion in her parting. They also purchased a sari for the *neet koney*, the little bridesmaid. Although special children's saris are available in Kolkata, on this occasion they bought a full-size sari so that the bridesmaid's mother, an important relative, could have it afterwards as a bonus.

They still had to buy several more, as they intended gifting the bride about sixty saris altogether, including a special one for her first night in their home, but they decided they would buy the rest of these later. They intended to take their purchases home, show them to their relatives, consult with them and then return a week later. By then, they hoped to have the list from the bride's house detailing the various relatives who needed to receive a gift from the groom's side.

The essential shopping done for the day, the parents then urged their daughters to buy saris for themselves to wear at the wedding. They had already bought one each, but this one was to be a present from their parents. The two sisters lived in the same household, as they were married to two brothers, and they liked to wear similar saris when they went out together. But as one was of a darker complexion than the other, they needed to find the right colour that would suit them both. They settled for slightly different shades of pink, but these cost a thousand rupees each, nearly twice the father's budget, so they postponed the purchase for another day.

These scenarios are, of course, just a few fragments from the complex world of sari buying. As already noted, many women, especially in villages, obtain almost all their saris as gifts. More affluent city dwellers, on the other hand, may have specialist sellers calling at their home, and we watched a team of Bengali handloom sellers doing the rounds of middle-class households in Delhi. After hearing many other middle-class households talking about obtaining their saris from 'exhibitions' we also visited one such exhibition, taking place in one of the up-market hotels. But these in turn represent just some more examples from what could never be a comprehensive account, given the vast number of regional differences and categories of sari buying and selling that might be encountered.

Despite this diversity of the sari economy, the scenarios that have been described lend themselves to some significant generalisations. These concern the movement away from a tradition where men took responsibility for the purchase of women's clothing. As we have seen, a man's first sari purchase is often a marker of his coming of age as an adult. For most sari purchases, and especially significant ones for special occasions, and for gifts outside of the family, men were formerly expected to make the choice and

Handloom sellers doing the rounds

conduct the transaction. However, they are increasingly having their confidence sapped by criticism from increasingly assertive wives and daughters, who point out both their lack of knowledge and the fact that they are not troubling to understand women's desires. Where women find that they have an independent income and greater mobility, they assert their wish to be more directly involved in buying their own clothes. Therefore, as in two of our three examples, there is increasingly equal gender participation. In such cases the role of 'desire' moves from periphery to centre stage, because the person involved in the purchase is likely to at least empathise with the individual who will wear the cloth. Men had previously argued that it was precisely their absence of desire which would ensure more objective and thrifty choices. These gradual changes in purchasing are reflected in the rise of modern advertising for saris, where companies such as Garden developed campaigns increasingly targeted at women themselves.[80] And with families and couples shopping together, the shopping expedition itself, which might be dismissed as merely an economic activity, becomes a moment of shared love and concern.[81]

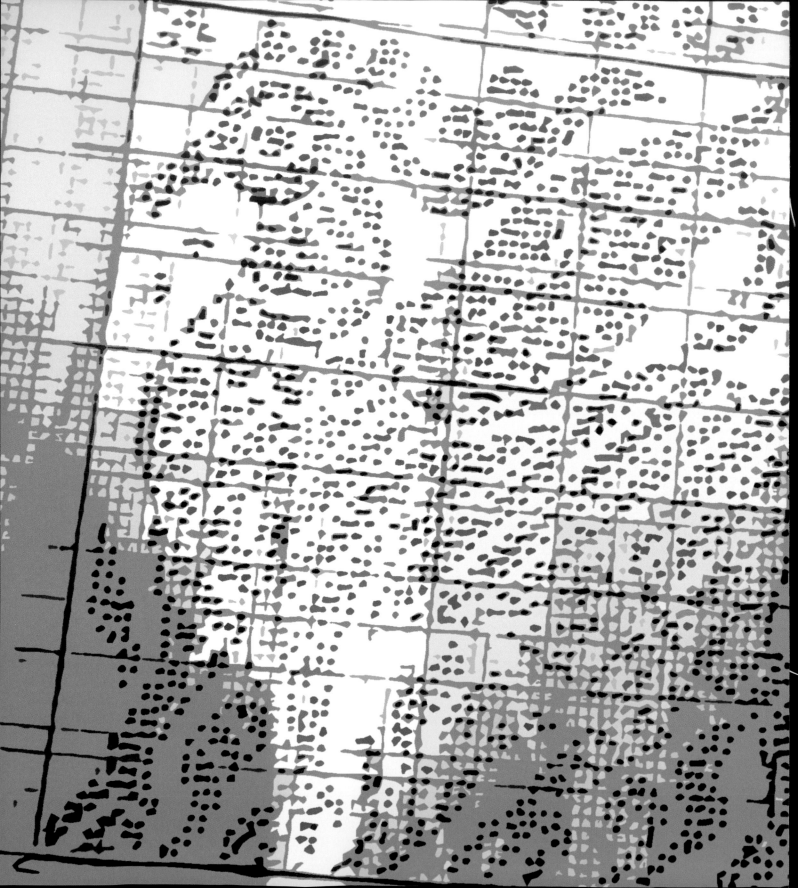

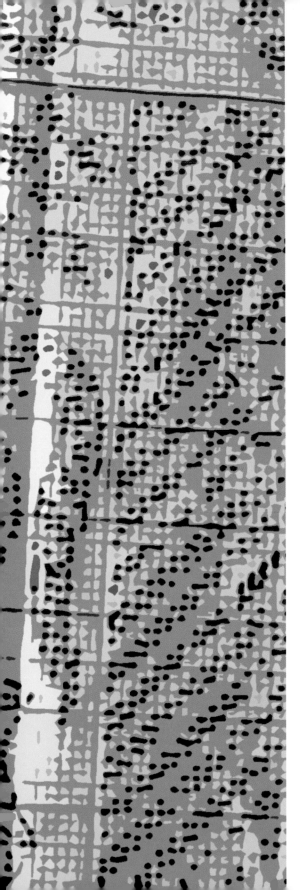

CHAPTER 10

Producers and Designers

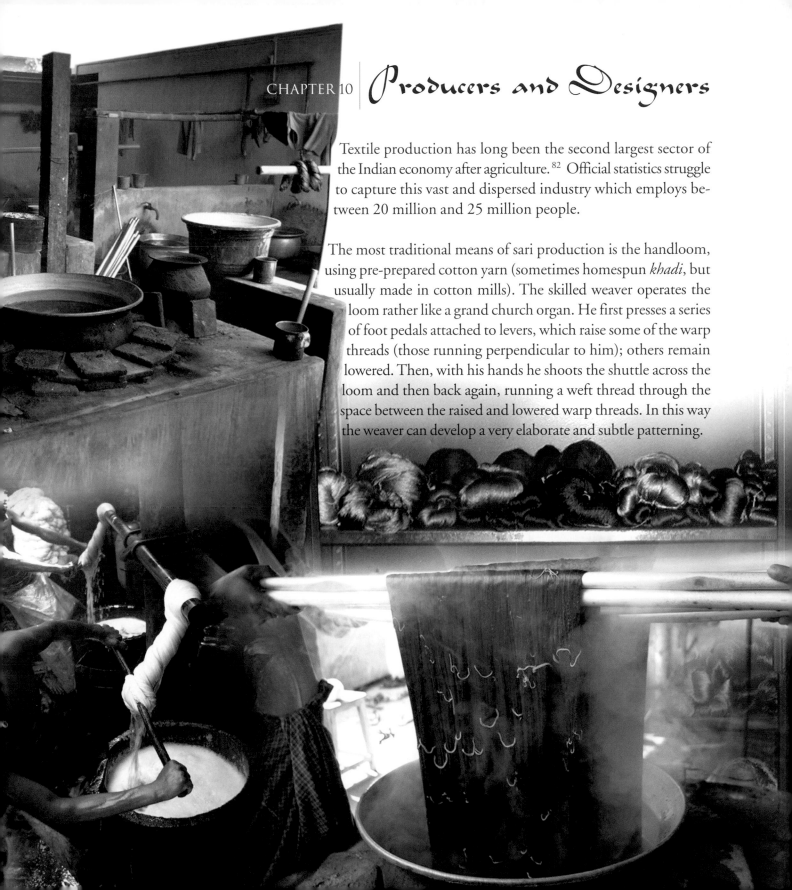

CHAPTER 10 | *Producers and Designers*

Textile production has long been the second largest sector of the Indian economy after agriculture. [82] Official statistics struggle to capture this vast and dispersed industry which employs between 20 million and 25 million people.

The most traditional means of sari production is the handloom, using pre-prepared cotton yarn (sometimes homespun *khadi*, but usually made in cotton mills). The skilled weaver operates the loom rather like a grand church organ. He first presses a series of foot pedals attached to levers, which raise some of the warp threads (those running perpendicular to him); others remain lowered. Then, with his hands he shoots the shuttle across the loom and then back again, running a weft thread through the space between the raised and lowered warp threads. In this way the weaver can develop a very elaborate and subtle patterning.

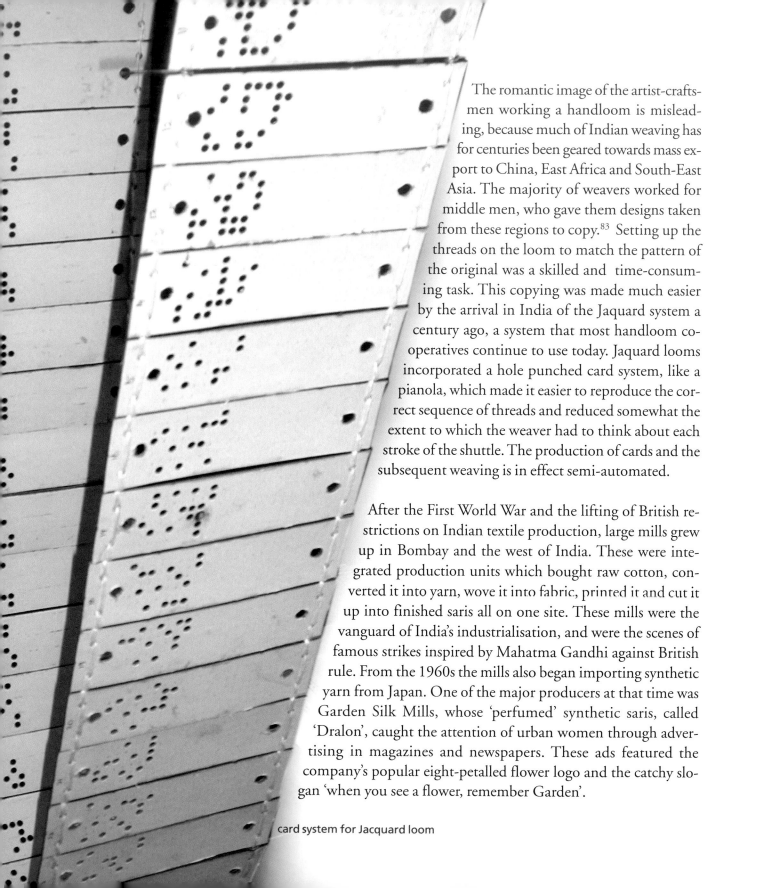

The romantic image of the artist-crafts-men working a handloom is mislead-ing, because much of Indian weaving has for centuries been geared towards mass export to China, East Africa and South-East Asia. The majority of weavers worked for middle men, who gave them designs taken from these regions to copy.[83] Setting up the threads on the loom to match the pattern of the original was a skilled and time-consum-ing task. This copying was made much easier by the arrival in India of the Jaquard system a century ago, a system that most handloom co-operatives continue to use today. Jaquard looms incorporated a hole punched card system, like a pianola, which made it easier to reproduce the cor-rect sequence of threads and reduced somewhat the extent to which the weaver had to think about each stroke of the shuttle. The production of cards and the subsequent weaving is in effect semi-automated.

After the First World War and the lifting of British re-strictions on Indian textile production, large mills grew up in Bombay and the west of India. These were inte-grated production units which bought raw cotton, con-verted it into yarn, wove it into fabric, printed it and cut it up into finished saris all on one site. These mills were the vanguard of India's industrialisation, and were the scenes of famous strikes inspired by Mahatma Gandhi against British rule. From the 1960s the mills also began importing synthetic yarn from Japan. One of the major producers at that time was Garden Silk Mills, whose 'perfumed' synthetic saris, called 'Dralon', caught the attention of urban women through adver-tising in magazines and newspapers. These ads featured the company's popular eight-petalled flower logo and the catchy slo-gan 'when you see a flower, remember Garden'.

card system for Jacquard loom

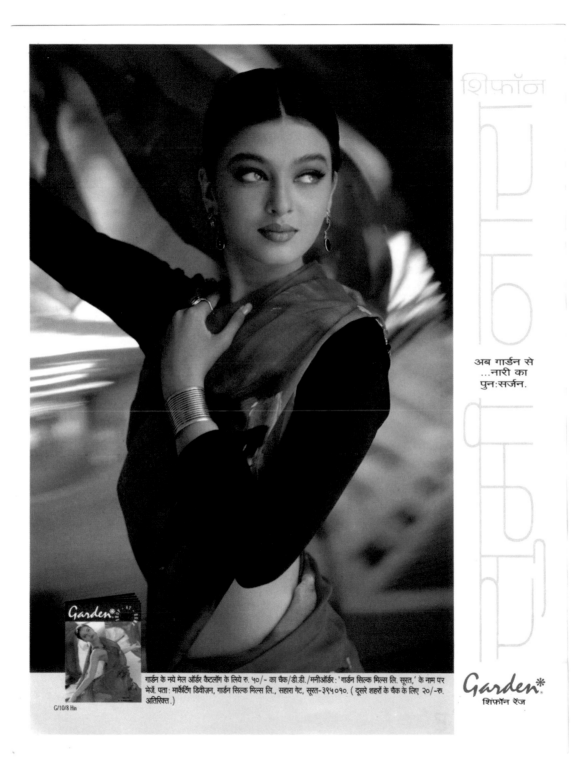

शिफॉन

अब गार्डन से
...नारी का
पुन:सर्जन.

Garden*
शिफॉन रेंज

G/10/8 Hin

Aishwarya Rai modelling a polyester *Garden* sari

In the 1970s, synthetics production advanced from spun yarn to 100 per cent polyester filament. This allowed for much sharper printing and high colour saturation, thereby offering a totally new look in saris. The new polyester chiffons and satins combined a low maintenance 'wash and wear' practicality with a silk-look-alike dressiness, making them suitable for both casual wear and smarter occasions. As Praful Shah, Garden's Manager Director, explained:

The sari was seen as a traditional costume. Garden wanted to present it as a modern garment, a contemporary form of fashion attire. 'Garden creates a new women' was the ad line for seven years in the 1970s. In a country where daylight is strong, the light, fresh and dainty florals became a runaway hit. The sari got redefined for the modern woman.

The new Garden look broke away from the traditional pattern of pallus and borders and instead introduced all-over prints in colours fashionable in the west. The pastel look, in a variety of floral prints, became the mainstay of 'that Garden look'. Garden, along with other companies such as Reliance (who launched their 'Only Vimal' brand), used the faces of well-known beautiful women to advertise its products. Through novel design and skilful marketing, the synthetic sari, previously thought of as a hard-wearing economy garment, became an expression of chic and modernity among the middle classes.

In the 1980s, however, there was something of a fashionable backlash against the mass-produced synthetic designs. This has been dubbed the 'ethnic style' revolution, and was influenced partly by Mrs Gandhi's own exquisite regional saris and the high-profile 'Indian Festivals' of fashion and trade she sponsored abroad, which depicted the handloom weavers as world-class craftsmen. Much of the educated middle class began to turn back to handloom cotton and silks.[84] These were distinguished by muted terracotta shades and vegetable dyes, with striking motifs drawn directly from specific regional styles, including tribal art. Those who favoured such saris were generally concerned to demonstrate aesthetic knowledge and discernment rather than wealth. In some cases, their enthusiasm reflected a left-wing political sympathy with the handloom weavers, or a pluralist vision of India that valued ethnic and religious minorities and diversities.[85]

From the purely fashion perspective, however, combining an informed ethnic taste with a sense of exclusivity became increasingly difficult as saris of this kind became widely available through handloom co-operatives, exhibitions and fairs, government emporia and specialist regional sari shops such as Nalli. The cognoscenti came under pressure to search for ever more obscure or unusual saris from specific villages known only to them, as one of them said:

'Something that people would like to be seen in, that is special, that makes you stand out. Such as handlooms from the North East. Lots of people still don't recognise them and I have one or two that I would feel very pleased to wear. If they don't know, they would ask – "where is this from" and if it is really obscure, like if it is from Manipur, then they would ask "how did you get hold of it?".'

The most enthusiastic supporters of ethnic style tended to be younger, professional, well-educated women. Other elements of the middle class, such as the speaker below however, were less enthusiastic about the purity of ethnic style:

I love the *kantha* work and the traditional *tangails* from Calcutta, and the Dhaka influences. But they can be a little monotonous, and with a bit of training the craftsman could make it better. I wouldn't want to eliminate tradition, but just a little introduction of the right shades of colour into the same designs can work a magical difference. My point about ethnic saris is that imitation is not what style is all about.

While the ethnic revolution turned attention back to handlooms, the mass market was being affected by the growing influence of the powerloom. These too use pre-prepared yarn, but are electrically powered and so work more rapidly, throwing the shuttle back and forth at great speed. The powerloom sector is extremely varied, however. The president of the Federation of All India Textile Manufacturers Association explained to us that it includes both extremely large operations with hundreds of modern machines and small rural houses containing just a couple of ancient rusty iron looms run by a ropey conveyor belt.

The government has not been enamoured of powerlooms, preferring handlooms and mills.[86] The powerlooms lack the prestige of tradition and craft and the philosophical and political approbation which Mahatama Gandhi gave to the handloom. The Handlooms (Reservation of Articles for Production) Act 1985 aims to protect the millions of handloom weavers from the competition of powerloom operators by reserving eleven categories of textile articles for exclusive production by handlooms.[87] The reason for favouring the mill sector is that the government finds the small and dispersed powerloom enterprises hard to keep track of, to tax and to monitor for compliance with labour laws.[88] Both the private sector and the state are increasingly concerned that the current modest technical base and highly dispersed and unregulated nature of the industry mean that India's weavers will struggle to compete in world markets. This is a particularly important consideration given that India will lift import barriers on textiles in 2004 under the terms of GATT, a change that some predict will have catastrophic effects.

Nonetheless, contrary to government intentions, the bulk of sari production is now firmly in the hands of the powerloom sector, much of it produced in tiny 'cottage industries' with no more than a dozen looms.[89] The handloom sector represents only 10 per cent of sari production while the mill sector has declined to just 5 per cent (down from 80 per cent in 1950, and 36 per cent in 1980). The number of powerlooms has increased from under 25,000 in 1951 to 850,000 in 1985, to well over 1.5mn today. Subject to little regulation, and often exploiting its workers,[90] the sector is anarchic but extremely flexible and is quick to respond to market trends and demand.[91] All manner of networks of production are being created by diverse entrepreneurs who cut their own deals linking spinning, designing, weaving and dyeing, with no one able to hold or enforce copyright or patent.[92]

Ahm

एकज़ म

Surat (B

Daman (

Surat: the Eldorado
of the synthetic sari

SAREES & DRESS MATERIALS

SAREES

Behind the politics and the statistics lie myriad small sites of production, such as the small town of Kanchipuram, renowned throughout India for its heavy traditional silk saris, often worn at ceremonial occasions such as weddings. Sari production in Kanchipuram could hardly be more domestic in scale. There is little indication that one is in a residential area for weavers until one crosses the threshold of a house. Immediately one sees a room entirely dominated by a large loom, the basis of the town's reputation. The looms are wooden and traditional in character. The weaver sits with his feet on the pedals sunk into a small pit. These pedals lift different combinations of warp threads (organised as 'sheds') to form a channel for the shuttle to pass through, which creates the particular pattern of the sari.[93] The loom is surrounded by the paraphernalia of family life, including pots, umbrellas and clothing, demonstrating that this form of sari production is still very much a domestic craft.

The principal threat to this system of production can be viewed just a few streets away, in another unmarked house. For here in the middle of Kanchipurum, the bastion of handloom production, is a powerloom weaver. His looms are producing cotton cloth for loin-cloths, so he is not an immediate threat to the silk sari weavers across the way, which is why he is permitted to work within the town. And this is certainly power technology with a small 'p'. The house contains a single electrically driven belt that lies in a trench dug from one end to the other. This single belt is enough to power up to six machines within the two main rooms, including not just looms but warping machines. The set-up bears no relation to the high-technology powerlooms found elsewhere in the powerloom sector: but it seems to 'do the business'.

The power looms have been able to take advantage of technological advances in the 1990s which further improved the quality of polyester yarn and made it cheaper. Their saris have found a ready market among the growing numbers of women working outside the home, who were demanding robust materials that could withstand rush hour commuting and frequent washing. At the same time, the mass-produced synthetic sari re-staked its claim to high fashion and glamour. With the liberalisation of the economy in the 1990s, a whole new range of international make-up and grooming techniques arrived in India, influencing ideas about desirable looks. Garden had their synthetic saris modelled by Aishwarya Rai, who subsequently, by virtue of her success in the Miss World competition, became not merely a beautiful local girl wearing national dress but a supermodel wearing an internationally fashionable garment. Such glamour not only boosted the mass market for synthetic saris, but wooed back some of the 'discerning middle class' from their handloom saris.

These new images and the increasingly sophisticated tastes of consumers led to growing expectations that even such mass-produced saris would display ever more unusual, interesting and distinctive designs. In response, the mass producers began to draw on the work of India's emergent *haute couture* fashion industry. That industry grew up rapidly in the 1990s, on the back of initiatives such as the National Institute of Fashion Technology, founded in 1991. An exceptional crop of creative designers emerged, including Ritu Kumar, Tarun Tahliani, Reena Dhaka and the Abu-Sandip team, setting up their own houses, brands, fashion shows and bespoke saris, which embraced a great sweep of ebullient non-traditional designs. For a price well in excess of most people's annual wage, each designer sari was guaranteed to be unique, and marked by its creative combination of old and new elements and motifs. As one affluent lady comments on the current exuberance:

Now chiffon is back in fashion. I have worn chiffons from the early 1960s and I still have those saris and in fairly good condition. Even though I have worn them plenty since. So chiffon is not something new for me, chiffon has always been there. But today it is combining kashida embroidery on chiffon and mixing it with a bit of a lace. If you go to the designer houses, they add on a pallu – a bit of intricate gossamer lace, delicately worked, very slim beading, just right there, on the border – the focus is just on the pallu. The influences are not very Indian, its an amalgam of East and West. These are enthusiastic young designers who sometimes go over the top. But when they can stay within the framework and can combine it with subtlety then it is a good piece. Otherwise it is only for the ramp.

These designers have come a long way since 1982 when Zandra Rhodes showed her collection of sari designs in New Delhi: 'Ripped, shredded at the edges, scattered with strategic holes, it constituted, people felt, not a design but an assault.'[94] More than two decades later, the new designers are again experimenting with the sari. As one of them, the well-known designer Tarun Tahiliani, commented, 'Many people think it is sacrilege to touch the sari. I think they are just stuffy.'[95] But perhaps mindful of earlier failed experiments with the hipster sari or the mini sari and the reaction to Rhodes, these new designers have done little to alter the integrity of the sari itself: it remains a five-metre piece of textile teamed with blouse and petticoat. Instead, they have used their imaginations to experiment with the cut of the blouse, the decoration on the sari and different draping styles. Given the importance of the film industry, a major shift came when

'Many people think it is sacrilege to touch the sari. I think they are just stuffy.'
– Tarun Tahiliani

the distinction between models and actresses and film stars became blurred. The entry of the beauty queens into Bollywood cinema meant that they began to serve as the clothes horse of designers, and their films served as fashion-shows.[96] The one-off designer pieces worn in films are quickly and illicitly copied and then mass-produced by the powerloom operators.

As well as internationally known names, there is a wide range of designers stretching from those working with block prints or silk screens to those in the computer-aided design laboratories of mills and co-operatives. At the mass-production level, Garden also employs fine art graduates rather than textile designers or commercial artists in an effort to secure greater creativity and imagination, with artists and computers together creating endless variations of modern geometrics and floral motifs to fill the seasonal collections.

a computer generated sari pallu design from Deepam, Bangalore

A sari designer in Delhi

Anita had set out to become a textile designer, and trained at a polytechnic for women in South Delhi. Her first job was with a small firm in Delhi that specialised in silk screens and block prints. She then went freelance before establishing her current design studio in 1990. Currently her offices have room for seven female designers. She employs another four male designers who work at a site 3 km away (she feels that working alongside men would not be suitable for her female employees), along with ten employees who produce the transparencies and silk screens. All the designers have diplomas in design from one of the polytechnics. They take around a week to produce a design, using ordinary poster colours and brushes like artists. Her team produces sketches, transparencies and screens which are given to her clients, printer-wholesalers who print around a hundred saris a day to distribute to retailers. In 2002 she had four such clients, all within Delhi.

The designers produce eighteen-inch screens, spanning the width of the sari. These are repeated along the sari's length. There will be different screens for the pallu, often reversed in a mirror image, and for the border. A separate blouse piece may require a fourth screen. They can make variants by re-combining these screens in different ways. For shalwar kamiz they make a screen for the body, but most of the work is spent on the design of the *dupatta*, although there may also be special work on the front of the *kurta*. While expensive pieces may be made with ten colours or more, the bread-and-but-

ter work seems to be moving from five to four colours in order to cut costs. A good six-colour design will sell for around 11,000 rupees. Most of Anita's work is done for silk crepes, chiffons and georgettes, although she is aware that there is an increasing synthetic element in these. She does not design for cotton or handlooms.

The annual cycle consists of two seasons, interrupted by the monsoon, whose high humidity prevents discharge printing. For the summer season, Anita starts in October, supplying the designs in December and January for printing in March and April, at which point she starts work on her winter collection. A typical client may want fifteen or twenty designs for a month's printing. In general, winter favours more traditional designs such as paisleys, while summer is suited to brighter and bolder colours.

Anita also has to have a sense of changing fashions. After a year and a half in which 90 per cent of her output was floral designs, she has seen a clear shift to abstract and geometric designs. She gains her sense of these trends from a mixture of national and international textile fairs, influential magazines and films. She also has her own preferences, which are for floral designs such as those by William Morris, reinforced by a visit she made to the museum dedicated to his work in North London.

She considers a design to be a hit if it used to print more than 500 pieces. Only a few will be printed at first, because the printers can quickly assess the likely demand. The printer/wholesalers sell onto boutiques around the country. Her company's name is never used even when her work is the sole basis of a retailer's 'designer' collection. She remains in the background, and is only known only through word of mouth.

A few years back Anita had ten clients and employed nearly sixty people. She feels the decline in her fortunes reflects a decline in the sari itself in Delhi. Her own production has moved from being based almost entirely on saris to being 60 per cent shalwar kamiz and only 40 per cent saris. The increase in Western clothes at the higher end of the market also suggests longer term problems. Equally important is the lack of effective copyright laws. Whole 'designer' collections can and have been directly copied by other retailers. There is little she can do, since she has heard that even India's most famous designer, Ritu Kumar, has had little success in trying to sue those pirating her designs. She suggests that some of the biggest textile producers in India don't bother employing designers, preferring to simply copy what they see in the market: 'they all have advanced technology, and are rampant copiers. The industry is absolutely disorganised at our level.' On the other hand she feels less threatened by computer design, citing several clients who found these ineffective and returned to her handmade designs. But computers may have more of an impact in production, as one of her clients has started using computer-generated embroidery in sari production, though she personally feels such work still looks clearly inferior to hand production.

As a result of these recent developments in powerlooms and design, the traditional divisions in the production chain are breaking down, being replaced by various arrangements for the connections between design, production and distribution. For example, Reliance Textiles, which produced one of the well known 'Vimal' brand of saris, closed its own mill for producing saris in 2001 and outsourced production to small-scale powerlooms based in Surat.[97] The Jaquard cards of the handloom co-operatives often now embody patterns generated from design software from the Chennai headquarters of Co-optex, one of India's biggest textile co-operatives. Today,

'with the press of a button and click of a mouse, you can now design the sari of your dreams. And Tamil Nadu textile giant Co-optex will weave that dream to life for you. A computer-aided design centre at the state-run textile corporation in southern India, popularly known as Co-optex, will let women design their own saris. The customer is able to sketch her own design at the centre in Chennai and Co-optex weavers will weave it to her specifications.[98]

In London many shops now offer this bespoke design facility, with the garments made up in India.

At the same time, designers working at the top end of the market are moving out to villages in order to be associated with traditional handloom production. They sit with weavers in the villages, translating their own designs into the weavers' terminology of sequences and warp and weft threads, in order to make garments that will be sold as expensive 'designer collections' on the Delhi market. The degree of confusion between once clearly demarcated categories of sari production is exemplified in a new hybrid – the 'handloom synthetic', produced by handloom weavers using synthetic yarn. At first sight a contradiction in terms, the handloom polyester expresses well the dilemmas of the contemporary handloom sector, caught between trying to serve a cheap mass market and a more expensive taste for craft saris.

This increasing fuzziness between the traditional distinctions on production is reflected in a corresponding fuzziness in consumers' knowledge about the fabrics they are buying. Almost any shop will set out its saris divided neatly into cotton, silk and synthetics. But with knowledge of actual production sites and processes, it becomes evident that neither the shopkeepers nor shoppers can be at all sure about what is being sold. For quite some time there have been artificial yarns such as 'art silk' or 'apoorva', which most (though not all) shoppers appreciate to be imitations of silk. In addition, many companies now produce yarn which is a mixture of synthetic and natural fibres. Since each potentially compensates for the deficiencies of the other, a mixed fibre can produce more satisfactory results. Some of this is quite above aboard, but there is growing evidence of silent adulteration. Within a garment that is supposed to be pure silk or cotton, synthetic fibres can be found, often deliberately concentrated in the centre of the sari, leaving the extremities – which is the part that most people touch and test – relatively pure. With new technology and better yarns, it is increasingly possible to fool even the professionals.

Not surprisingly, we struggled in our conversations with people to pin down the precise meaning of terms such as 'crepe', 'chiffon' and 'georgettes'. The following is a typical example:

We used to have silks, chiffons, dasheen crepe. That's made of... what is that? I really can't say – it's man-made, not pure, a mixture, something like Mysore(?) crepe. Mysore is more expensive, more pure – pure means more silk, well, artificial silk – they don't take the silk out of silk worms. The average person wouldn't be able to tell. They will know the basic distinction. For them this is all 'silk' in their language. Silk is silky texture, the feel – that's the main thing. So then I can say it is a kind of silk, a variety of silk.

As this suggests, what at first appear to be technical terms are in reality descriptive ideas, with no more specificity than 'floral print' or 'a sort of green'. Consumers' primary distinctions, of handloom v. mill, silk v. synthetic, *zari* v. plastic, chiffon v. crepe, are at heart relative terms that distinguish what are seen as better or worse products within a given context. So 'pure silk' can designate a genuinely expensive sari, but is also likely to be used to refer to more expensive end of a cheap range of goods. It does not necessarily designate what the fabric is actually made of.

There are similar doubts over *zari*. This is the term once given to gold-covered silver thread that was used to embroider fine saris. There are many testimonies to its authenticity in the 'old days' in stories about the puddles of molten metal found after a fire in a sari shop. Today, almost every establishment concerned with saris claims that the higher end of its stock is made with 'real *zari*'. Certainly the weavers in Kanchipurum were convinced that the bobbins they were using, which came with a government stamp indicating their weight and place of origin, were of real *zari*. However, these were

a fusion design: Sambhalpuri weave (Orissa) on *tussar* silk

sold to the weavers at such a low price that they could not possibly be genuine metal. It is likely that only the most expensive saris (over ten thousand rupees) contain *zari* made of silver and gold.

Branding has also become an issue. Earlier, with handloom saris, the names of saris were associated with the particular regions where they were made: for example, *leheriya* saris came from Rajasthan, *paithani* saris came from Maharashtra, *Kanchipuram* from Tamil Nadu and so on. These saris had distinctive weaves, colour combinations and quality of yarn used which were signified by their regional names as labels. Various categories were matched to particular demands, such as the Benares sari being a frequent choice in North India for a Hindu bridal sari. However, in recent years, the production of handloom saris has become somewhat more eclectic, such that Sambhalpuri weaves (from Orissa) are being innovatively produced on cheaper *tussar* silk, and Bengal weavers are incorporating 'temple' designs from southern saris. While motifs and patterns have always travelled in the textile world, the rapidity of this movement in the contemporary market makes it hard for even shopkeepers to keep pace or invent a new nomenclature for these hybrid handloom saris. But they insist the hybrids have been good for sales, since they are usually much cheaper than the original. So, for example, while Sambhalpuri silks were prohibitively expensive for most customers, the reproduction of Sambhalpuri designs on cheaper silk have made these saris relatively affordable.

zari yarn

In the case of powerloom synthetic saris the story of brand names is quite different. Most of these saris have names printed in small letters at one edge. Names like 'Praful' and 'Parag' are common. These names might correspond to a unit of production, but often are associated with a particular distributor or some aspect of marketing. The more popular names come to represent a reliable quality of the fabric, excellence of design and fastness of colour. But, on account of the lack of effective regulatory measures or law, these names can easily be stolen and mis-used by other companies producing inferior goods. As a result, while there are a growing range of brands in the market, it is extremely difficult to establish with confidence where any given sari was produced. When asked by gullible customers or anthropologists where a certain sari was from, shopkeepers simply make apparently confident claims about their origins in 'Surat', the centre of the powerloom industry.

Most customers do not, however, ask for synthetic saris by name. As one villager put it:

On television there are lots of names of saris: silk, tant, Kohinoor brand – now these are all new names for saris and we cannot remember all of them when we go to buy we try to remember these names and the shopkeeper also uses these names. But in the end we have to rely on the shopkeeper to tell us whether is something of good quality or not and what the best is that we can afford in our budget.

Even the more savvy and streetwise shoppers prefer to ultimately be guided by price and their own assessment of quality than specific brand names. Shopkeepers have their own tricks to demonstrate the undoubted quality of a sari. The 'knee test' was a particularly endearing one, whereby the shopkeeper nimbly bends his knee and pull the sari across it to demonstrate its strength and crush-proof quality. The 'flame test', holding matches to fibres taken from the sari to obtain an organic residue (and so prove its natural composition) is another dramatic display. Where demands from customers were less driven by

expectations of quality than by the desire for new designs and colour combinations, retailers tried to be first to spot these as new consignments arrived at the wholesale markets from distributors and producers. These skills of shopkeepers and the larger personal relationship between buyers and sellers remain important, since in this still largely unregulated and unbranded market, issues of trust and persuasion remain the critical factors in linking the industry with its consumers.

the 'knee test'

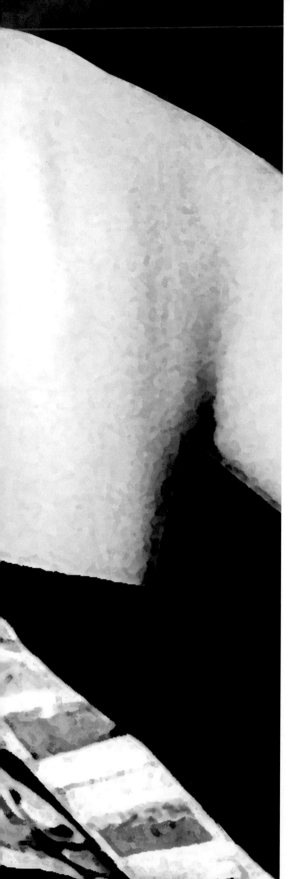

CHAPTER 11

Arbiters of Fashion

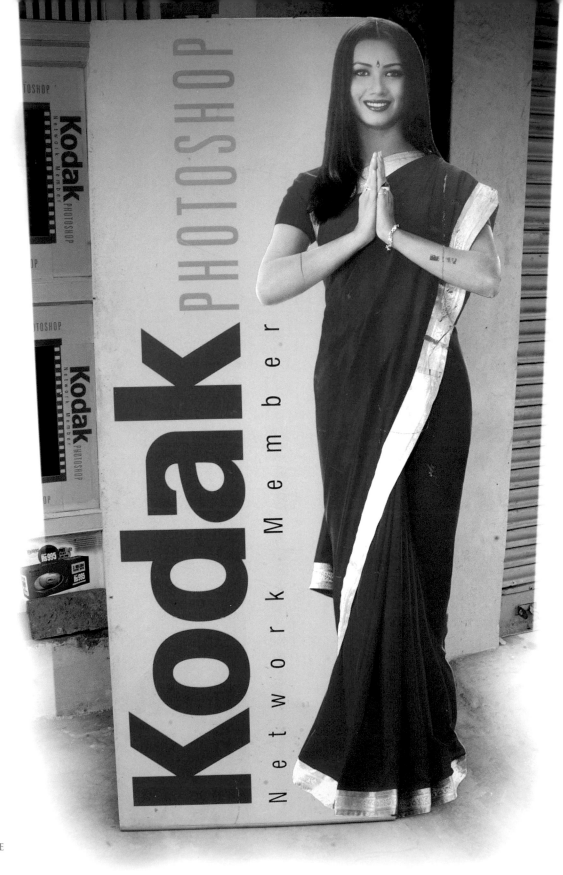

Arbiters of Fashion

The contemporary sari is as much a product of new developments in fashion and publicity as it is of powerlooms and companies. The Nivi style of draping the sari was invented in the nineteenth century (see note 6) and in the following decades became fashionable among the growing numbers of women beginning to appear in public life, including those active on the platforms and demonstrations of the anti-colonial movement. Their images became widely known through the press coverage of their political activities. The Nivi style also featured in iconic nationalist propaganda images, such as the sari unfurled as the map of Mother India, by Raja Ravi Verma.[99]

Following independence, the sari's popularity was further boosted by government information posters, film stars, politicians and ambassadors. It was adopted as an official uniform in the army, police and national airline, and as an unofficial one for teachers and bureaucrats. Many traditional alternative ways of draping the garment began to fade from view or remained confined to the domestic space, as did non-standard fabric lengths. The ultimate result was a self-consciousness that what one was wearing was not simply the traditional local draped garment of a region (described in several languages simply by the local word for 'cloth') but rather 'the Sari', the emblem of the new nation as a whole.

This provided the foundation for the adoption of the sari as a symbol of India itself. This association was cemented when, under the guidance of that consummate politician, Mrs Gandhi, the sari for a while became central to the construction of a visual image of India both internally and abroad. This nationalist appropriation of the sari was confirmed

a sari unfurled as the map of Mother India

in the popular mind by Mrs Gandhi's triumphant visits to the USA in the 1970s, which many women still recall. In the context of the Cold War and India's close economic and diplomatic links with the USSR, and the subsequent political tensions, these visits were of great importance. For the American audience, she coiffured her hair with its distinctive streaks of white, and wore lipstick to complement the silk saris she had chosen, which were far more luxurious and colourful than her usual handlooms. Long gone were her younger days travelling in Europe. when she sometimes felt self-conscious in her saris and switched to wearing Western clothes. Now, her brilliantly judged ensemble delighted the cameras and exuded a cool authority that greatly helped her official mission of conveying to the USA the notion that India was not to be treated lightly.

Back home, however, her saris were always handloom cotton, which identified her with the *swadeshi* and *khadi* campaigns of her father, Nehru, and of Mahatma Gandhi. In reality the fabric was more expensive, the weave unique, the creases fewer. Indira wanted to look like an ordinary Indian woman, but as the quintessence of such womanhood, not merely an instance of it. She was well aware that, as Nehru's heir, she held a special place in the popular imagination. Her task was to maintain the delicate balance between sharing a familiarity with the mass of her supporters while retaining the special mystique which made her revered. This she achieved, for women still recall the effortlessness with which she always wore the most apposite and exquisite saris. In public she never fidgeted, touching the pallu only to pull it over her head or hitching it up if the hot sun or muddy lanes demanded it. She moved in a fluid way that made you believe she was totally at home in a sari. She was the epitome of the carefully casual, power-dressing sari wearer, maintaining an apparently effortless perfection, conspicuously too busy with Affairs of State to worry about her appearance. Equally, the modest way in which she usually covered her head with her pallu in public satisfied the popular

Indira Gandhi abroad (compare with Mrs. Gandhi at home on page 128)

expectation concerning a widowed mother of two sons, and did much to obscure her cynical and ruthless use of power.

For many middle-class women Indira Gandhi was thus a trend-setter, a modern professional woman who wore traditional saris. She also contributed to the growing taste for the ethnic style, which she herself promoted through her patronage of festivals of India abroad where the work of Indian weavers was showcased. One of the hallmarks of her public appearances around the country was that she always wore a sari made in that region: a *tangail* in Bengal, a Coimbatore cotton in the south, the distinctive *sanganer* print in the western states. By appearing in these saris and greeting the crowds in the local language, she instantly established a rapport.

The most dramatic example of her astute sense of occasion was in 1972 when she addressed a gathering in the newly independent nation of Bangladesh. Thousands turned up to see the Prime Minister of India who had supported their struggle by sending Indian troops. The memory that most took away with them was of her sari, in traditional Bengali white with a red border. The sari conveyed a vivid message of solidarity with the region. By seeing the Prime Minister of India clothed in such a sari, the local gained national legitimacy and a powerful neighbour offered its respects to the new nation.

Even today, Mrs Gandhi's is by far the most commonly cited sari wardrobe, having becoming almost legendary in extent. Following her example, other women too aspired to collect saris from all over India, buying them on their holidays, asking fathers and brothers on business trips to bring back something 'typical', and educating themselves about the differences in weaves and sari names. More generally, women noted how Indira was always dressed in appropriate colours for specific occasions: white on a condolence visit, an auspicious *lal-pila* (maroon and turmeric) for a Hindu festival, a muted cream for a university convocation. The unusualness of the weave each time made up for the predictability of the colours, as one woman put it:

Indira Gandhi had the perfect collection of saris. Her aesthetic judgment was always unerring, you would want to wear any of them yourself, the variety was infinite, she rarely repeated a sari, the colours always suited her (that may have been because of her fair skin and the muted colours she wore) and she always looked elegant in them.

The message for many women was that it was possible to be elegant in handloom cotton and that the height of taste was a sober and restrained beauty. Most of all, one could justify buying exquisite saris by reminding oneself that one was supporting the handloom weavers who would otherwise become extinct. If the nationalist movement determined a new pan-Indian style of wearing the sari, Mrs Gandhi set the trend for their enthusiastic acquisition.

Although Mrs Gandhi was the professional politician whose image transcended any specific media, her kind of careful manipulation of image has come into its own with the rise of the modern media. Indeed, India has seen an increasingly close relationship between the film industry and politicians: there are several examples of the latter who either transferred from the cinema or who had simultaneous careers as film stars and political figures.[100] With television sets rare until well into the 1970s, films also provided most people's main exposure to glamour and fashion.[101] While there are prolific and influential cinema industries in India's regional languages, it is the Hindi cinema made in Mumbai (Bollywood) which is most widely distributed and understood across the country. In a nation of such great cultural variety, Bollywood is a common subject which people of all backgrounds and regions can share and discuss, in college canteens and railway carriages. Everyone has their favourite star, and many have a specifically remembered screen sari, drawn from this common stock of images. These often hark back to the avidly

watched classics of the black-and-white era. From the 1960s, people recall Nutan's playfulness with her pallu, the impossibly low hipline of Sharmila Tagore, the hourglass effect of Asha Parekh's tightly draped folds, or the natural, indescribable elegance of Waheeda Rehman. The 1970s belonged to Rakhee, who was famed for wearing her own beautiful saris in films. These names are always mentioned when men and women seek to describe their ideal of a beautiful Indian woman in a sari. Whatever else they wore on and off screen, there was consensus that they looked best in their saris. As Dwyer comments, 'the sari is heavily laden with cultural meanings of nostalgia, tradition, womanhood, nationalism and social status, the full range of which are developed in the Hindi movie'.[102]

The bias toward older movies reflects a nostalgia for moments which irresistibly combined modesty and glamour. Without colour to distract them, the viewers focused on the

Vayjanthimala, a star of the black-and-white era

varying textures of the saris and the way these wrapped and embraced the actress. The clothes worn by those stars were much like those of ordinary women, as was their behaviour: legs were not revealed, cleavage and arms were only hinted at. As the writer Nabanita Dev Sen put it: 'The only time you glimpsed a bit of ankle was when a woman walked along the beach. And that was erotic because it was illicit. But now everything is bared all the time.' In the last two decades the clothing of Bollywood stars has become increasingly divorced from reality, as the films have grown into ever-grander fantasy spectacles. The key sequences now are the musical numbers where typically the actress dances her way through a whole series of rapidly changing clothing, against a background of changing landscapes. Deena Pathak suggested that while during the rest of the film the heroine is a figure such as a poor villager or gangster's moll, these sequences represent a kind of dream state. The effect is to concentrate on the actress herself as an embodiment of beauty. Just as the viewer becomes mesmerised by a sheer green chiffon, we are taken to the next outfit in pink, and then the next in turquoise, and so on. The intention is that just when we feel the star could not look anymore beautiful, the next image reveals her as still closer to the ideal of beauty. These saris worn by the heroine are designer creations which increasingly fashion the whole look and wardrobe of a character for the entire duration of the film, rather than just for a particular scene. Such star wardrobes typically include a whole range of clothing, and are used by fashion designers when making their pitch to their wealthy clientele.

It is perhaps for this reason that Rekha is admired and talked about as the last of the classically glamorous stars in a sari. In the 1980s she refused to follow the trend towards greater exposure of flesh and wider choice of garments. Instead, she chose ever more conventional saris, such as the heavy silk Kanjivarams, wearing them with a distinctively cut blouse which millions of women sought to emulate. Knowledgeably choosing her own saris, there are stories of her refusing to come to the set until she had got her way over the choice. She wore her saris in austere styles, elevating them to a pinnacle of beauty.

the incomparable Rekha

Among the later stars, some such as Madhuri Dixit, Karishma Kapoor and Kajol are considered to carry off a sari better than their contemporaries. A public judgment seems to have been made that they can never be iconically glamorous in the manner of the past stars, just as today's Hollywood heroines can never recapture the magic of Audrey Hepburn wearing Givenchy for the first time (though there is an abiding legacy in the 'little black dress').[103]

Despite the growing variety of clothes in the movies and the constant designer showcasing, the sari retains an integral place in the morality and narratives of Bollywood. Until the early 1990s the wardrobe of the heroine was distinguished from the 'vamp', the anti-heroine with loose morals and dubious virtue. The latter wore the more Westernised outfits, while the heroine dressed in Indian clothes throughout as a symbol of incorruptibility. Since then, however, the wardrobe of urban elite women has expanded to include more and more Western fashion. As a result, the movies could no longer sustain a straightforward association of jeans with vampishness, and heroines too could now wear Western clothes.

Nonetheless, the sari is still seen as a significant marker of growing virtue, maturity and stability. The standard plot lines see poor/rich boy meet rich/poor girl, fall in love and want to marry; families oppose the match; the couple elope and are chased by villains; then there is the death of the villain in a fight, a resolution and reconciliation of all parties, and a wedding to celebrate it all: '(T)he heroine…is a perfect woman at least by the end of the film if not the beginning…She may begin the film by wearing western clothes or a loose interpretation of the *salwaar-khamees*, but by the end of the film will most likely wear a sari, if only for her wedding which ends the film'.[104] The writer Javed Akhtar commented on this persistently reactionary quality of current Bollywood portrayals of female characters by pointing out:

The 1990s screen heroine is extremely tradition-bound. She may be wearing a mini-skirt, but the moment she falls in love she starts wearing a sari. This means if you are a good girl, you wear a sari; if you are not a good girl, then you can wear a skirt.[105]

sari box with film title

Thus the transition in the woman's status is marked by her wearing a sari after marriage. This transition is particularly marked in some recent films such as *Hum Dil De Chukey Sanam, Kabhi Khushi Kabhi Ghum*, or *Humraaz* where the marriage takes place mid-movie and the plot follows post-marital tribulations.

Blockbuster films can still on occasion set trends. After *Kuch Kuch Hota Hai*, many women sought out the plain chiffon sported by Kajol in the film. More recently, *Kabhi Khushi Kabhi Ghum* re-popularised chiffons with intricate *zari* embroidery. Sari boxes in shops have the names of films and the photos of the heroine printed on them for easy recognition by shoppers. However, the very emphasis on the ideals of glamour and fantasy tend to mean that these saris are worn only for special occasions. In terms of mass sales of everyday wear, it is the television soaps that now exert the dominant influence.

Television and soap opera

By contrast to the film industry's transcendent images, television series claim to portray mundane middle-class life and mores. Family dramas are set in recognisable public and private spaces, and are populated by formidable female characters, what one woman called the '*bindi* brigade' (referring to the traditional mark on the forehead of Hindu women). A sari is essential to these portrayals of 'ideal' mothers, wives and sisters. In the serials, these women are always immaculately turned out, even inside the home; their blouses and saris are perfectly matched and draped as if constantly at an official function. Against the backdrop of a Hindu fundamentalist government, some commentators express exasperation at what they see as an absurd and reactionary portrayal of domesticated womanhood.[106] On the other hand, the influential television fashion stylist Nim Sood argues that the immaculate saris are only there to entertain:

People enjoy domestic dramas, but they don't necessarily enjoy the scruffiness that goes with it - they want to see people and settings which are perfect. So our actresses are beautifully groomed, to make it pleasing to the eye.

Our conversations with villagers in Bengal suggested she might be right. They said they often preferred to follow the Hindi language soaps rather than those in Bengali. Though the Hindi was hard for them to follow, the Bengali productions were insufficiently slick, and 'looked too grim', too much like the constrained life they saw around them. Nonetheless, despite the perfect grooming, the soaps stick to conventional clothing, to saris, shalwar kamiz and occasionally trousers, avoiding the innovative 'costumes' of the movies. This means that the stars are wearing recognisably the same clothes as the viewers; just doing it a little better.

advert featuring popular soap stars

Nim Sood is currently the single most powerful influence on women's choice of saris in India. She neither produces nor sells saris, but instead selects the clothing for the major Star TV soaps, including *Kyunki Saas Bhi Kabhi Bahu Thi* (KSBKBT) and *Kahin Kissii Roz,* which have by far the highest viewing figures on Indian television. It might be assumed that she is pressured by writers, directors and even outside commercial interests; but in practice she seems to have considerable autonomy in deciding the style of the characters presented to her by the script.

'Let's take Tulsi from KSBKBT. She was the young daughter of a priest and I gave her at that stage a very simple, cotton shalwar, because she would not have looked right if she was too flamboyant. Then when she got married, we gave her a look that was different from the other daughters-in-law. They had a lot of jewellery, but she remained a little subdued. Now, twenty years later in the serial, she has become more confident, she has been accepted as the daughter-in-law of the house, everybody listens to her. So the look has totally changed; she is into the beautiful saris, a lot of jewellery. Quite different from what she was originally.'

For more peripheral characters, the clothing may be used to illustrate broadly their background and context. If the character is wealthy, Nim might consider 'chiffons, chamois satins, more chiffons and

very nice benaresi borders, embroidery, all sorts of things. Anything new that I can think of. New fabrics keep coming out of the market so when I go there I check whatever is new.' More specifically, a wealthy Punjabi character might have silk or chiffon with pearls or crystal jewellery. If an ethnic look is required, as in the case of a character who was a dancer, she might construct this out of short kurtas with jeans or traditional mirror work suits. 'We do have one character who is totally ethnic, she wears oxidised silver jewellery and she only wears the kurtas with black rims and mirror work and *jutis* on her feet.'

Nim has no particular opinion with respect to the sari itself, preferring to follow what she sees around her. For example, 'If she is a married women, then she probably wears saris, but married women do also wear shalwar kamiz sometimes. It depends upon the family background. We use a lot of Western clothes for the younger generation, for the college going generation. They do not wear saris. In the Indian community saris are worn when we get to about twenty, twenty-one. You only wear a sari when you tend to look a little older. So the girls stick to the jeans, tops, T-shirts.' It seems she can influence fashion precisely because she does not attempt to be a voice in support of any particular mode or garment. Instead, she tries to keep a feel for what is happening 'on the street', while nudging it very gently in the direction of

KUSUM

sari named after soap opera star

her personal taste; taste which millions of women seem keen to follow.

Nim is aware of her influence on the retail market. 'A character in KSBKBT was wearing Bandani saris throughout and because of that, because I was doing Bandani in different colours, Bandani caught on in the market so fast – everybody wanted to buy Bandani! That was her character and we didn't want to shift from it, but there was starting to be a Bandani drought! So as soon as any Bandanis arrived shops used to call me. I would go and pick the lot up straightaway before they were snapped up by everyone else! Maybe there would be just one, a new colour, a new combination that I could use.'

Sood goes out herself to select and buy the clothes the actors wear. She tries for authenticity, so if a character should wear an eleven thousand rupee sari, she buys an eleven thousand rupee sari for them. 'If the quality is no good you would notice it on television. I am really critical myself, I watch really carefully if I know something is not looking good.' She favours relatively colourful saris, because of the need for things to stand out on the small television screen.

In a typical episode there may be three or four changes of sari, but the sari will be worn again in subsequent episodes to create the sense that the character has a genuine wardrobe from which she selects each day. These are typically imagined to contain around forty or fifty saris. As with an ordinary wardrobe, these are divided into 'saris for the home, saris for party wear, saris for functions, at different sort of rituals, *pujas* that go on in the house'.

But there is a limit to this realism, because viewers expect the characters to look better than real people do. ' I don't know why, but if you show a typical character, for example, if she is in a regular job, or in an ordinary sort of house, and you give her a typical dress, then the audience doesn't want to see that. The audience doesn't relate to it. If she is a pretty girl, they want to see her wear something nice – it can be simple, but should be something that makes her look even prettier.'

This point is critical to understanding Nim Sood's great influence on women's wear. She provides a *slightly* idealised version of the ordinary and quotidian. The characters and their clothes are realistic enough for ordinary viewers to identify with them; but they have been made to look their best through the choice of clothing and grooming. And that optimisation makes the clothes desirable to the viewer, for it promises to make them look their best too. Nim Sood recognises the importance of dovetailing with these everyday aspirations. As she puts it: 'if you notice carefully, even the average girl who goes to the office likes to wear something nice. She wears nice cottons, and she won't wear very ordinary cottons – she is living in a very ordinary place but she likes to be slightly glamorising – though not too much!'

Her selections also influence the sari market through the increasing use of her characters as models. During our fieldwork there was a ubiquitous street advert for Kodak that featured the actress Naushin

Sardar Ali from the serial *Kkusum* in an eye-catching red sari. While sari designers tend to team up with a film actress, the advertising of mass market products lends itself more to the use of soap actresses, who may well be portrayed in the image that Nim Sood has constructed for them.

Commercial bodies are increasingly aware of Nim Sood's impact. She recently had complaints from jewellers that people were buying an increasing amount of artificial jewellery because it was being worn by her characters. Other retailers try and draw her attention to their new designs. But, contrary to our own expectations, there was no evidence for direct 'product placement', though she said this may well occur in other soaps. From her perspective, this would considerably curtail her creative freedom. As things stand, she can simply go out and purchase whatever she needs on an ad hoc and immediate basis – she has no desire to be involved in complex procedures for obtaining and returning garments to particular firms. But she is also aware that a number of firms now label their saris as *Tulsi* or *Kkusum* saris after the characters who wear them, because as many shopkeepers confirmed, customers are increasingly asking for such saris by name. Given the lack of effective copyright laws, she can gain no financial advantage from this, but it obviously adds to the glamour and significance of her characters and of the television company she works for.

Recently her influence has spread even further thanks to

the popularity of the soaps abroad. An example of this was the construction of the 'one shoulder blouse'. Sood described the circumstances under which she created this innovation: 'The writer presented me with a character who is very, very modern. Very much into clothes and she is a slightly negative character, a bit of a bitch, yeah, and a bit of a slut. And she leaves her hair open. So I let her wear all her saris with blouses that are body hugging, with a strap only on one shoulder, and with transparent sleeves. She looked amazing - the single shoulder strap is located under the pallu, giving the illusion that both shoulders are bare. Loads of people called me and said "where did you get those blouses?". I had actually re-cast a stretch fabric halter-top as a blouse piece.' Soon other people in the media such as television anchors were wearing these apparently shoulderless blouses on air.

The soaps exert an influence on current fashion, an influence that is even wider now that television has become available to much of rural India. Mannequins in local markets are often now draped in saris similar to those worn by stars on television, and to make brand recognition even easier, the names of the characters such as Tulsi and Parvati are pinned to them. Inside the shops, boxes of saris are marked with the same names. Shopkeepers also talk about the frequency with which customers come in and specifically ask for saris as worn by a particular character in a particular show, and so knowledge about the soaps becomes central to the production and distribution of saris.

sari label with soap stars dressed by Nim Sood

This chapter has surveyed some of the major arbiters of taste, from politics, film and television soap opera. These complement the development of branding and the impact of major companies discussed in the previous chapter. The big players in the commercial sector seek to influence what people wear through manufacturing, advertising and sponsoring powerful and seductive images that people want to emulate. Nevertheless, their hold remains a relatively flimsy one. Production at present is becoming more dispersed rather than more centralised, and there are simply too many individual designers and too many small producers to establish a real monopoly of taste. The eccentric sari shopper is never likely to encounter the kind of fashion hegemony which means that in Western markets flares or long jackets may disappear entirely if they are not part of that season's styles.[107] While 'fashions' in saris do happen, they are likely to guide only a small proportion of new sari buying each year.[108] Women may buy one sari which is 'trendy', but will usually ensure it is inexpensive in case it is no longer wearable the following year. More expensive saris are rarely bought according to such short-lived trends, for as we have seen, the influences on taste go far beyond the latest soap operas to include fondly remembered national leaders and the timeless classics of a vast legacy of films, as well as regional, family and personal traditions.

the new brands: saris named after soap opera characters

CHAPTER 12

Modern Clothes

Suddenly, across the years, she heard Uma's voice, explaining the evolution of sari-wearing. It gave Jaya a thrill, even after all those years, to recall how astonished she'd been when she'd first heard the story. She'd always imagined saris to be a part of the natural order of the Indian universe, handed down from immemorial antiquity. It had come as a shock to discover that the garment had a history, created by real people, through human volition.

— THE GLASS PALACE by Amitav Ghosh

Modern Clothes

The elevated sari

Perhaps the most striking feature of contemporary clothing in India is the difference between the two sexes. Over the last two centuries, men's appearance has become dominated by a version of 'Western dress' (mainly trousers and shirts), while women have retained a non-Western clothing tradition. It could be argued that this largely reflects a basic inequality of power in South Asian society. Men's clothing attests to their involvement in what have become global powers and ideologies, that give them access to forms and forces that perpetuate their overarching control in society. By contrast, women in their saris are in danger of being left behind as merely symbolic figures, the representatives of 'tradition' or 'authenticity'.[109] They have been elevated, put on a pedestal, but may thereby also be removed from access to the levers of power.

Yet as has been clear throughout this book, it would be quite wrong to think of the contemporary sari simply in terms of continuity with the past. Just as with men's clothing, it too is the product of a history. Starting from a long tradition of unsewn and draped clothing, during the twentieth century the sari has been radically changed by additions of sewn garments. It is dominated today by the mass production of powerlooms rather than individual handlooms. The method of wearing the sari has also homogenised around one particular style of draping, the Nivi, which has been plucked from amid hundreds of others and elevated to a position of respected uniformity. This began as an accident of high society fashion, but received most of its momentum, wittingly and unwittingly, from the members of India's political and opinion-forming class as they tried first to forge a unified fight for freedom from colonial rule, and then to bind together in a newly formed nation the vast mix of regions, languages and cultures which lay within India's borders. Subsequently, this style was embraced by both rural migrants to towns and the growing middle classes emerging from the burgeoning state bureaucracy and new industries. Rich and poor alike watched these saris adorn the nationally loved film stars of those years. In the process, the sari was elevated from the diffuseness and variety of its historical origins into a precious and precise national emblem[110].

As a result of this process, women working in the fields and those relaxing on New Delhi verandahs today both wear what is recognisably the same garment. The former may tend to cite the sari's adaptability as perfectly suited to their lives, a cheap and flexible item of clothing that facilitates an instant transformation from fieldworker, with sari hitched up around squatting thighs, to respectable villager with legs fully and modestly covered. The latter might tend rather to see their lives enhanced by the sari as a thing of beauty, offering endless variations of colour, decoration, texture and mood, or as a faithful ally in projecting authority across a meeting table. Nonetheless, this sharing of the sari by women otherwise separated by vast gulfs of circumstance is precisely what makes it a plausible emblem of India itself, something that can transcend the myriad differences and tensions of wealth, class and religion. This emblematic status creates pride and expectation and hence also, for many, anxiety. The sari is a garment that people feel they have to 'live up to'. As we have seen, this involves not only the technicalities of subtly re-engineering one's basic movements of walking, sitting, bending and veiling, but learning to become the kind and quality of person that the sari now requires and stands for. It is not just a thing of casual habit, but something they feel they have to learn to 'inhabit' in order to fulfil all that it represents.

This 'elevated sari' has a vastly enhanced capacity for good and for bad. Perhaps the single most common comment we heard about the sari was that it makes a woman the most beautiful she could ever become, a view reiterated by women from every kind of background and region. In a society where power itself is generally thought of as having a female aspect, in the form of *shakti,* the sari simultaneously augments, combines and 'totalises'[111] the possibilities of aesthetic beauty, female mastery,[112] sexuality and the cult of the maternal. As a symbol of Indian-ness itself, it represents not a compact nationality so much as an aspiration, what Khilnani has called 'the idea of India', which people struggle to live up to as worthy inheritors of a great and ancient culture, an India that transcends regions and diversity to reconstitute itself at a higher plane. As a result, and as one fashion commentator perceptively put it, to violate the integrity of the sari is akin to 'burning the American flag'.[15]

Understandably, then, the sari is being adopted by those for whom it was not traditional garb but who wish to show their loyalty to India. The most visible example is Sonia Gandhi, who, like other foreign women married to Indian men, has tried to display her commitment to her adopted culture through her Indian clothes and her gradual mastery of the sari. As the leader of the opposition to a ruling government associated with a right-wing Hindutva ideology, this has helped her to counter political criticism of her alien origins. More widely, the same impulse is reflected in the shift from dresses to saris by Anglo-Indian women (the descendants of mixed race liaisons from the Raj) who are now abandoning their parents' aloofness from India in favour of greater Indianisation. Elsewhere the sari has spread to become formal wear in some regions where it was not previously used, to the resentment of some. As one lady put it, 'saris are not the only Indian dress but they have become the only "formal" Indian dress'.

The elevated sari has become the means by which the person wearing it also hopes to become elevated, achieving a higher dignity, a power and beauty, a maturity and a sense of their Indian-ness or of their own professionalism, depending upon the context. Wearers aspire to reach a position that they feel they could never have reached if they had not managed to inhabit the sari. To go from being merely 'an Indian' to becoming the glamorous embodiment of India becomes, for some, a life's ambition, and for many more, a heavy and only dimly perceived burden of expectation. The perfect posture, precise make-up, pasted smile and policed sari of airline staff or hotel receptionists is the most obvious example of this, but nearly every woman, reaching for her sari, will share this duty. It is this power that men sense when they complain of the unfair advantage of women in senior jobs in corporations or in the bureaucracy, since men have nothing that can intimidate and impress to the same degree. It is also the power that a fully eroticised sari can have when a woman uses the ambiguity of being simultaneously covered and uncovered to become unbearably attractive and desired.

With such an elevated status, it is little wonder that so many feel they fail to achieve a sense of mastery or of comfort within the sari. Just as learning to drive a car can lead to one being stigmatised as a bad driver, so one can become known as 'uncomfortable in a sari' however often one wears it. A garment that seems sometimes to possess its own agency because it is so dynamic can easily become something that oppresses the wearer. The sari exposes the body, and reveals its blemishes. Sweat stains the blouse, the pleats can unravel, the base ride up too high, adding high heels is an invitation to trip and stumble or fall. Thus even rural women, who after puberty never wear any garment other than the sari, may spend their lives oppressed by their inability to inhabit it properly as their own, and the sense that the sari will betray and humiliate its wearer. Yet this difficulty merely vindicates and confirms the sari's iconic status. Once elevated above the pragmatic world of everyday life, it becomes appropriate that the task of inhabiting the garment of India should not be at all easy. Not everyone should be able to do it well. It should demand considerable skill, effort and practice, and impose expectations of beauty and skin colour that not all can fulfil. With elevation comes the potential for a fall.

The functional shalwar kamiz

So far we have concentrated on the dynamics of the sari itself, culminating in the development of the elevated sari. But to appreciate the deeper significance of these changes, we need to consider the main parallel development in women's clothing in India, the rise of the shalwar kamiz. The relationship between the sari and the shalwar kamiz should be understood as a conflict, firstly over how clothing is rationalised as sensible or appropriate, but ultimately as part of a deeper conflict over the nature of 'rationality' itself in modern India.

The history of clothing in India is nothing if not unpredictable. With respect to the sari, its prevalence among, and association with, the rural and the poor did not make it an obvious candidate for securing elevated status amongst the middle class, who might easily have turned to the dresses of the West. Equally, there are many reasons why one would not have predicted that the shalwar kamiz would have developed more recently as the sari's main rival. One might have thought that the previous associations of the shalwar kamiz, originally with Punjabis and then increasingly (as it became the national dress of Pakistan), with Muslims more generally, would have made it a highly unlikely candidate as the acceptable dress of ordinary Hindu Indians.[114] This is especially the case given the drift towards nationalism in India and the recent election of Hindu fundamentalist governments. And it is surprising too that Christian-run schools should have been so keen to embrace the 'Muslim garb'. In order for this change to happen, people have had in effect to 'forget' a great deal of what they knew about these garments.[115]

This rather surprising story seems to have begun at the moment when women, particularly in towns and cities, began to be married at an older age than was traditionally the case. Two generations ago, most Indian girls would switch to wearing saris at puberty. The sari was the marked garment for the female sexualised body. Many women also married early, between eleven and seventeen, or even younger in rural areas. At this time, adolescence were usually marked by a suitably liminal garment: one which was not quite a sari but not a frock or shorts either, such as the half-saris in South India, or the *gharara* and *dupatta* of the north.

With the shift in the age of marriage, several things could have happened. Women *could* have remained for longer in their frocks, half-saris or regional childhood clothing. However, the exposure of legs and arms which such garments typically allowed seems to have been viewed intuitively as incompatible with the kind of coverage and modesty expected of sexually mature womenfolk. Alternatively, women *could* simply have continued to turn to saris after puberty by severing the link and association between saris, sexuality and marriage. There seems however to have been a general reluctance to make that severance. Instead, women began to turn to a garment that was viewed as solving these problems because it hid rather than revealed the sexually blossoming body, an asexual but grown-up garment.

Increasingly, the shalwar kamiz has become the uniform for girls aged 12–16 in government schools, succeeding the skirts and blouse of the under-twelves.[18] This change occurred mainly during the 1980s, and appears to have proved popular with the schools, parents and girls alike. The latter, cycling to school, often see themselves as far more free and more 'modern' than their mothers, and feel this is well expressed by the shalwar kamiz. The shalwar kamiz also appealed widely across the social spectrum. In some cases, rural parents, aware through television of metropolitan developments, petitioned their own local schools to introduce the shalwar kamiz instead of the sari as uniforms for their adolescent daughters. Meanwhile, elite Anglicised private schools in the cities were also turning to the shalwar kamiz to replace the skirt and blouse which pupils had traditionally worn even in their senior years. For the Catholic nuns and Jesuits who often ran such institutions, the shalwar kamiz freed them from the growing battles they had to fight with their pupils concerning inappropriate skirt length. The change initially met a storm of protest from parents who wanted their girls to continue to look different from students at the free government-run schools (which the children of their servants attended). This, after all, had been part of the attraction of such English-style medium education. The girls were also resistant, assuming (correctly) that it would become harder to flaunt their figures and indulge in competitive games of adolescent sexuality. Nonetheless the changes were imposed, adhered to and, over time, accepted.[19]

Increasingly, girls voluntarily maintained shalwar kamiz even in the more free regimes of colleges and universities. The natural modesty of the garment, which had put off some girls, appealed to many others, especially to those entering adulthood and leaving the relatively sheltered world of school or college. They saw its stitched and constant nature as very much less sexualised than the sari, leaving little scope for either deliberate flirtation or accidental revelation. Countless adult women explicitly ground their choice of the shalwar kamiz in its ability to hide the body, rather than reveal it. The shalwar kamiz's growing acceptance as part of schooling and further education also meant it was increasingly associated with the modern ethos of the 'college girl', an ethos very different from traditional assumptions concerning the role and control of women.

The shalwar kamiz was now the garment of young women who were not married at an early age, and not confined to the world of the domestic hearth. When Tarlo was conducting her fieldwork in a Gujarati village in 1988, it was clear that while older people still perceived a somewhat problematical association of the shalwar kamiz with Islam, their main reservations concerning it were focused upon its more recent association with college girls. That is, they were less concerned that wearing shalwar kamiz would make their daughters turn to Islam, than that they might start to acquire what was perceived as the immodest licence and freedom of city college girls.

These educated cohorts and those who aspired to be like them thus took the shalwar kamiz out into the wider world, to the offices and laboratories they came to occupy. As well as the shalwar kamiz's sexual modesty, many now saw the sari as unwieldy and inconvenient, ill-suited to the apparently more dynamic life of the modern working woman.

Subsequently, this attitude has begun to permeate the wider strata of urban women who have little education but who do work outside the home. They too began to see the shalwar kamiz as best suited to the social and physical demands upon them. Just as previously they had embraced the pragmatic benefits of synthetic saris over cotton, now they have begun to embrace the convenience of the shalwar kamiz over the sari. The trend is often remarked upon: 'Today even women who haven't travelled much and would not be described as cosmopolitan and well travelled are making the switch to shalwar kamiz. That's why it is so amazing a change.' Foreign anthropologists remarked that in the 1980s they themselves *had* to wear the sari if they were married, whereas now in the twenty-first century they are accepted if wearing a shalwar kamiz.[118]

Many urban women are starting to make assumptions about the obvious superiority of the shalwar kamiz as the dress of modern India, and this creates an illusion that this has already become the assumed dress in those areas that stand for Indian modernity. However, the picture is rather less cut and dried than this might suggest. We carried out counts of clothing worn in various other cities and rural areas. Overall, these indicated that the distribution of shalwar kamiz was still a variable minority, being outnumbered 5:1 by the sari in Chennai, 4:1 in Kolkata, 3:1 in Mumbai, and 2:1 in Bangalore. Only in Delhi was it something like 50:50. Only in Mumbai did Western dress make as a significant contribution, though even there it was limited to around 7 per cent for Central and South Mumbai. Clearly, then, one should avoid exaggerating the effects of such trends. What these observations confirm is that for the moment, the numerical dominance on the streets still remains clearly with the sari, and this is even more the case for rural areas where any challenge from the shalwar kamiz in traditional sari-wearing areas is negligible; the proportion of women wearing the shalwar kamiz remains at barely 1 per cent.[119] Nonetheless, it is important to note these discrepancies between what people actually wear and what different people in India *think* they 'see'. Their perceptions reflect their expectations, but also their desires. Those who see a marked increase in shalwar kamiz and Western dress take this as evidence for the emergence of the kind of modern India that they espouse. By contrast, those who oppose them are offended precisely by such presumptions about what their clothing represents.

Similarly for Western dress a senior professional woman in Chennai described nearby Bangalore as the new 'Western' cityscape of India. She assured us that as soon as one leaves the airport one would be amazed at the prevalence of Western dress, including items such as spaghetti straps, unimaginable in a less Westernised city. Hers was only the most extreme example of comments often made about Bangalore. To check this, we decided to make a count of clothing worn starting from outside the airport and continuing through the town and the suburbs. Yet the number of women we saw wearing Western dress during this tour of Bangalore was absolutely zero. There are two or three key streets in the middle of the town and the hi-tech stations outside of town where Western dress is in fact common. But this is a city of eight million people, where these centres of Western dress represents a tiny enclave culture. For journalists and the elite, however, it is the enclave that is visible and the rest is shrouded into the background. Many anthropological accounts of Indian society remark on the ability of elite groups or high castes to effectively screen out from view what is happening within the mass population.

In general, the most common ways in which women argue about the superiority of one or other garment are not based on fashion or claims about the elevation of the sari or the modernity of the shalwar kamiz. Their arguments are based much more on a common sense pragmatism and assumptions about the functional advantages of the clothing in question. Claims about these functional advantages are constantly being asserted in both villages and towns. After hearing many such conservations, we observed that one of their most striking features is that exactly the same claims are made for both the sari and the shalwar kamiz, as illustrated by the following examples.

AGAINST SARIS	FOR SARIS
(1) A sari is inconvenient because while I am working in a lab I have to carry stuff in my hand. I have to move with different instruments and while climbing the stairs holding the stuff in my hands. I need to hold the sari as well. The most inconvenient thing about the sari is that I tend to trip over it when I am walking fast. I can't afford to do it if I am carrying things in my hand (micro-biologist).	(1) Saris are better to wear when doing manual work, like when you are harvesting grain, or putting cowdung up to dry, or carrying bricks on your head, since you can tie the sari tightly around yourself and carry on working, while other clothing might get in the way. You can tuck a sari in and you can shorten it. With a shalwar kamiz, the *kurta* flaps at the back when you are sitting down, you need to have your waist tightly bound when you are working to support the back, and in a shalwar kamiz you can't squat and bend unless it is tied at the waist with something. When occasionally you see women in shalwar kamiz working in the fields they have to get *gamcha* and tie it on top to keep the waist tight (Bengali rice farmer).
(2) In the heat, when one sweats the sari wraps itself around the legs, around the arms. If I had total freedom, I would prefer *churidars* (maid).	(2) I feel a little breathless in an shalwar kamiz, it is tight (hospital cleaner).
(3) I think a *dupatta* is more versatile because it is detachable. If I have to sit on a dirty place, you can take it off and sit on it. If I have to board a bus and the bus is very crowded then a sari becomes difficult to handle, but with suits, you can manage (university lecturer).	(3) I have always done housework in a sari. One can pick it up and pull it and then tuck the pallu into the waist. It is more uncomfortable in an shalwar kamiz, one is worried about it getting wet (low income urban schoolgirl).

(4) If my daughter goes out in a hurry she prefers shalwar kamiz, she says it takes less time (maid).

(4) I also have a little girl. It is difficult to breast-feed her in anything but a sari. I can just tuck her head into my breast and cover it with my pallu. In a *kurta* one has to lift the whole thing and bare the body totally (chauffeur's wife).

(5) Maybe because in the lab I am more worried about the work. It is really important work and I have to apply my whole mind to it. I don't want to have one additional thing which I have to think about like holding my sari (student).

(5) People in towns wear shalwar kamiz more since they have less work to do, but we sow grain, we transplant it, harvest it. You can't do any of this wearing a *churidar* because it can get wet in the water in the fields. A *kurta* is hanging loose on all sides of the body and if you sit down to boil rice then these bits that hang around your body can so easily catch fire (Tamil rice farmer).

(6) A shalwar kamiz is more economical as you can wash and iron them yourself. A sari is more costly to maintain because you have to have it ironed by the presswallah and that costs Rs 6 every time (housewife).

(6) Saris are so much cheaper than a shalwar kamiz. An average shalwar kamiz can cost anything between 350–500 but I can have a sari for 140, blouse for 30 and petticoat for only Rs 50 (villager).

In general, the defence of the functionalism of the sari tends to come from those involved in heavier labouring work, such as agricultural or building labourers, while the defence of the shalwar kamiz is spearheaded by those in less onerous urban occupations. But the similarity between their claims suggests that these reasons are as much post-hoc rationalisations as the reasons behind a choice, if indeed any active choice has been made. In many cases, it is custom or conformity that determines an individual's actions. For both sides, claims of comfort and convenience are above all statements of familiarity, involving intimate feelings about ways of walking and sitting, the climate, and also the sense of modesty with which one has been brought up. The larger picture includes the relative price, the difficulty of maintaining various textiles and of controlling one's appearance. As such, 'feelings' about function are closely aligned with class and status; but only aligned, not determined. Village girls may accept their mother's claim for the functionalism of the sari, but adopt the shalwar kamiz in emulation of the more fashionable urban girls.

Even if we cannot take the idea of the shalwar kamiz's greater convenience at face value, the reasons for such claims being made are themselves interesting and important, touching on deeper issues that wearers themselves may be only dimly aware of. That give us clues about a wider debate that is taking place, a debate about the nature of modern India more generally.

Rationality and modernity

A suitable starting point for this investigation into the deeper implications of this choice of clothing are those women who have retained an unquestioned relationship to the sari, such as many villagers, manual workers, and especially older women. For them, the legitimacy of the sari is not partitioned into separate practical and symbolic aspects. Rather, they un-selfconsciously but inextricably interweave considerations of function and appearance. They defend the sari in terms of its practicality in the fields, its convenience when having to pee or to cook; but equally and simultaneously they praise it for its capacity to quickly veil oneself when someone enters a room, or to look attractive to a prospective husband. They stress the easy availability of the pallu to clean something, but also to change one's appearance or expression. They tend to talk in terms of what might be called 'tasks of life', rather than just work. For these women, having to look appropriate at a wedding is just as 'practical' a matter as having to keep one's legs free when weeding a field. Managing one's family, reputation and neighbourly relations are just as much tasks as doing one's laundry. The propensity of a pallu to fall and graze a latrine, thereby becoming polluted, is just as much a practical problem as when it threatens to catch on a nail.[120]

The sari fully accommodates the requirements of these varied demands. The same gesture with the pallu protects from the sun and from the male gaze; the same adjustment of the petticoat helps one feel both modest and in control. The sari's layers can simultaneously suggest one is both covered and uncovered, as its asymmetry makes vulnerability a matter of perspective. 'The cloth is in constant motion, being drawn, adjusted, withdrawn and redrawn in such a variety of ways that it seems almost like a part of the female body.'[121]

The resulting ambiguity of the sari harmonises with deep-rooted aspects of Hindu religion and philosophy. While monotheistic religions stress a basic dualism of good and evil, male and female, the gods in India are understood as an incorporation of both male and female aspects, while power is a property that

is both good and bad.[122] This is a complex bi-polar world that women know well, where to be married or have a child is simultaneously a huge gain and a burden, a loss and a becoming. Such ambivalence is not a failure to understand the world and its proper divisions, but a realistic representation of a world that is itself full of contradictions. These complex properties of the sari are not hidden, nor were they excavated by us through some difficult or devious analysis. We are merely commenting upon the things most women say most of the time when asked about the sari. The potential ambiguity and transformative ability of the sari were often the first things that women commented upon spontaneously.

Significantly, however, no one spoke in such terms of the shalwar kamiz. The latter, as a tailored garment, is experienced as a form of effective closure around the body. One of the most common comments made by those wearing shalwar kamiz is to point out this feature. An accountant described the shalwar kamiz thus: ' it sort of covers from head to toe, it covers your body. It makes you look good, presentable, it does not over-do it, nor under-do it.' This garment represents a divided dualistic relationship to the world; it either covers the body or it does not. This dualism is understood as part of its clearer rationality and convenience. Likewise, when one asks about the *experience* of wearing the shalwar kamiz, people do not discuss its flexibility of appearance, or its symbolism. They talk only about its functional advantages. And where discussions about saris commonly revolve around what fabric it is made of – a cotton, a silk, etc. – discussions about the shalwar kamiz rarely touch on this.

In all these respects, the shalwar kamiz seems to be experienced as a simple garment, without the ambiguity and dynamism of the sari. Young woman talk of its day-to-day convenience, its absence of pins and perils. Indeed, it seems reasonable to infer that at least part of what motivates them to wear suits is the long memories of youthful nerves and anxieties over wearing a sari correctly. All can remember their various 'driving tests', while learning to wear them and the occasional haunting failures. In their modern shalwar kamiz they are suddenly free of all the historical associations that come with wearing a sari. As a teacher notes: 'Saris are a very traditional dress and you associate it with India. It brings a sort of belongingness to the country. It is very modern to have a sari from each and every state. In shalwar kamiz there is none of this regional association. I don't think of shalwar kamiz as either religious, or regional, it is about functionality.'[123]

Thus, socially the shalwar kamiz is unhampered by judgement of skills of wrapping and draping. Therefore when many women talk of its greater comfort, it is clear that much of what they mean is the psychological freedom that comes with it, that allows them to focus on the efficiency with which they carry out a particular role as good managers or mothers. As a result, what previously was a single form of rationalising that did not separate out functional and symbolic aspects, is becoming, especially in the towns, two increasingly distinct forms of legitimacy. One, the shalwar kamiz is couched in terms of function and efficiency as modern; the other, the sari, is viewed in terms of symbolic and social effect as an elevated garment.

But this focus on such specific, separable domains of function and symbol embodies a very particular perspective on the world. One of the many approaches to understanding the concept of 'modernity' centres on the role of rationality, and is most closely associated with the writings of Max Weber.[124] He suggested that being modern has become associated with just one version of being rational. This version tends to be secular, functional and associated with the kind of formal systems of utility and calculation that one finds in economics, ideas which are first taught through the school system. What is eliminated by this dominant version of rationality are more qualitative values, and also attitudes such as ambivalence, subjectivity, emotion, or holistic vision, all of which are assumed to be old-fashioned or vaguely mystical alternatives to the pragmatic. To be truly rational is to separate out the precise interests or factors relevant to a decision and use only these to calculate the correct course of action. Science subsequently took its place as the quintessence of this system of thought, a belief in the distillation of the purest essence of order and reason based on the objective recording of the rule-based behaviour of the natural world. But it is the education system more generally that has been the means by which these beliefs about objective rationality have become so widely held and so powerful.

From this perspective, when we turn back to the developing relationship between the sari and the shalwar kamiz, what we find is evidence for the way ordinary clothing seems to have been a major player in the attempt by this narrow version of rationality to become dominant. The shalwar kamiz has become the garment that stands for functionalism and the power associated with pragmatism and efficiency. It is the clothing identified by that sense of order and reason that is associated with science and modernity.

The workers in two of the sites of our fieldwork, a microbiological laboratory in Bangalore and a data-processing company in Mumbai, made this very clear. A few women wear saris in the laboratory, but this is seen as the retention of something slightly awkward and inappropriate. In a very short time, the natural garment of the scientist has thus become the shalwar kamiz. In turn, the scientist as a vision of the modern woman stands at the pinnacle of what has been achieved for Indian women more generally through the growth of education, such education generalises the ideals associated with science from the laboratory technique of unambiguous observation and analysis to the overall preference for clear distinctions, functionalism and efficiency.

As the shalwar kamiz takes over the mantle of rationalism and modernity, the sari, by virtue of its uncontested superiority as the elevated symbol of various aspirations and ideals, thereby cedes any claims to be a serious contender as a rational garment of the modern world. It too occupies a pinnacle, but in this case one that seems to stand for a very different world of symbolic values. Its triumph as an elevated form could well sow the seeds of its own downfall in the longer term. While the sari is constantly used to proclaim itself as an alternative to 'the West' it seems predictable that this will be claimed increasingly in terms of what is being called 'culture', where the word culture comes to stand for a kind of remnant symbolic identity that stands against the encroachment of modern rationality. The same people who argued that a shalwar kamiz is simply easier to maintain, and that it removes the sense of anxiety about how one looks and which bit of one is being looked at, also assert that to be truly beautiful, to look radiant, there is nothing like a sari. The awe and aura of the sari is constructed precisely by its separation from the mere dross of utilitarianism and pragmatism. In this story, then, to see oneself as modern means subscribing to the values embodied by the shalwar kamiz; a superior, dualist rationality based on the separation of the symbolic and the practical. By contrast, the ambiguity of the sari renders it a kind of worrying and obsolete hybrid.

This separation between the rational shalwar kamiz and the symbolic elevated sari may appear increasingly 'natural' and 'obvious': but it is not. We can be helped in resisting this claim to 'common sense' by the work and writings of Bruno Latour. Latour developed his ideas as an anthropologist, studying how science actually operates in both the laboratory and the field. On the basis of these observations, he

argued convincingly that any story about the existence of a pure rationality of science is largely misleading. The activity that is science in practice never becomes a pure abstracted pursuit separated off from the much more muddied waters of interpretation and society. He argues rather that almost everything we do, whether in science or in everyday life is a complex hybrid that cannot be divided into the objective and subjective, or nature against society. We actually live in a world of hybridity, ambiguity and messy compromises.

From this point of view, Latour argues in the title of his best-known book, *We Have Never Been Modern*, that we have allowed ourselves to be lulled into a story about being modern, based upon a much narrower version of rationality than that which we actually live by. It is no better a description of how scientists work in laboratories than it is of how villagers work in fields. Consequently, Weberian rationality should not be assumed to represent how we actually act in the world, but be viewed as merely an idealised model of one version of what being modern might look like.[125] From this broader perspective of modernity and rationality, could not the sari, rather than the shalwar kamiz, be the natural 'modern' garment suited to the new problems associated with living a 'modern' life? Indeed, in its responsiveness to functions which cannot be separated out as instrumental or symbolic it seems ironically 'tailor-made' for this role.

The use of the term 'modernity'[126] is generally associated with a decline in relatively fixed forms of identity and social position. This includes the breaking down of customary and clear-cut roles and expectations, and subsequently an increasing experience of ambiguity. It is often argued that for many women, the problem of contemporary living is that an individual finds herself having to identify with a growing variety of different roles and situations during the course of a day. Under these circumstances, women need all the support they can find in order to deal with the contradictory demands that they often face at home and at work. From this perspective, it seems *highly* efficient and sensible to adopt a garment, the sari, which allows one to be wife, mother, professional, carer, boss and flirt; this single item of clothing has the flexibility and ambiguity to adapt to this growing plurality of social roles. It is not that the sari has failed to change in relation to these demands: as we have seen, the development and adoption of the Nivi style and the way it releases the pallu has certainly enhanced the ability of the sari to

be manipulated. In retrospect, the sari can be seen to have provided a dynamic response to the need for ambiguity and more nuanced and plural expressions of the self. From the perspective of this alternative 'modernity', it is the sari that now appears as the perfect modern garment.[127]

Anthropologists have constantly noted that the terms 'modern' and 'modernity' are highly problematic.[128] There is no one modernity, any more than there was ever a static 'tradition'. Indeed, the point Latour is making is that if being modern is based on the claim to actually live according to the clear demarcated rationality of science, then no one is really modern. What the study of clothing makes clear, however, is that there is a constant struggle between competing imaginations of being modern which fight for legitimacy and hegemony.

However, at present, it seems that the word 'modern' is more likely to be captured by the shalwar kamiz than the sari. On the other hand, in those moments when women wish to look special, or beautiful, or dutiful, a sari is preferred. For the middle class, if the current turn to the shalwar kamiz continues apace, there is the possibility that the sari will lose completely that part of its dual rationale as a 'sensible' and taken-for-granted garment of everyday life, work and comfort. It could then become restricted to highly formalised representations of ceremonial nationhood, as has arguably happened to some other distinctive forms of national dress. The sari then risks becoming just a formal garment for special occasions.

Will the sari turn into the kimono?

Among urban elite women, we were asked from time to time, 'do you think that the sari is going to become like the kimono?' Their question implied that the sari will cease to be worn as an everyday garment and become reserved solely for ceremonial use. Fortunately this question can be examined in some detail by comparing our findings to those of an excellent book on the kimono by the anthropologist Liz Dalby, in particular, the chapter entitled 'Women who cross their legs – kimono in modern Japan'.[129] Thanks to Dalby's work, it is possible to draw up a kind of checklist of the similarities and differences between the history and possible fate of the two garments.

It appears at first that the kimono has gone through a process of 'elevation', to a much further degree that has the sari. Dalby notes that at one stage in its recent history there was an attempt to adapt the kimono and reconcile it to a growing everyday functionalism, but that this failed. Instead, the kimono abandoned functionalism to Western dress and became itself a symbol of national identity. Today, 'Even though most women wear kimono a few times a year at most and men rarely, if ever, don one, Japanese regard kimono as the most beautiful native dress in the world. In its fabric is expressed the Japanese aesthetic sensibility to season and colour; in its folds is layered the soul of Japan.'[130]

Another parallel is that this elevated kimono has become an icon to be inhabited in the way we have suggested for the sari: 'if anything the new self is a stylised Japanese self a woman may not be fully conscious of possessing until she wears kimono'.[131] Finally, as with the sari there was a particular relationship to marriage, with the kimono becoming important to the transformation of women from the freedom of youth to the demure responsibility of marriage.

On closer inspection, however, the differences between the two garments are perhaps more striking. Firstly, the path of elevation was rather different, for the kimono was always an aristocratic dress. It is primarily the rise in the standard of living that has allowed the mass population to aspire to this highly costly garment, so that today some women wear the kimono come from families that never in the past imagined that they would achieve this level of wealth and status. By contrast, in India the lower the income the more likely the individual will be found wearing a sari for everyday use, and it is unlikely that this will change quickly.

Secondly, there are striking differences in the nature of the garment itself that suggest divergences in their future trajectories. The kimono is an elaborate sewn garment with a number of formal rules. One chapter of Dalby's book is a structural analysis that documents an amazing number of variants of sleeve details set against social parameters such as age, gender and the formality of an occasion.[132] As it became fixed as a symbol of Japan, wearing the kimono lost its spontaneity and hardened into an entirely ritualised formal procedure: 'its cultural mission is to reflect constructed yet traditional notions of genteel femininity. It is intolerant of variation and inimical to experiment.'[133] The sari could hardly be more different. As an unsewn draped garment, it could never be dissected into component parts as Dalby has done with the kimono.

According to anthropologist Inge Daniel,[134] another important difference lies in what has become the absolute rigidity of the kimono, in that an individual can wear it well simply to the degree to which they conform to the fixed shape and size of the kimono. By contrast, this book has demonstrated that wearing a sari well depends upon creating something more like a partnership between person and cloth. Indeed the most modern change, the rise of the Nivi style, has increased this possibility of flexibility and performance. Inhabiting a sari properly means transforming the sari into that which is appropriate for the individual, whereas inhabiting the kimono completely subsumes the individual within that which is represented by the clothing.

According to these anthropologists, there is no comparable sense of the kimono as ambiguous and the possibility of allure has become largely restricted to the equally ritualised role of the geisha. The sari also has the potential for a certain degree of ritualised formality, as in the heavily pleated style with a long pallu worn as uniforms, what we have called the

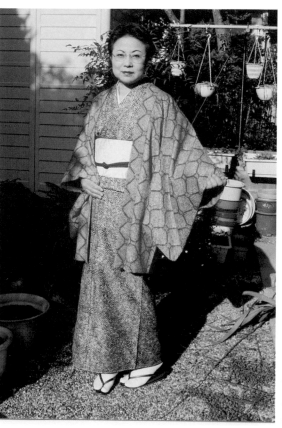

policed sari. But this was exceptional rather than signifying a trend. In its rise to elevation, the sari develops rather than loses its capacity for empowerment through the creative and dynamic use of ambiguity. It is also very hard to imagine that the sari would lose its capacity for allure as well as for modesty, and the sheer simplicity of its form means it cannot be entirely separated from fashion and is unlikely to develop the kind of rule-like status that makes a structural analysis so convincing for the kimono. The sheer expense and the dependence upon professional seamstresses also restricts the kimono in a very different manner, since as a simple length of cloth there will always be versions of the sari that resist both extravagant expense and professionalisation.

When we started our research we were dismissive of the idea that the sari – still worn by the vast majority of women most of the time – was likely to go the way of the kimono and become a largely ceremonial dress. Now we are not so sanguine, and have to acknowledge that for some urban women this has already happened and that it will undoubtedly become more common. But while this may be possible for the elevated sari of the middle class, we would not like to make any such prediction as to the fate of the sari for the majority of rural women. One reason why prediction is so difficult is that there is an extraordinarily important difference between the dynamics of modern clothing in India and in Japan. The kimono simply ceded the functionalism of everyday wear entirely to Western dress. By contrast, in

India by far the most important alternative to the sari is another Indian dress, the shalwar kamiz. As we have seen, both the sari and the shalwar kamiz have been radically transformed in recent years. The former has become 'elevated' as an emblem of culture and tradition; the latter has been adopted as everyday wear associated with education and modernity, but significantly also with functionality.

In their relationship to Western dress, the fact that the sari and the shalwar kamiz have evolved this vertical hierarchy between function and elegance may prove to be more important than the fate of either clothing style in isolation. The sari alone looks increasingly unable to deflect the attraction of Western dress since, as with the kimono, it may fail to compete at the level of the mundane. In Japan the effect of the elevated kimono was to allow Western dress free range to emerge as functional and everyday. A simple dress, jeans and a T-shirt seem much more effective as embodiments of the ordinary. This path is effectively blocked in India to the degree to which the shalwar kamiz, in its opposition to the sari, is affirmed precisely as a functional everyday form of modern dress. The shalwar kamiz has been constructed as a viable alternative to Western dress in the guise of a modern functional garment, but only by relegating it under the elevated beauty and integrity of the sari. Few Indian women would ever suggest that Western dress could look as beautiful or elegant as a sari, and this seems unlikely to change. Our admittedly limited statistics suggest the penetration of Western dress in contemporary India is well below that which most Indians claim to be the case. So when the shalwar kamiz and the sari are viewed as complementary rather than as opposed, it seems we can afford to be far more sanguine about the possibilities for these two together acting to represent Indian dress, and thereby constituting a continuing viable alternative to what elsewhere has become the inexorable spread of generic Western dress.

From the perspective of the spectre of Western dress that is haunting India, the relationship between the sari and the shalwar kamiz is suddenly no longer one of opposition but rather of complementary development, better considered together than apart. If we think in terms of the general dullness of contemporary male Indian urban dress, the hundreds of millions of white and off-white shirts and brownish trousers, then the two forms of women's dress suddenly have a great deal more in common. In terms of their colours, diversity of styles and general exuberance, there is absolutely no danger of incipient global blandness.

Conclusion

We have argued in this final chapter that contemporary Indian women seem to be wearing their philosophy on their sleeves. This is not a given property of the clothes, nor of Indians. A discussion about clothing in contemporary Europe would probably bring up few, if any, of the same issues. There is no reason to expect to find a similar clash in the fundamental nature of rationality expressed through clothes elsewhere.[135] Similarly, a study of the sari in India two hundred years earlier would have very little in common with the claims made for the sari in this book. In most important respects, we might as well be talking about a different garment. Certainly, many of our observations relate to the sari as a draped garment, but other draped garments are used very differently and with different effects.[136]

The arguments made in this book arose from a decision to enquire first into the most intimate aspects of a woman's relationship to her clothes and then to explore, within the same volume, how these micro observations about individuals might be related to macro changes in the way populations relate to issues as profound as being modern and being rational. A study of clothing should not be 'cold'; it has to be involved in the tactile, sensual, emotional, intimate world of feelings. The task of an anthropological account is firstly to convey these feelings empathetically: that is, to try to experience the sari from the point of view of the various women who wear them. But while empathy is the starting point, it should not be the ending point of anthropological enquiry. Its necessary corollary is to ask the analytical questions: why should these particular people be experiencing the world in the way they do? Why does ambiguity or a particular distinction in texture seem to matter for this population but demonstrably not for other societies? Why are feelings about formality or about beauty taking this form at this moment and not previously?

So, our ending point has been a chapter where some broad claims have been made about what is at stake in the choice of contemporary clothing, based on documenting a remarkable and unexpected history of shifts in both the sari and other clothing in India. In this history, the women wearing these clothes are as active a force as the producers of garments. The intimate and the general are also best understood in relation to each other. It is the very same ambiguity of thin cloth partially wrapping the body, of the dynamics of the pallu as a 'semi-detached' self and a shifting sense of comfort and confidence that has proven to be both the experience of individual women within the home and as a thought and felt encounter with the world. In the hybrid world of everyday life, it is often these intimate and sensual realms that are most effective in determining the acceptability and plausibility of the regimes of thought that we call reason and rationality. Through the realm of clothing, we can see how for most peoples, systems of thinking about the world also have to 'feel' right.

NOTES

[1]   Boulanger (1997) records ninety-seven different styles.

[2]   In a recent book on drapery in general, Gen Doy (2002) suggests a very specific 'Western' history of drapery. Her starting point is that 'aestheticisation is associated with civilisation, and drapery is the aestheticisation of cloth' (2002: 230) She suggests that drapery which was once associated with the classical has developed a more recent association with the barbaric. Her work would suggest that it would be quite misleading to consider the sari in terms of a word with such connotations. Doy also notes that in European traditions there may be associations that derive from drapery in home interiors (Sparke 1995) or window dressing (Zola 1992), none of which would have any resonance in India. So while the sari is draped, it should not be viewed as part of this Western history of drapery.

[3]   Chishti and Sanyal (1989, 1995); Lynton and Singh (2002).

[4]   Banerjee (2000)

[5]   Miller (1995); Clarke and Miller (2002)

[6]   The Nivi style of draping is attributed by historian Krishna Dutta to Jyananda Nandini, the wife of Tagore's (the Nobel Prize-winning writer) older brother (Dutta, personal communication). The story is that Jyananda Nandini developed the Nivi style under the influence of the Parsi ladies she had come to befriend in Bombay in 1864. Her husband, Satyanendra Nath, was a liberated man who, to the chagrin of his family insisted his wife accompany him on being transferred to Bombay rather than be confined to the women's quarters in Calcutta. Jyananda Nandini was faced with the dilemma that women wore saris without a blouse or petticoat inside the house, and this would be clearly unsuitable in public. For her journey to Bombay she wore an 'Oriental' costume, a cumbersome dress held together with many pins and tucks made to resemble a sari, acquired in Calcutta. But in Bombay she noticed that her Parsi hosts wore saris with a blouse and petticoat and draped it in the style of the *seedha palla*, i.e. with the pallu brought over from the back over the right shoulder, in the manner of Gujarati women. Finding the pallu flapping against her right arm inconvenient, she a brought the pallu around her body and threw it over her left shoulder (similar to the style of local fisherwomen), thus giving birth to the 'Nivi' style of draping which went on to become the ubiquitous outdoor style for all women in India. In 1866 the press reported on this original attire as worn by her at a Christmas party hosted by the Governor-General, John Lawrence. It can be assumed the style became adopted over the next few decades, alongside the involvement of women in public life. It appears in images of women in the nationalist movement in the early years of the twentieth century, and from there it developed a mass appeal.

[7]   For early sources on the development of the sari and Indian clothing see Ghurye (1951).

[8]   Inevitably, much of this book represents an artificial separation of clothing from its accessories. To be well dressed in India is to be as concerned as much with matters of jewellery, shoes, hair, make-up and the figure as with clothing. A person's appearance is always an assemblage of these things. But by the same token, each of these deserves a book in its own right, whether on hair (see the rich discussion of hair in Olivelle (1998)), on jewellery (see Pandya (2002) for a study of just one item of jewellery, and also Dwyer (2000a), especially pp.187–8). There are countless texts available on other aspects of appearance: indeed, one can imagine a very good book just on the plait alone. Unfortunately, to write a book on any one topic creates a focus on that topic at the expense of others. In this volume the emphasis is clearly on the sari, and these other elements of appearance are not considered even though they are clearly closely related in the world of practice.

[9]   We have edited out some sections of this transcript in order to shorten it, but have not interrupted the narrative by indicating the subsequent gaps.

[10]   'Suit' is a common term used for the three-piece garment, consisting of tunic, trousers and scarf. In this book we shall refer to this mostly as the shalwar kamiz, although a variant of the trouser may be called *churidar* and the top may be called a *kurta*. The most common term for the scarf is *dupatta*, but *chunni* is also used.

[11]   A chiffon can mean either silk or synthetic.

[12]   The pallu is the end of the sari usually draped over the shoulder, and is commonly marked by distinct and heavier decoration from the rest of the sari.

13 Kota is a particular style, which as Mina suggests consists of small squares.

14 The rate of exchange during fieldwork was 70 rupees per pound sterling.

15 This book is based on several pieces of work. At its core was fieldwork conducted in March–April 2002 jointly by the authors. For domestic reasons, we had far less time than is usual for such a project. To compensate, we maximised our time carrying out over a hundred interviews and visiting most of the major cities as well as some rural sites. It was the most intensive work either of us has ever carried out. Most of the material describing village life is taken from Banerjee's fieldwork in two villages in West Bengal, which has been conducted during several visits over the last five years. In addition, information of topics such as advertising campaigns and politicians' clothing were accumulated on the basis of Banerjee's own experience of growing up in India and research on Indian democracy. It should be stressed, however, that any previous knowledge was radically re-thought in relation to the recent fieldwork, as is shown by the many differences between what both of us anticipated would be the story of the sari and the story as finally told in this book. Some of our encounters were contrived. Asking different people to spend more than three hours describing an act of getting dressed, which takes them ten minutes, is hardly natural to them, but was essential for us.

We clearly recognise that all generalisations are in some sense false. Yet this is intended as a work of anthropology, not of fiction, so we hope that every one of the implicit generalisations made is also in some sense true, at least to the individuals we have encountered and listened to and who then come to represent larger categories of people. Of course, a maid cannot stand for all maids in India. The traditions of relationship between maid and mistress vary between Bengal and Kerala, between the very rich and the lower middle classes. But even if we were to eschew all labelling and categories and claim to only represent an individual, this would remain a false act. Any individual we talked to was affected by the circumstances in which we talked to her and self-reflexive about her appearance as (for example) a maid. As an individual, the opinion she expressed may have been quite different than it would have been a year before. Indeed, individuals in India as in every other country are often unsure about their own opinion. They may say something and at the same time there is a cautionary voice in their heads saying, 'is this really what I think or am I just saying that'. So our approach to truth starts from our rejection of any ideal of pure objectivity. If even an informant can never know if they are telling the truth about themselves, how could an academic ever make such a claim?

If we are prepared to acknowledge this fundamental uncertainty behind all representations of people, then we should be spared a kind of false holy grail that implies that there is clear truth out there if only our methods are careful and precise enough, while at the same time we strive to live up to accepted standards of scholarship. Freed of this false goal, we can then take responsibility for those generalisations that appear to us warranted by what we feel we have learned through undertaking this research on the one hand, and to be worthwhile as part of a striving for knowledge and understanding on the other. What appears in this book is, then, not truth, but rather something we hope was true to our encounter with an extraordinarily diverse range of individuals.

16 *Zari* is embroidery, originally made using metal thread, usually gold covered silver, but today mainly made with fake metal thread or plastic.

17 After it is purchased but before it is worn, the sari is often taken to a tailor and strengthened in various ways such as adding a fall (a two-yard strip of cloth about five inches wide) to the bottom border of the sari, turning in the ragged ends of the pallu and in some cases protecting the embroidery of the pallu with a piece of net.

18 Winnicott (1971). For a general argument with respect to textiles and transitional objects see Attfield (2000: 121–3).

19 Iyengar (1992).

20 In recent years, inflationary demands for large dowries that parents of daughters are unable to provide has let to the phenomenon of 'dowry deaths' of young brides who are punished by their in-laws for their failure to arrive with the promised dowry.

21 We can gain a further understanding of the specific nature of this dynamic relationship between sari and wearer by comparison with other garments. A recent academic study of the Victorian corset (Summers 2001) has suggested that it also possessed considerable agency of its own and in relationship to women. She notes that the corset created an intense hybridity between the body and clothing. It affected considerably women's sense of their sexuality and their self. But also it was a powerful

instrument used by women to change their social position and alter the way they were seen in society. Summer's thereby contradicts the idea that it was a symbol of passivity amongst women. But what is immediately striking is that this argument is being made for a garment that in other respects appears to be the precise opposite of the sari. The corset is the most extreme example of highly fitted clothing, with the emphasis upon the body having to be adjusted to fit the clothing itself. The effect is to make us aware of two highly contrastive forms of agency. While the sari is constantly dynamic and presents a relative equality of relationship between wearer and clothing, the corset is rigid and only gives agency at the expense of being also highly oppressive.

22 See Norris (2003).

23 Tarlo (1996: 180).

24 See Hoskins (1998: 5) for the visual memory box.

25 See Chapter 5.

26 See especially Bourdieu (1984).

27 Described in Miller (1985).

28 See Chapter 7.

29 We return to these difficult choices in Chapter 8.

30 Though Indira Gandhi seemed almost to manage it; see Chapter 11.

31 See also Kamala Markandaya's moving story 'Hunger' (1997), set among paddy growers, in which a woman is forced to sell her treasured wedding sari for money during a terrible drought.

32 Caroline and Filipo Osella, personal communication.

33 The *shalwar* is usually a loose baggy trouser tapered at the ankles and tied at the waist with a drawstring, while the *churidar* is a long tight fitted trouser with close gathers from knee to ankle.

34 Benei (2002).

35 See Sunder Rajan (2001).

36 See Tarlo (1996: 185–6).

37 Sunder Rajan (2001) explores the cultural resonances between the forceful disrobing of women in contemporary Indian cinema and Draupadi's disrobing in the *Mahabharata*.

38 See Guha-Thakurta (1999:174–5) for her examination of the legacy of Raja Ravi Verma's paintings on popular calendar art.

39 ibid.

40 Dwyer argues, for example, that portrayals of the iconic 'wet sari' scene, an enduring element of cinema of recent decades using monsoon showers, ocean waves and forest waterfalls, 'can provide a particular celebration of the erotic rather than the pornographic body…The erotic body here is fully clothed, but totally sensualised to the point of being orgasmic…' This orgasmic nature of wet sari sequences is seen most clearly she suggests in the song 'I Love You' in *Mr India* where the invisible Mr India apparently makes love to the writhing heroine. Despite its conspicuously erotic nature, this film was still regarded as family viewing which did not transgress any of the censors' codes on sexual display. She argues therefore that Hindi films 'show how female sexuality is a crucial part of the semantics of the sari, and how sexuality is woven into the bourgeois notion of the ideal woman who represents the nation, Mother India.' Dwyer (2000a: 159).

41 See Nanda (1999).

42 Banerjee (1989: 132).

43 Guha-Thakurta (2002: 13).

44 For the contemporary power of this story see Mankekar (1993).

45 A more general potential in the gifting of cloth was noted by Bayly. He argues that clothing was central to the relationship between the people and the king in India. It went upwards in the form of tribute, but then in turn the king bestowed garments upon his people, thereby symbolically enveloping and encompassing them: 'The king was pledging protection and incorporating the subject into his royal body through the action of the royal charisma that was immanent in the cloth' (1986: 299), see also Cohn (1986).

46 See Werbner (1990) on the bride as the final wrapped and dazzling gift in this sequence of exchanges.

47 The average monthly income of such a rural family would be about Rs 4000.

48 The week-long celebration and worship of the ten-armed goddess Durga in eastern India.

49 See Tarlo (1996: 182).

50 Tarlo (1996: 168–74) also recounts a story in which a village father-in-law criticises his new daughter-in-law in similar terms for wearing an 'urban' cardigan over her sari.

51 See Chapter 6 for further discussion of such pollution.

52 See Leslie (1992).

53 ibid.

54 See Jeffrey (1979).

55 See Pande (1986).

56 See Dumont (1972); Marriot (1976).

57 See Kaviraj (1997), specially pp. 91-94 for a discussion of the distinction between outside and inside in an Indian home.

58 See Bayly (1986), especially pp. 288–93 for a discussion of the relationship between the texture of cloth and bio-moral substance.

59 See Loomba (1997) for a controversy over police uniforms.

60 See Young (1999) for some very different contradictions in the clothing of police in the UK.

61 See Entwhistle (1997).

62 For the wider possibilities of an anthropological study of women's clothing at work, see Freeman (2000: 213–52).

63 Joshi (1992: 226).

64 See Chapter 10.

65 See Bean (1989); Tarlo (1996: 62–93).

66 Tarlo (personal communication) noted that visitors to Mrs Gandhi's museum tended to linger longest at the exhibit of her bullet-ridden sari, worn at the time of her assassination.

67 See Bate (2002).

68 See Banerjee (1999 and in press).

69 Frank (2001: 259).

70 The sari as a garment has its own complex story of death, and in some cases quite surprising instances of re-birth. A fascinating and meticulous study of the fate of used saris, the way these are exchanged for steel utensils, the huge market in second-hand saris and the re-manufacture of goods from both parts of used saris and recycled imported clothing as well as the recycling of saris has been carried out by Lucy Norris at the Department of Anthropology at University College London, for her PhD thesis (2003). Her work contributes an extraordinary additional story to the tale of the sari as told here.

71 The way in which widows are expected to demonstrate the waning of their desires is well described by Sarah Lamb (2000) in her ethnography *White Saris and Sweet Mangoes* and by Gita Hariharan (1992) in her short story 'The Remains of the Feast' in her collection *The Art of Dying*. See also Lawrence Cohen's excellent *No Aging in India* (1998), especially pages 116–20 and 205–8 for an analysis of widowhood, aging and pathology.

72 Parry (1994:174).

73 ibid. 174.

74 ibid. 284.

75 Kak (1992).

76 In Britain, by contrast, the world of clothing creates anxiety far more because individual women feel they don't know what the socially appropriate clothing is, and subsequently are uncertain as to what they should wear. See Clarke and Miller (2002).

77 In fact in India, this combination of formal rules and constant social critique make clothing into an instance of what one of the founders of modern sociology, Emile Durkheim, called a 'social fact'. In Durkheim's definition, social facts are general (they apply to everyone), they are exterior (to the individual) and they are constraining (they restrict the expression of personal

desire and taste). For Durkheim, such social facts serve as a kind of cement, serving the necessary role of educating, moderating and binding together the forces of individual consciousness and volition, and forging them into a stable enduring entity that avoids anarchy and collapse (Durkheim 1938).

[78] Compare Vickery (1993: 282–4) for a parallel custom of giving second hand clothes to maids in eighteenth-century England.

[79] For an example, see Viswesaran (1996: 170–1).

[80] See also Nag (1991).

[81] Compare Miller (1998) for shopping in London.

[82] We could find no clear or convincing descriptive account of the modern textile sector in India. Verma (2000) does, however, provide a snapshot. Currently this sector employs around 20 million persons. It has radically decentralised over the last 50 years. Verma notes that in 1950 the organised mill sector accounted for 80 per cent of textile production but by 1980 this had fallen to 36 per cent and by 1998 to a mere 5.4 per cent. Powerlooms, by contrast, increased from 23,800 in 1951 to 836,000 in 1985 to an estimated one and a half million in 1998 (2000: 2). Overall this is seen as part of a fairly disastrous situation in which the industry has failed to modernise as fully as its overseas competitors. For example, in 1996 only a fifth of looms in India were of the modern form, without shuttles, while for the rest of the world the statistics are reversed in that only a fifth still have shuttles. There is also said to be massive overproduction, 38 square metres per person in India as against domestic demand of only 18 square metres, and exports are unlikely to amount to more than 10 per cent of production. Worst of all, it is predicted that when the protectionism provided by the current agreements on the textile trade runs out after 2004, Indian industry will be engulfed by a flood of imported textiles. The disorganised and decentralised nature of the industry is reflected in the difficulty of finding accurate academic information. Much of the concern today is with the comparative costs, wages and competitiveness of the two main sectors, that is handloom and powerloom (for which see Misra (1993: 89-120), Sinha and Sasikumar (2000), and Uchikawa (1998)). Figures for employment are also provided by the Ministry of Textiles and echoed by FAITMA, the Federation of All India Textile Manufacturers.

[83] See note 92

[84] See Tarlo (1996: 284–317).

[85] It is probably not possible to distinguish between what might be thought of as 'good' and 'bad' aspects of this appropriation. On the one hand it may seem exploitative, turning such people into reservoirs of authenticity to be used by a metropolitan elite. On the other hand many of those involved are, like the mistress figure of Chapter 8, working for NGOs and other such organisations with genuine concern for the welfare of such people. Indeed, the situation is not particularly different from the 'left' clothing of groups in many societies whose attitudes and effects are inevitably ambiguous, since their concerns may be genuine but their positions are very different from those they claim to represent.

[86] See Mehta (1997).

[87] See http://texmin.nic.in, the website of the Government of India's Ministry of Textiles.

[88] The debate between the legal status of a sari as 'textile' or 'apparel' was settled by the Punjab and Haryana High Court in the case of Subhash Embroidery Works *v.* Union of India (33 ELT 267) which ruled that a sari is a piece of fabric rather than clothing, as it becomes apparel only after it has been fortified by the addition of the `fall' which is a strip of cloth stitched to the base of the sari. This decision explains why saris are cheaper to produce than ready-made clothing, as they are exempt from Sales Tax under the Bombay Sales Tax Act 1959. Most saris do not attract Luxury Tax either (which can be levied on fabrics and textiles) because they usually cost less than the taxable rate of Rs 1,000 per metre (*Apparel Magazine*, March 2001 vol. 7, no. 3).

[89] Things would look different if we isolated other parts of the process. Apart from a very small *khadi* sector, almost all the yarn used by the handloom producers comes from the organised mill sector.

[90] In this book we have not tried to present a picture of the lives of workers in this industry, but many accounts are available. See Kumar (1988), or for sari embroidery, Wilkinson-Weber (1999). For a portrayal of exploitation and corruption in both the handloom and powerloom sectors, see Shyam Benegal's film *Susman* (1986).

[91] Swallow (1982) provides a well-researched precedent for the success of informal unregulated weaving enterprises over those with fixed assets.

[92] Most contemporary commentators discussing the state of the textile industry tend to assume that this is the outcome of very recent trends in the export of neo-liberal capitalism. To generalise such conversations, it is assumed that the nascent independent state of India under Nehru favoured both paternalism and protectionism, but these have now been broken down by the combined efforts of bodies such as the IMF, World Bank and WTO, whose strictures have been incorporated (though in a particular fashion) by the BJP government, partly in repudiation of the socialism associated with the previous Congress governments. Although this story is undoubtedly part of the explanation for the current situation, these assertions about neo-liberalism seem to ignore the very long and significant history of one of the major industries of the ancient world. Certainly prior to colonialism there existed a system whereby traders dominated a network of 'putting out' production, where orders were given out to various workers often supplying materials in advance that kept them in debt. This highly flexible and exploitative network seems to have constantly defeated more regulated alternatives. So far from being the pinnacle of modern capitalism, it is important to understand textile production in India as in some ways pre-capitalist or even non-capitalist. Capital is often still tied to mercantile rather than industrial interests, leaving producers largely responsible for their own costs and assets. This limits the capital available for investment in production itself. Most likely there have been fluctuations over a very long period. When there was a strong state such as during the Mauryas, the Gupta dynasty or post-independence one sees control being established through state-supported systems such as guilds or cooperatives. At other times merchants and middlemen flourish, profiting from highly dispersed producers who rise and fall with a demand over which they have no control, while the traders themselves incur far less by way of costs and risk. Though recent research suggests this might not have been quite as controlling as the European 'putting out system of production', where capital rather than materials was advanced to the weavers (see Arasaratnam (1993: 87); Chaudhuri (1993: 52–6)). This history has not been gathered together in any one source but a sense of the repetition of this theme at different periods may be garnered from sources such as Chaudhuri (1990), Naqvi (1968) and Perlin 1983. For the twentieth century, see the extensive volumes on production that were researched in association with successive censuses of India, and also Swallow (1982) for a more recent case study.

[93] For production see Kumar (1988); for a highly elaborated form of handloom see Bühler and Fischer (1979).

[94] Khan (1993: 61).

[95] ibid. 62.

[96] In a discussion of clothing in Indian cinema, Dwyer comments that: 'The totality of costume is similar to the fashion show, in which the Indian designer is required to present all types of clothes, from Western to a whole range of Indian (especially the wedding ones) although she/he may specialize in one' (Dwyer 2002: 93).

[97] Mr. Narayan, CEO, Reliance Textiles, personal communication.

[98] The Indo-Asian News Service, 7 May 2002.

[99] See Bean (1989); Tarlo (1996).

[100] See Dickey (1993); Pandian (1992).

[101] See Liechty (2003: 126–35) for an example of this, including crucially the impact of films on the seamstress.

[102] See Dwyer (2000b), 'Bombay Ishtyle', pp. 183–6

[103] See Edelman (1998).

[104] See Dwyer (2000b).

[105] Kabir (2001: 74).

[106] See Rajagopal (2001) and Ohm (2002) on television soaps.

[107] We recognise that this simplifies a dynamic industry in the West, much of which no longer accords with this image given, for example the decline of influence of *haute couture* and the rise in influence of certain elements of the retail sector; see Entwhistle (2000: 208–36); White and Griffiths (2000).

[108] For this reason the blouse is often remarked upon as more subject to Western-style fashion trends than is the sari itself. See Liechty (2003: 124).

[109] See Chatterjee (1992).

[110] The story of the Nivi style parallels that of other aspects of everyday life such as cricket and cooking, which Appadurai (1988, 1995) has shown contributed to the development of a pan-Indian public culture.

[111] In the sense of Sartre (1976).

[112] See Wadley (1975); Das (1981).

[113] Khan (1993: 62).

[114] In fact, one strain of opinion among habitual sari-wearing Muslim women in Bengal was that perhaps the shalwar kamiz may be better suited for Muslim notions of modesty rather than the more revealing sari.

[115] For an example of resentment by people in the south to this 'northern' garment see Viswesaran (1996: 177) 'It was thus that I witnessed a tired office worker in crumpled sari give a literal dressing down to the student [in a shalwar kamiz] who had stepped on her foot: "Look at you," she declared angrily. "You are living in the South and haven't even the decency to wear a sari".'

[116] This causes great discomfort to girls who fail to gain promotion at the end of the academic year. The poverty of their academic record is punished by trapping their growing bodies in infantile clothes.

[117] Compare Arthur (2000), Kinsella (2002) and McVeigh (2000) for the troubled relationship between school, uniforms and sexuality in Japan.

[118] Caroline Osella, personal communication.

[119] The counts were all made during March and April 2002. Those in town were conducted while travelling slowly by car and reflect commuter-belt areas, that is, streets which include people waiting for buses, walking to and from work, as well as some who work on the street itself. They also include some shopping areas. The count only included adults aged (on the basis of an instant guess), to be eighteen and over. Under this age the proportions would be entirely different, since the sari is not usually adopted until after college age for urban dwellers and puberty/marriage for rural dwellers. Clearly this survey also does not include any rural region where the sari is not the traditional dress.

[120] See Pfaffenberger (1990) for an analysis of religion as form of technology.

[121] Tarlo (1996:160).

[122] See Fuller (1992), specially chapters 1, 2 and 8.

[123] Clearly none of this would necessarily be the case for those regions where it is the shalwar kamiz and not the sari which is traditional, although even there young women may today relate to the shalwar kamiz more in terms of this generic modern aspect rather than as part of their family traditions.

[124] For an introduction to Weber's ideas see Weber (1964). For very different but also influential versions of the history of modern rationality, compare Foucault (1970) or Polanyi (1957).

[125] See Latour (1993, 1999). A similar point has been made within material culture studies: see Büchli (2002).

[126] For a general discussion of approaches to modernity and an attempt to use these in comparative anthropology, see Miller (1994: 58–81); for the philosophical basis of these arguments see Habermas (1987).

[127] The recent history of these two garments is even harder to simply take for granted when we remember just how little any of the discussion within this chapter has to do with any intrinsic feature of the clothing in question. On a London street the shalwar kamiz has very little in its appearance that seems to make it the embodiment of functional rationalism. The shalwar with its flowing trousers tapered tight at the ankles is a very particular style, its gathers and flows are quite distinct from trousers elsewhere. The garment is also just as subject to fashion as the sari, with the length of the *kurta* constantly moving up and down with the seasons. If anything the long scarf-like *dupatta* appears even less obviously functional as an aspect of clothing than does the pallu. It looks as though it was made to be trapped in car doors or escalators. But then one has to remember that the first movement to create modern 'rational' dress in nineteenth-century Britain, known as the dress reform movement, managed to see ties and waistcoats as emblematic of the new functional rationality! (See Wigley 1995) So there should be no temptation to ground these discussions in any claim to some trans-cultural functionality or rational dress. We are not dealing here with the 'natural' propensities of dress. Otherwise we might have predicted that the *dupatta* would become some kind

of extension of the pallu. The greater detachability of the *dupatta* seems to represent a further movement in the potential for separation already evident in the partial separation of the pallu. It would have been very easy to make such an argument. But that is not what emerges from a study of conversations about the *dupatta* or observations of how they are worn. The strength of ethnographic fieldwork likes in the fact that we cannot extrapolate anything merely from our expectations about what we think clothing should mean or be good for. Similarly, much of this chapter represents a struggle against the sense that these histories of clothing were either natural to the form of the clothing or predictable. Our point is that they are radical and surprising.

[128] See Kahn (2001); Marcus (1992).

[129] Dalby (2001: 125–59).

[130] ibid. 125.

[131] ibid. 131.

[132] ibid. 183–239.

[133] ibid. 128.

[134] Inge Daniels, personal communication.

[135] Clothing may at times form part of such struggles over systems of thought and legitimacy, but at other times may be quite irrelevant. One obvious example of deliberate and explicit political usage in India is that associated with Gandhi (Bean 1989). To cite just one example elsewhere, the Comaroffs (1985, 1996) describe the complex relationship between the ideals of covering, of civilisation and of Christianity during colonialism. It is, however, important to recognise that we cannot assume any such role for clothing in all places and at all times.

[136] As shown by the entirely unrelated history of draped garments in the West. See Doy (2002).

BIBLIOGRAPHY

Appadurai, A, (1988) How to make a national cuisine: cookbooks in contemporary India. *Comparative Studies in Society and History*. 30 (1): 3-24

— (1995) Playing with modernity: the decolonisation of Indian cricket. In C. Breckenridge (ed), *Consuming Modernity: Public Culture in a South Asian World:* Minneapolis/London: University of Minnesota Press.

Arasaratnam, S. (1993) 'Weavers, merchants and company: the handloom industry in Southeastern India 1750–90), in T. Roy (ed.), *Cloth and Commerce: Textiles in Colonial India*, New Delhi: Sage, 85–114.

Arthur, L. (ed.) (1999) *Religion, Dress and the Body*, Oxford: Berg.

— (2000) 'School uniforms as a symbolic metaphor for competing ideologies in Indonesia', in L. Arthur (ed.), *Undressing Religion: Commitment and Conversion from a Cross-Cultural Perspective*, Oxford: Berg.

Attfield, J. (2000) *Wild Things: The Material Culture of Everyday Life*, Oxford: Berg.

Banerjee, M. (1999) 'Mamata's *khomota' Seminar* August: 30–35

— (2000) *The Pathan Unarmed*, Oxford: James Currey.

— (in press) 'Populist political leadership in West Bengal and Tamil Nadu: Mamata and Jayalalitha compared', in R. Jenkins (ed.), *Regional Reflections: Comparing Politics Across India's States*, Oxford: Oxford University Press.

Banerjee, S. (1989) *The Parlour and the Streets: Elite and Popular Culture in Nineteenth-Century Calcutta*, Calcutta: Seagull Books.

Bate, J.B. (2002) 'Political praise in Tamil newspapers: the poetry and iconography of democratic power', in D. Mines and S. Lamb (eds), *Everyday Life in South Asia*, Bloomington, IN: Indiana University Press, 308–25.

Bayly, C. (1986) 'The origins of swadeshi (home industry): cloth and Indian society, 1700–1930', in A. Appadurai (ed.), *The Social Life of Things: Commodities in Cultural Perspective*, Cambridge: Cambridge University Press, 285–321.

Bean, S. (1989) Gandhi and Khadi, the fabric of Indian independence', in A Weiner and J. Schneider (eds), *Cloth and Human Experience*, Washington, DC: Smithsonian Institution Press.

Benei, V. (2002) '*Mother-India* at school: nation, family and gender in Marathi-speaking primary schools', paper presented at SAAG conference, Edinburgh.

Boulanger, C. (1997) *Saris: An Illustrated Guide to the Indian Art of Draping*, New York: Shakti Press International.

Bourdieu, P. (1984) *Distinction: A Social Critique of the Judgement of Taste*, London: Routledge and Kegan Paul.

Buchli, V. (ed.) (2002) *The Material Culture Reader*, Oxford: Berg.

Bühler, A. and Fischer, E. (1979) *The Patola of Gujerat*, Basle: Krebs A.G.

Carrier, J. (1995) *Gifts and Commodities: Exchange and Western Capitalism since 1700*, London: Routledge.

Chatterjee, P. (1992) *The Nation and its Fragments: Colonial and Postcolonial Histories*, Delhi: Oxford University Press.

Chaudhuri, N.K. (1990) *Asia before Europe*, Cambridge: Cambridge University Press.

— (1993) 'The structure of Indian textile industry in the seventeenth and eighteenth centuries', in T. Roy (ed.), *Cloth and Commerce: Textiles in Colonial India*, New Dehli: Sage, 33–84.

Chishti, R. and Sanyal, A. (1989) *Saris of India: Madhya Pradesh*, New Delhi: Wiley Eastern.

— (1995) *Saris of India: Bihar and West Bengal*, New Delhi: Wiley Eastern.

Clarke, A and Miller, D. (2002) 'Fashion and anxiety', *Fashion Theory* 6: 191–214.

Cohen, L. (1998) *No Aging in India: Modernity, Senility and the Family*, Delhi: Oxford University Press.

Cohn, B. (1986) 'Cloth, clothes, and colonialism: India in the nineteenth century', in A Weiner and J. Schneider (eds), *Cloth and Human Experience*, Washington, DC: Smithsonian Institution Press.

Comaroff, J. and Comaroff, J. (1985) *Body of Power, Spirit of Resistance*, Chicago: University of Chicago Press.

Comaroff, J. (1996) 'The empire's old clothes: fashioning the colonial subject', in D. Howes (ed.), *Cross-Cultural Consumption*, London: Routledge.

Dalby, L. (2001) *Kimono: Fashioning Culture*, New York: Vintage/Random House.

Das, V. (1981) 'The mythological film in its framework of meaning: an analysis of Jai Santoshi Ma', *India International Centre Quarterly* 8(1): 43–56.

Dehejia, V. (ed.) (1999) *Devi: The Great Goddess Female Divinity in South Asian Art*, Washington, DC: Arthur M. Sackler Gallery.

Dickey, S. (1993) *Cinema and the Urban Poor in South India*, Cambridge: Cambridge University Press.

Doy, G. (2002) *Drapery, Classicism and Barbarism in Visual Culture*, London: I.B. Tauris.

Dumont, L. (1972) *Homo Hierarchicus*, London: Paladin.

Durkheim, É. (1938) *The Rules of Sociological Method*, 8th edn, trans. S.A. Solvay and J.H. Mueller, ed. G.E.G. Catlin, Glencoe, IL: Free Press.

Dwyer, R. (2000a) 'The erotics of the wet sari in Hindi films', *South Asia* 23 (2): 143–59.
— (2000b) 'Bombay ishtyle', in S. Bruzzi and P. Gibson (eds), *Fashion Cultures: Theories, Explorations and Analysis*, London: Routledge, 178–90.
— (2002) *Cinema India: The Visual Culture of Hindi Film*, London: Reaktion Books and the Victoria and Albert Museum/New Brunswick, NJ: Rutgers University Press/Delhi: Oxford University Press.

Edelman, A. (1998) *The Little Black Dress*, London: Aurum Press.

Entwhistle, J. (1997) '"Power dressing" and the construction of the career woman', in M. Nava, A. Blake, I. MacRury and B. Richards (eds), *Buy this Book*, London: Routledge.
— (2000) *The Fashioned Body*, Cambridge: Polity.

Foucault, M. (1970) *The Order of Things*, London: Tavistock.

Frank, K. (2001) *The life of Indira Nehru Gandhi*, London: HarperCollins.

Freeman, C. (2000) *High Tech and High Heels in the Global Economy*, Durham, NC: Duke University Press.

Fuller, C. (1992) *The Camphor Flame: Popular Hinduism and Society in India*, Princeton, NJ: Princeton University Press.

Ghurye, G.S. (1951) *Indian Costume*, Bombay: Popular Book Depot.

Guha-Thakurta, T. (1999) 'Clothing the goddess: the modern contest over representations of Devi', in V. Dehejia (ed.), *Devi: The Great Goddess Female Divinity in South Asian Art*, Washington, DC: Arthur M. Sackler Gallery.
— (2002) *Visual Worlds of Modern Bengal*, Calcutta: Seagull Books.

Habermas, J. (1987) *The Philosophical Discourse of Modernity*, Cambridge, MA: MIT Press.

Hariharan, G. (1992) 'The remains of the feast', in U.Butalia and R.Menon (eds) *Other Worlds: New Writing by Indian Women*, Delhi: Kali for Women

Hoskins, J. (1998) *Biographical Objects: How Things Tell the Stories of People's Lives*, London: Routledge.

Iyengar, V. (1992) 'No letter from Mother', in U. Butali and R. Menon (eds), *In Other Words: New Writing by Indian Women*, Delhi: Kali for Women.

Jeffery, P. (1979) *Frogs in a Well: Indian Women in Purdah*, London: Zed Press.

Joshi, O.P. (1992) 'Continuity and change in Hindu women's dress' in R. Barnes J.B. Eicher (eds), *Dress and Gender: Making and Meaning in Cultural Contexts*, Oxford: Berg.

Kabir, N.M. (2001) *Bollywood: The Indian Cinema Story*, London: Channel Four Books.

Kahn, J. (2001) 'Anthropology and modernity', *Current Anthropology* 42: 651–80.

Kak, M. (1992) 'Twilight', in in U. Butali and R. Menon (eds), *In Other Words: New Writing by Indian Women*, Delhi: Kali for Women.

Kali for Women (ed.) 1986 'Tragedy in a minor key' in *Truth Tales: Contemporary Stories by Women Writers of India*, New York: The Feminist Press at the City University of New York.

Kaviraj, S. (1997) 'Filth and the public sphere', *Public Culture* 10(1): 83–113.

Khan, N. (1993) 'Asian women's dress: from burqah to bloggs – changing clothes for changing times', in J. Ash and E. Wilson (eds), *Chic Thrills: A Fashion Reader*, Berkeley and Los Angeles: University of California Press.

Kinsella, S. (2002) 'What's behind the fetishism of the Japanese school uniform', *Fashion Theory* 6: 215–37.

Kumar, N. (1988) *The Artisans of Benaras: Popular Culture and Identity 1880–1986*, Princeton, NJ: Princeton University Press.

Lamb, S. (2000) *White Saris and Sweet Mangoes: Aging, Gender, and Body in North India*, Berkeley, CA: University of California Press.

Latour, B. (1993) *We Have Never Been Modern*, Hemel Hempstead: Harvester Wheatsheaf.
— (1999) *Pandora's Hope*, Cambridge, MA: Harvard University Press.

Leslie, J. (1992) 'The significance of dress for the orthodox Hindu woman', in R. Barnes and J.B. Eicher (eds), *Dress and Gender: Making and Meaning in Cultural Contexts*, Oxford: Berg.

Liechty, M. (2003) *Suitably Modern: Making Middle-Class Culture in a New Consumer Society*, Princeton, NJ: Princeton University Press.

Loomba, A. (1997) 'The long and saggy sari', *Women: A Cultural Review*, 8(3): 278–92.

Lynton, L. and Singh, S. (2002) *The Sari: Styles, Patterns, History, Techniques*, London: Thames and Hudson.

Mankekar, P. (1993) 'Television's tales and a woman's rage: a nationalist recasting of Draupadi's "disrobing"', *Public Culture* 5: 469–92.

Marcus, G. (1992) 'Past, present and emergent identities: requirements for ethnographies of late 20th century modernity worldwide', in S. Lash and J. Friedman (eds), *Modernity and Identity*, Oxford: Blackwell.

Markandeya, K. (1977) 'Hunger', in S. Rushdie and E. West (eds), *Mirrorwork: 50 Years of Indian Writing in English 1947–1997*, London: Henry Holt and Co.

Marriott, M. (1976) 'Interpreting Indian society: a monistic alternative to Dumont's dualism', *Journal of Asian Studies* 36(3).

McVeigh, B. (2000) *Wearing Ideology: State, Schooling and Self-Presentation in Japan*, Oxford: Berg.

Mehta, D. (1997) *Work, Ritual, Biography: A Muslim Community in North India*, Delhi: Oxford University Press.

Miller, D. (1985) *Artefacts as Categories: A Study of Ceramic Variability in Central India*, Cambridge: Cambridge University Press.
— (1994) *Modernity: An Ethnographic Approach*, Oxford: Berg.
— (1995) 'Style and ontology in Trinidad', in J. Friedman (ed.), *Consumption and Identity*, Chur: Harwood.
— (1998) *A Theory of Shopping*, Cambridge: Polity Press/Ithaca, NY: Cornell University Press.

Mines, D. and Lamb, S. (eds) (2002) *Everyday Life in South Asia*, Bloomington, IN: Indiana University Press.

Misra, S. (1993) *India's Textile Sector: A Policy Analysis*, New Delhi: Sage.

Nag, D. (1991) 'Fashion, gender, and the Bengali middle class', *Public Culture* 3(2): 93–112.

Nanda, S. (1999) *Neither Man nor Woman: The Hijras of India*, Belmont, CA: Wadsworth.

Naqvi, H. (1968) *Urban Centres and Industries in Upper India 1556-1803*, London: Asia Publishing House.

Norris, K.L. (2003) The life cycle of clothing: recycling and the efficacy of materiality in contemporary urban India. Submitted for PhD. University of London.

Ohm, B. (2002) '"East" and "West" within the East: television in Turkey and India', paper presented at EASAS Conference, Copenhagen, August.

Olivelle, P. (1998) 'Hair and society: social significance of hair in South Asian traditions', in A. Hitebeitel and B.D. Miller (eds), *Hair: Its Power and Meaning in Asian Cultures*, New York: State University of New York Press.

Pande, M. (1986) 'Tragedy in a minor key', in Kali for Women (ed.), *Truth Tales: Contemporary Stories by Women Writers of India*, New York: The Feminist Press at the City University of New York.

Pandian, M.S.S. (1992) *The Image Trap: M.G. Ramachandran in Film and Politics*, New Delhi and Newbury Park, CA: Sage.

Pandya, V. (2002) 'Nose and eyes for identity: accoutrements and enumerations of ethnicity among the Jatha of Kachchh', *Journal of Material Culture* 7: 295–328.

Parry, J. (1994) *Death in Benares*, New Delhi: Foundation Books.

Perlin, F. (1983) 'Proto-industrialization and pre-colonial South Asia', *Past and Present* 98: 30–95.

Pfaffenberger, B. (1990) 'The Hindu temple as a machine, or the western machine as a temple', *Technique et Culture* 16: 183–202.

Polanyi, K. 1957 *The Great Transformation.* Boston: Beacon Press.

Rajagopal, A. (2001) 'Thinking about the new Indian middle class', in R. Sunder (ed.), *Signposts: Gender Issues in Post-Independence India*, New Brunswick, NJ and London: Rutgers University Press.

Roy, T. (ed.) (1993) *Cloth and Commerce: Textiles in Colonial India*, New Delhi: Sage.

Sartre, J.-P. (1976) *Critique of Dialectical Reason*, London: Routledge.

Sinha, A.K. and Sasikumar, S.L. (eds) (2000) *Restructuring of the Textile Sector in India*, New Delhi: Vikas.

Sparke, P. (1995) *As Long as it's Pink: The Sexual Politics of Taste*, London: Pandora.

Summers, L. (2001) *Bound to Please: A History of the Victorian Corset*, Oxford: Berg.

Sunder Rajan, R. (2001) 'The story of Draupadi's disrobing: the meanings for our times', in R. Sunder Rajan (ed.), *Signposts: Gender Issues in Post-Independence India*, New Brunswick, NJ and London: Rutgers University Press.

Swallow, D. (1982) 'Production and control in the Indian garment export industry', in E. Goody (ed.),. *From Craft to Industry*, Cambridge: Cambridge University Press.

Tarlo, E. (1996) *Clothing Matters*, London: Hurst and Co.

Uchikawa, S. (1998) *Indian Textile Industry: State Policy, Liberalization and Growth*, New Delhi: Manohar.

Verma, S. (2000) 'Restructuring the Indian textile industry', in A.K. Sinha and S.L. Sasikumar (eds), *Restructuring of the Textile Sector in India*, New Delhi: Vikas, 1–23.

Vickery, A. (1993) 'Women and the world of goods', in J. Brewer and R. Porter (eds), *Consumption and the World of Goods*, London: Routledge.

Visweswaran, K. (1996) *Fictions of Feminist Ethnography*, Delhi: Oxford University Press.

Wadley, S. (1975) *Shakti: Power in the Conceptual Structure of Karimpur Religion*, Chicago: University of Chicago Press.

Weber, M. (1964) *The Theory of Social and Economic Organization*, New York: The Free Press.

Werbner, P. (1990) *The Migration Process*, Oxford: Berg.

White, N and Griffiths, I. (eds) (2000) *The Fashion Business*, Oxford: Berg.

Wigley, M. (1995) *White Walls and Designer Dresses: The Fashioning of Modern Architecture*, Cambridge, Massachusetts: MIT Press.

Wilkinson-Weber, C. (1999) *Embroidering Lives: Women's Work and Skill in the Lucknow Embroidery Industry*, New York: State University of New York Press.

Winnicott, D. (1971) *Playing and Reality*, London: Tavistock Press.

Young, M. (1999) 'Dressed to commune, dressed to kill: changing police imagery in England and Wales', in K. Johnson and S. Lennon (eds), *Appearance and Power*, Oxford: Berg.

Zola, E. (1992) *The Ladies Paradise*, Berkeley, CA: University of California Press.

GLOSSARY

almirah	Cupboard
alna	Open rack for storing clothes
bindi	Forehead decoration
buti	Small recurring motifs
churidar	Trousers fitted from knee to ankle in close gathers
chunni/ chunri	Scarf worn with shalwar kameez or ghagra
dan	Charity
dhoti	Draped lower body garment for men, tied at waist.
dupatta	Scarf worn with shalwar kameez
gamcha	Cotton towel
gharara	Flared culotte-like trousers
ghagra	Flared full-length skirt
jutis	Shoes traditionally worn in Northern and Western India
kamiz	Long tunic
karhai	Wok
khadi	Handspun, hand-woven cloth
kurta	Long tunic
lojja bostro	Modesty garment used by Bengali bride to cover face
lungi	Sarong
maya	Illusion or materiality
neet koney	Lit. 'little bride,' a Bengali bridesmaid
pallu	The end of the sari usually draped over the shoulder, and is commonly marked by distinct and heavier decoration from the rest of the sari
prasad	Sacred food blessed by being first offered to deities
pucca	Baked/cooked
puja	Prayers
purdah	Socially prescribed veiling
seedha pallu	Draping style with pallu over the right shoulder
shakti	Female aspect of power
shalwar	Baggy trousers caught at waist with a drawstring and tapered at the ankles
sindoor	Vermillion paste in hair parting, mark of marriage in some parts of India
stridhan	Lit. 'woman's wealth', given to a bride at her wedding
swadeshi	Home produced with nationalist overtones
tilak	Caste or religious mark on forehead
zari	Silver thread covered by gold

modesty
    and eroticism 86, 89
    expectations of women 102, 103, 160,
        220–1, 239
    and glamour or allure 222–3, 251
    patriarchal enforcement of 82, 105
    role of pallu 36–7, 38
    shalwar kamiz 240
    see also purdah
Monsoon Wedding (film) 96
monsoons 114, n.40
moral concerns
    anxieties about dress 144
    rules of cosmology 119
Morris, William 207
mothers
    aspirations 158–9
    breastfeeding 243
    and children's experiences of the sari 32–
        4, 67, 69
    criticism of daughters' saris 146–7
    gathering together of trousseau 95
    men choosing and buying first sari for
        72
movement 26, 28, 160, 236
    see also dynamism
Mumbai 27, 102, 104, 130, 165, 222, 241,
    247
Muslims
    beliefs and traditions 36, 48, 57–8, 96–
        7, 139
    new saris for festivals 56–7, 174, 175
    shalwar kamiz 238, 240
    see also Islam
Mysore 210

nail polish, 'Auntie' and her advice 77, 78
nakedness 81
Nalli (shop) 198
Nandini, Jyananda n.6
National Institute of Fashion Technology
    203
nationalism 238
    appropriation of sari 219–20, 221, 249
    Japanese kimono 249
    see also BJP
Nehru, Pandit 128, 220, n.92
neo-liberalism n.92
Neruda, Pablo, poem 145
net saris 78

New Delhi 204
New Year 72
Nivi style 5, 25, 102–3, 111
    flexibility 248–9, 251
    origin of 219, 235–6
    uniform saris 122
Norris, L. n.70
North East India, handlooms 198
nuns 140
nurses 119
Nutan 222
nylon saris 81, 113

older women 7, 103–4, 244
    Chandra's story 145–7
    expectations 138, 139, 143
    gifting by daughter 162
    in rural villages 27, 28–9, 143, 161
    see also widows
Orissa 13, 155, 211
ornaments 140
    see also jewellery

paithani saris 211
Pakistan, shalwar kamiz 5, 238
pallu
    actresses' use of 29–31
    adopting styles 67, 74, 77, 78, 116
    ambiguous qualities 36–7, 253
    between self and world 29–41
    catching fire 16, 40
    chiffons 114
    children's encounters with 32–4
    compared with *dupatta* n.127
    covering of head with 15, 16, 102
    criticisms 146–7
    designer saris 204
    intimacy 23, 24, 25, 26, 81
    Mina's experiences 13, 15, 16, 80
    Mrs Gandhi 220
    Nivi style 103, 248–9
    pinned style of hotel receptionists 125
    potential for beauty 34–6
    practical concerns and uses 37–8, 159,
        244
    problems and betrayal by 160, 244
    Reshma's story 142
    silk screens 206
    synthetics and cottons 160
    uniform saris 120, 251

as unpinned on power sari 125–6, 127,
    128, 157–58
Pande, Mrinal, short story 111
Parekh, Asha 222
party wear 51, 78, 79, 138, 227
Pathak, Deena 23, 30–1, 223
patriarchy 1, 80–1, 104–6
patterns
    abstract and geometric 183, 205, 207
    advice and disdain 73
    buti 52
    ikat 1
    kota style 13, 155
    regional designs 211
    rules and traditions 53, 164
    see also printed saris
Peanuts (cartoon) 33
personal aesthetics 1
    comparisons between saris 114
    'ethnic' saris 154, 198
    sari wardrobe 51, 52–3
    see also aesthetic concerns
personality, Chandra's view of sari 145
petticoats 5, 24, 25, 26, 27, 81, 85, 104,
    244
    Mina's experiences 14, 15, 16, 17, 27
    styles of wearing 75, 78, 157
pinning 70, 102, 130, 157–58
    uniform saris 120, 122
playfulness 37, 85–6
pleats and pleating 24, 25–6, 67, 70, 114,
    116, 130
    adopting styles 78, 157
    kota saris 155
    men's anxieties 87
    Nivi style 25, 102–3
    policewomen's uniform saris 120
policewomen 119, 120 2, 219
political issues
    anti-colonial movement 219, 235–6
    ethnic values 198
    Mrs Gandhi's visit to USA 220
    and the shalwar kamiz 5
    see also nationalism
politicians 33, 128–30, 131, 183, 219, 222
    see also Gandhi, Indira
pollution
    dangers of pallu 244
    fears and prevention of 49, 103, 117–
        18, 119
    through recycling 58

images of goddesses 85
 men's fantasies 87, 88–9
 new bride 139
 and patriarchal control 80–1, 105
 potential of the sari 82, 85, 87–9, 236
 power sari at work 127–8
 and touching the pallu 37
Shah, Praful 198
shakti 236
shalwar 66
shalwar kamiz (or suit)
 college girls 82, 240
 comparisons with sari 27, 113, 127, 128, 240, 242–4
 complementary relationship with sari 252
 contest with sari 5, 7, 238, 242, 247–8
 functionality 27, 240–1, 245–6, 247, 252
 hiding the body 80, 240, 245
 Mayawati 129
 Mina's story 14, 15, 16, 18, 95, 99, 101
 modernity 239, 241, 242, 246, 247, 249, 252
 Muslim dress 238, 240
 as rationality 246–7
 rural villages 176, 239, 240
 school 238, 239
 survey of urban and rural areas 241
 in TV soaps 226
 work of designer 206, 207
 worn by girls and young women 2, 66, 96, 123, 165, 239–40, 243
 worn by urban women 98, 102, 104, 153, 177, 240–1
shawls 2
sheets 158–9
shoes
 jutis 226
 party wear 78
 sandals 112
shopping 7, 99, 212–13
 branding and film celebrities 183, 225, 228
 three scenarios 173–88
 for TV soap styles 228
 for wedding saris 96
 see also buying saris
silks 69, 78, 113, 114, 124
 artificial yarns and mixing fibres 209, 210

designer saris 207
 handlooms 198, 202, 211, 220
 Mina's wedding 13
 South Indian 95–6
 village women 49
 for weddings 5, 97, 98, 183
 worn by stars 129, 223
sindoor 14, 159
sleeping 14–15, 27, 185
soap operas
 actresses' use of pallu 29
 influence on fashions 163, 225, 227–8
 power of Nim Sood 226–8
social concerns 7, 54, 125
 in activity of buying 173
 comparisons between saris 113–14
social facts n.77
social hierarchy, decreasing extent of 165
social pressures
 and control over clothing 144
 on older women 143, 145
social roles 68, 70, 72, 155
 and modernity 248
Sood, Nim 225, 226–8
South Asia
 draped and unsewn clothing 2
 gender inequality 235
South India 37, 95–6, 138, 221, 238
special occasions 51, 54
 see also festivals; weddings
spiritual life 138, 153
Sridevi 83
starch
 from boiled rice 1, 17, 28–9, 112–13, 153
 kota cloth 155
starching 17–18, 28, 120
state bureaucracy 236, 237
 dress codes 123
stitched clothing
 additions to sari 235
 contrast with unstitched clothing 27, 40, 71, 113
 kimono 250
 nature of shalwar kamiz 113, 240
stories and histories 48–9, 50, 158–9
Stridharmapaddhati 105
studies
 of clothing 4, 47
 poverty, wealth and possessions 59

styles 1
 advice of 'Auntie' 79
 college girls 74–6
 and independence 102–3
 and individual choice 137
 maid's dilemma about urban and village wear 163–4
 Mina's preferences 138
 modern and traditional 159
 Mrs Gandhi's influence 221
 pallu 18, 77, 78
 Shona's problem of what to wear 154–58
 uniform saris 122
 worn by Rekha 223
 see also fashions; *kota* style; Nivi style
Subhash Embroidery Works v. Union of India court case n.88
Sufi poetry 147
suicide, of brides 40
suit *see* shalwar kamiz
Surat 208, 212
Swaraj, Sushma 130
sweepers
 Banno at work and home 115–16, 117, 119
 servants 104
symbolism
 Japanese kimono 250
 and rationality 247–8
 of sari 219–20, 235, 236, 246, 247
synthetics 52, 112, 113, 114
 Bimla's story 160–1, 161, 163
 fashions 198, 203
 for maids 163
 mixing with natural fibres 209
 production and design 196–8, 203, 207, 212
 worn by politicians 129

Tagore, Rabindranath, story 145, n.6
Tagore, Satyanendranath n.6
Tagore, Sharmila 222
Tahiliani, Tarun 204
Tamil Nadu 2, 129, 208, 211
Tamils 13, 15, 143, 243
tangail, handloom saris 97, 199, 221
Tarlo, Emma 47, 80, 102, 240
teachers *see* lecturers; schoolteachers